THE WORLD'S BEST HOTELS 2008/09

THE WORLD'S BEST HOTELS 2008/09

To obtain preferential rates and amenities at the hotels featured in *The World's Best Hotels*, please register online at: www.theworldsbesthotels.com

FIRST PUBLISHED IN 2008 BY	Nigel Bolding THE WORLD'S BEST HOTELS The Studio, 27 High Street, Godalming, UK GU7 1AU Tel: +44.560.115 3892 Email: nigel.bolding@theworldsbesthotels.com Website: www.theworldsbesthotels.com
DESIGNED & PRODUCED BY	EDITIONS DIDIER MILLET PTE LTD 121 Telok Ayer Street #03-01, Singapore 068590 Tel: +65.6324 9260 • Fax: +65.6324 9261 Email: edm@edmbooks.com.sg Website: www.edmbooks.com
EXECUTIVE EDITOR	Melisa Teo
EDITOR	Suzanne Wong
ASSISTANT EDITOR	Meia Ho
WRITERS	Hallie Campbell Paul Mooney Yu-Mei Balasingamchow Brandon Lee
DESIGNER	Annie Teo
PRODUCTION MANAGER	Sin Kam Cheong
DESIGN CONCEPT BY	Nuts Ideas
COLOUR SEPARATION BY	SC Graphic Singapore
PRINTED BY	Star Standard Singapore

PREPARED IN COLLABORATION WITH	INSTITUTIONAL INVESTOR Special Projects Department 225 Park Avenue South, New York, NY 10003, USA Tel: +1.212.224 3000 • Fax: +1.212.224 3704 Website: www.institutionalinvestor.com
EDITOR & PUBLISHER	Ernest S McCrary
NEWS EDITOR	Marilen Cawad
ART DIRECTOR	Francis Klaess
DIRECTOR OF SALES & MARKETING	Douglas Campbell
COORDINATOR	Jill Michalek

The article "Where Luxury Lives" and all rankings are reproduced courtesy of *Institutional Investor* magazine. The rankings were compiled by staff under the direction of Director of Research Operations Group Sathya Rajavelu and Senior Editor Jane B Kenney.

© 2008 Euromoney Institutional Investor plc

ISBN 978-981-4217-57-6

THE WORLD'S BEST HOTELS 2008/09

Institutional Investor

Gilt at The New York Palace Hotel balances old-world grandeur with sexy modern art sensibilities.

A welcome basket of tea and cookies awaits each guest at Hotel Bel-Air, Los Angeles.

Contents

Introduction

Congratulations to The Ritz-Carlton New York, Battery Park, voted the world's best hotel by *Institutional Investor* magazine subscribers in its 27th annual hotel survey. Looking back, it's hard to believe that this all started back in 1981 when 120 bankers attending a conference in the south of France thought an informal hotel poll might be a bit of fun. Well, it's a lot more serious than that these days. The great thing about this survey is that it compares apples with apples—its where bankers stay on business. No cruise ships, no resorts—this ranking gives you the definitive list of where to stay if you are a financial traveller.

Welcome to the 2008/09 edition of *The Worlds Best Hotels*. Apart from profiling some of the very best hotels in the world, we also offer some great ideas on how to escape the world of finance when some extra time is at hand. Does the perfect gap year actually exist? Our feature on 12 Great Escapes offers the closest thing to it—one ideal hotel destination for each month of the year. Read on as well for our special report on family travel. Tip from my own personal (and expensive) experience: don't let the kids near the minibar. And have you noticed how the Meetings Industry has changed? Its not just boardrooms and dingy exhibition halls anymore—find out more as we cast the spotlight on this side of business travel. The city on everyone's lips this Olympic year is Beijing, epicentre of China's growing influence around the world. Eye on Beijing puts the focus on what is now more than ever one of the world's most important cities.

I look forward to hearing from you about what makes a great hotel. In these pages you will see a definitive collection of exceptional establishments, but we all have our own idea of what makes one of the world's best hotels. Its a lofty definition, and for me is often a decision made within minutes of stepping into the lobby. For many, its the location, and in this regard there is no doubt that The Ritz-Carlton New York, Battery Park has been the preferred home of the international financial community whenever they visit New York.

Nigel Bolding, Publisher
nigel.bolding@theworldsbesthotels.com

Lanson Place exhibits a masterful blend of understated luxury and quality service.

He's a fan.

MANDARIN ORIENTAL
THE HOTEL GROUP

To find out why Dennis Hopper is a fan visit www.mandarinoriental.com BANGKOK • CHIANG MAI • GENEVA • HONG KONG • KUALA LUMPUR • LONDON • MACAU • MANILA • MIAMI • MUNICH • NEW YORK • PRAGUE
RIVIERA MAYA • SAN FRANCISCO • SINGAPORE • TOKYO • WASHINGTON D.C. • OPENING 2008: BEIJING • BOSTON • SANYA

Where luxury lives

New York glitters with thousands of electric lights as night falls over this international financial capital.

As the demands of business travel keep intensifying, so do the demands of business travellers. Today's high-level executives require seamless wireless connections, top-notch meeting facilities and instant limousine service. For pleasure or entertaining, they relish luxurious spa facilities, sumptuous dining and a knowledgeable concierge. The ideal package combines efficiency and luxury with the pampering of attentive and highly personalised service.

These days more hotels than ever seek to fill that bill. As they expand, luxe chains and boutiques are competing with established landmark properties to cater to the various needs of pressured but well-heeled executives. To stand out, hotels need to offer a certain *je ne sais quoi*— a distinction that may say as much about the fickleness of client tastes as it does about a particular establishment's amenities or style.

Institutional Investor's annual ranking of the World's Best Hotels features significant changes at the top, reflecting the fluid but exacting nature of the market. Our voters rate The Ritz-Carlton New York, Battery Park, at the southern tip of New York's Manhattan island, as their favourite hotel. The hotel, the first luxury accommodation to open in Wall Street's vicinity, is far from the established bastions on Park Avenue and Central Park South and has been open for less than six years. Indeed, it's of such recent vintage that it didn't even make the top 100 a year ago. But the hotel's combination of traditional comfort and service, modern facilities and a convenient location with stunning views of New York Harbor certainly appeals to discriminating travellers.

The top-rated hotels in Europe and Asia are also relative newcomers that offer time-honoured luxury with a modern twist. Berlin's Adlon Kempinski was erected a decade ago on the ruins of a cherished Weimar-era institution. Today it beats with the pulse of Germany's new-old capital. In Bangkok, The Sukhothai offers exquisite Thai service in a distinctively relaxed and private setting in the capital's financial district.

Scores of other hotels are also satisfying the needs and whims of travelling executives. To compile our ranking, *Institutional Investor* surveyed senior executives in the financial services industry, asking them to rate hotels they had visited recently on a scale of 1 to 100. The scores were averaged and ranked according to a formula that assigns greater weight to those panelists who are the most frequent travellers. And frequent they are: Our voters spent an average of 41.12 nights in hotels last year; the busiest road warrior logged a daunting 165 nights.

THE RITZ-CARLTON NEW YORK, BATTERY PARK

The West Side Highway empties into the Brooklyn Battery Tunnel 200 yards from The Ritz-Carlton New York, Battery Park's front door. But fumes and gridlock seem a universe away as you settle in for evening cocktails at the 14th-floor Rise Bar, where a Wall Street crowd works off the adrenaline of the trading day and, outside, the Statue of Liberty glows in the sunset and looks almost close enough to touch.

In the 1980s, artists and other urban homesteaders began to form a neighbourhood amid the loading docks and office buildings of Manhattan's southern tip. Tribeca's coming of age received a seal of approval in the mid-90s when The Ritz-Carlton and premises owner Millennium Partners broke ground on a new flagship hotel. The project got off to an inauspicious start, however, when terrorists destroyed the World Trade Center a half mile to the north on September 11, 2001, just two months before the hotel was due to open.

The opening was delayed until January 2002. Today the property stands unrivalled for the top-scale traveller who prefers hip downtown to the usual midtown lodging, or who wants to walk to the New York Stock Exchange. Then there is the view. Polshek Partnership, the New York architectural firm whose credits include the William J Clinton Presidential Library and Museum in Little Rock, Arkansas, and the restoration of Carnegie Hall, cleverly curved the hotel's building "to resemble a 1920s ocean liner", as hotel general manager Richard Evanich puts it.

The design assures that two thirds of the guests face the harbour, not the highway. The fitness centre and Prada-operated spa share the top-floor vista with the bar; US$200 buys a 75-minute Harmonising Wrap skin treatment—with the view of the Verrazano-Narrows Bridge thrown in for free.

With the new location comes a new aesthetic for the venerable luxury hotel operator. "This is not your father's or your grandfather's Ritz," proclaims Evanich's deputy, hotel manager David Chase. "Manhattan luxury has almost by definition been old and dark. We are new and light."

Mahogany wainscoting and crystal chandeliers are out at the Battery Park hotel. Instead, designer Frank Nicholson has gone for clean lines and sparse, art

Artwork in shades of rose and fuchsia brings a clean-lined modernism to The Ritz-Carlton New York, Battery Park.

The Ritz-Carlton New York, Battery Park is bringing new vitality and elegance into lower Manhattan.

deco–inspired spaces, accented by granite counters and subdued abstract paintings by New York artists.

Even in the US$7,500-a-night Ritz-Carlton Suite, the earth-toned sofas and armchairs are modern and functional rather than ornate and fussy. The point, the managers explain, is to appeal to the rising generation of business leaders who like their comforts to be direct and informal. "Business travellers are not as old as they used to be, whether from the emerging markets, Europe or America," Evanich says. "They want luxury where they feel comfortable coming down in jeans and having a steak."

Executive chef Jacques Sorci serves a menu of seafood and grilled meats in the restaurant, 2 West, where a roaming saucier offers a choice of 10 sauces, including truffle, red wine and peppercorn gravy. For a quicker, less formal meal, guests can hit the New York Hot Dog Cart, a posh version of the city's ubiquitous street-corner stand, replete with oversize pretzels and steaming pots of sauerkraut.

In keeping with modernity, the hotel allows clients to specify their preferences on its Web site, which managers use to provide staff with an individualised scouting report on who likes to be checked in without fussing at the front desk or who had a housekeeping dustup on their previous stay and needs to be fawned over immediately upon arrival.

Such dedication pays off in compliments lavished on the hotel on feedback sites such as Tripadvisor.com. One couple from New Jersey who splurged on a night in town to celebrate their 20th wedding anniversary were delightfully surprised to have the reception staff congratulate them on the occasion when they walked in.

Respondents to *Institutional Investor*'s survey suggest that the 21st-century Ritz is getting the mix right. So do the occupancy numbers. Evanich notes with satisfaction that his house was 98 per cent full on a typical Wednesday last month and has more than enough second honeymooners and other weekend visitors to keep overall rates north of 80 per cent.

Success is spawning the sincerest form of flattery: as many as 3,200 new hotel rooms are scheduled to open over the next few years in lower Manhattan. The added rooms will more than double the area's current total of 2,200, according to the Downtown Alliance civic group. The W chain is set to challenge The Ritz-Carlton in the luxury niche with a hotel-condo complex a few blocks north, scheduled to open late next year.

Evanich professes to be unconcerned. "The more competition down here, the more buzz around the whole area, and the better it is for everyone," he contends. In any case, there will

The Oberoi Udaivilas, Udaipur
Rated the best hotel in the world by *Travel + Leisure* in the 2007 Readers' Poll.

WELCOME TO THE WORLD'S BEST

Oberoi Hotels & Resorts welcome you to the finest experiences at some of the best hotels in the world.

Travel + Leisure, USA, World's Best Awards, Readers' Poll 2007

1. **The Oberoi Udaivilas, Udaipur, India**
2. Singita Sabi Sand/Kruger National Park, South Africa
3. The Oriental, Bangkok
4. Four Seasons Hotel Istanbul at Sultanahmet, Turkey
5. The Milestone, London
6. Relais Il Falconiere, Cortona, Italy
7. Sabi Sabi Private Game Reserve, Sabi Sands, South Africa
8. Mandarin Oriental, Munich
9. Four Seasons Resort Hualalai, Hawaii
10. **The Oberoi Amarvilas, Agra, India**
11. **The Oberoi Rajvilas, Jaipur, India**
12. The Peninsula, Bangkok
13. Château Les Crayères, Reims, France
14. Jumby Bay, a Rosewood Resort, Antigua
15. Four Seasons Hotel Gresham Palace, Budapest

Condé Nast Traveler, USA, Readers' Choice Awards 2007

1. La Scalinatella, Capri
2. **The Oberoi Udaivilas, Udaipur, India**
3. **The Oberoi Vanyavilas, Ranthambhore, India**
4. The Peninsula, Hong Kong
5. Burj Al Arab, Dubai
6. **The Oberoi Amarvilas, Agra, India**
7. Four Seasons George V, Paris
8. Banyan Tree, Phuket
8. Table Bay Hotel, Cape Town
10. Four Seasons Gresham Palace, Budapest
10. Mombo and Little Mombo Camps, Botswana
10. Ritz Carlton, Berlin
13. Il San Pietro di Positano
14. Four Seasons Bali at Sayan
15. Four Seasons Maui at Wailea
15. Khwai River Lodge, Botswana

Oberoi Hotels & Resorts

Information and toll free reservations: USA 1 800 562 3764, UK 00 800 1234 0101, UAE 800 065 0551, Singapore 800 189 1009
E-mail: reservations@oberoigroup.com or visit us at: www.oberoihotels.com

Tranquillity pervades The Sukhothai's
open spaces, accented by stone features
reminiscent of Buddhist stupas.

likely be no match for The Ritz-Carlton's place at the foot of West Street with its unobstructed views in three directions—a virtual corner office for the whole of New York.

THE SUKHOTHAI, BANGKOK

Founded in the 13th century as the very first independent Thai kingdom, Sukhothai— whose name means "dawn of happiness"— was a centre of learning, commerce and culture. History has it that King Ramkamhaeng erected a bell at one of the capital's gates so that even a commoner could summon him for help. In modern Thailand the kingdom of Sukhothai is viewed as a golden age—a Thai ideal.

In the realm of the hospitality industry, general manager George Benney and the staff of The Sukhothai Bangkok are striving to create a similar ideal. Since its establishment 15 years ago, the 210-room Sukhothai has established a reputation as one of the finest hotels in a metropolis that boasts some of the world's best. This year the Sukhothai ranks as the top hotel in Asia in *Institutional Investor*'s annual survey. "Being number one is dangerous," says Benney, a 30-year industry veteran. "The last thing we want is complacency. You can't stop trying to be better."

For design, ambience, location and service, it's hard to do better than the Sukhothai. Its lobby and gardens are decorated with red-

Materials such as traditional fabrics, teak and rosewood convey a subtle atmosphere of Thai heritage underscored with luxury.

brick stupas, stone friezes depicting images from Buddhist mythological epics, and iridescent silks that conjure the hotel's namesake kingdom. Its stylishly appointed rooms blend traditional style with high-tech modernism. The furnishings have clean lines and make liberal use of Thai fabrics, teak and rosewood; vases and decorative plates in the pale green ceramic known as celadon adorn the rooms. Flat-screen televisions hook into sound systems outfitted with iPod ports. Even the hotel's new fleet of Mercedes S-class limousines has iPod-friendly sound systems. Wireless Internet access is available throughout the grounds.

In a city known for sumptuous dining, the hotel's Thai restaurant, named Celadon after the ceramic, is consistently rated as one of

Warm, rich colours highlight the faultless hospitality at The Sukhothai.

the most splendid. The extravagant delicacies on offer at the buffet in the Sukhothai's Colonnade restaurant—from omelettes and pastries to curries and seafood—make it the capital's prime destination for Sunday brunch. And the recently opened Spa Botanica is an oasis—a garden spa with outdoor pools and walkways that offers a full range of pampering from aromatherapy and East/West massage to herbal baths and facials.

Situated on Sathorn Road and surrounded by many leading financial firms, The Sukhothai is a favorite for executives from the likes of Goldman, Sachs & Co, JP Morgan Chase & Co, Pricewaterhouse-Coopers and other such top firms. Benney says guests really appreciate the residential feel of the low-rise hotel. Its rambling villas and four- and five-story wings afford the kind of privacy that allows guests to "just chill", in Benney's words—as France's Zinedine Zidane did following the frenzy of the 2006 World Cup—or rival corporations to hold meetings without worrying about what their competitors are up to. Many a hotel company would have been tempted to maximise the property by throwing up a 30-storey building, but such a structure would stand very little chance of drawing the elite clientele that repeatedly chooses The Sukhothai: an astounding 43 per cent of its guests are return customers.

Personal attention is also a major part of what sets The Sukhothai apart. "Service is an individual thing—doing the little things with love," Benney says. "If a guest eats only the mango on the fruit platter we send up, you can be sure the next one we send will be heavy with the best mangoes we can find." The hotel has recently upgraded its extensive computer system, giving its staff more space to record the various likes, dislikes and tiniest preferences of each guest, and also to include photographs so staff can address guests by name on sight.

This personalised approach even extends to the range of business services available at The Sukhothai as well. The hotel's facilities include a 240-seat ballroom and more than a dozen tastefully appointed meeting and conference rooms, including four Garden Villa meeting rooms surrounding a courtyard brimming with orchids, bamboo and palms.

With such lavish settings and service, Benney is determined to make the Sukhothai a new Thai ideal.

ADLON KEMPINSKI, BERLIN

History looms large at the Adlon. Even to this very day, nearly two decades after the Berlin Wall came down, Mikhail Gorbachev still gets a standing ovation whenever he strolls into the hotel's plush lobby.

IN OVER 53 DESTINATIONS, 12 COUNTRIES, 5 CONTINENTS, 77 HOTELS, 7 AUTHENTIC PALACES, 6 PRIVATE ISLANDS,

12 RESORTS AND SPAS, 3 PERSONAL JETS AND 2 LUXURY YACHTS, YOU'LL FIND A HOTEL CHAIN THAT IS

UNCHAINED BY CONVENTION, UNBOUND BY THE USUAL AND UNHINDERED BY ROUTINE.

TAJ NO ROOM FOR THE ORDINARY

Hotels Resorts
and Palaces

The Adlon Kempinski Berlin cuts a dramatic silhouette in the evening light.

More than a Berlin landmark, the Adlon is a constant reminder of Germany's painful past and the enormous promise of its rebirth after the fall of the Wall, which used to stand just a stone's throw from the lobby.

General manager Stephen Interthal knows full well that it is this historical aura that distinguishes the Adlon from the 224 other five-star hotels in Germany. He points toward the bustling crowds on Pariser Platz, the public square that separates the hotel from the Brandenburg Gate. "There were land mines out there," he says, his English tinged with a slight British accent. "Sometimes you have to take a moment to think about what kind of historical responsibility we have managing this hotel on this location."

Similar thoughts may have crossed the minds of the US presidents and Middle Eastern sheikhs who have peered out of the bulletproof windows of the Presidential Suite toward the floodlit gate.

Lorenz Adlon, a successful Berlin wine merchant, could never have foreseen the dramatic historical events that would play out here when he had the hotel first built back in 1907. Protocol obliged him to step aside and allow Kaiser Wilhelm II, the last German Emperor, be the first person to enter the new hotel building. This year the hotel celebrates its centennial, and the lobby is lined with photographs of illustrious past guests, including Marlene Dietrich, Charlie Chaplin, Herbert Hoover, Enrico Caruso, George Bush—both father and son—Vladimir Putin and Michael Jackson.

The old Adlon was a celebrated meeting place for the Weimar-era rich and famous. Journalists would hang out there because of the hotel's proximity to the British Embassy, next door, and the Reichstag, a 10-minute walk away. The hotel burned down just days before the Germans surrendered on May 8, 1945. Local lore has it that Red Army troops, while looting the wine cellar, set the hotel ablaze as they left. When East Germany erected the Berlin Wall in 1961, the ruins of the hotel wound up on the wrong side of history. For a brief period, East Berlin used one remaining wing of the hotel as a hostel. But in 1984 the last walls of the original hotel were razed, leaving an empty lot.

"When I came here in 1992, there was nothing," says Interthal.

The new hotel, a marriage of modern efficiency and old-world elegance, opened in 1997. The façade, a six-story yellow limestone exterior with a squat green roof, is a replica of the original. Some interior features have been designed from photographs of items in the old Adlon, such as an Indian sculpture with elephants and what appears to be a climbing lotus, the centerpiece of a lobby fountain. Other fixtures, such as the art deco–inspired lamps hanging from the hallway ceilings, merely seek to evoke an earlier style.

The spirit of the old Adlon has been revived as well in the latter day. Journalists, politicians and high-flying diplomats all meet in the spacious lobby, which with its marble floors, broad Oriental carpets and leather sofas and chairs is once again a favoured gathering place for Berlin society. The hotel is situated at the very crossroads of a vibrant and unified modern capital, just a few steps away from the British and French embassies and the brand new US embassy which is currently under construction on Pariser Platz, and less than a brisk 10-minute walk from the rebuilt Reichstag.

The hotel is one of the preferred lodgings for American executives who want to stay where the president stays, says Fred Irwin, head of Citibank in Germany and chairman of the country's branch of the American Chamber of Commerce. The Lorenz Adlon restaurant, which under chef Thomas Neeser has earned a prestigious one-star rating from Michelin, offers such delicacies as caneton à la presse Lorenz Adlon, or duck in blood sauce with truffles. The exclusive restaurant, which seats only about 30 people, is in the Library room overlooking the Brandenburg Gate.

Notwithstanding the resurrection of some of the original hotel's features, there is a distinctly modern feel to the Adlon today, especially when entering the rear of the hotel, where there are sleek meeting rooms for business gatherings and two ballrooms with the capacity for as many as 400 guests.

The residential wings boast 304 rooms, 75 suites and junior suites and no less than three presidential suites. The latter are aptly named, with each one offering 240 sq m (2,600 sq ft) of space, which includes two bedrooms, dining and living rooms, a sauna, an office complete with Internet access and fax, four flat-screen TVs and butler service. One of the three, the Security Suite, can have its entire floor sealed off, which raises the price to €20,000 a night. "You tell us what you want, and you'll get it," says Anne Martinussen, the Adlon's director of sales. Butler and limousine service is available to all guests, on request, as are the hotel's six private dining rooms, sauna, indoor pool and fitness room. Massages and cosmetic treatments can be ordered in-room.

The typical hotel guest, says Interthal, is a wealthy traveller who comes to enjoy Berlin's new energy and international flair. "Berlin was not on the map for many years," he says. "When you come here, we offer a great atmosphere, a certain elegance and European hotel tradition."

The Adlon Kempinski Berlin is a hotel alive with history, with the landmark Brandenburg Gate aglow in the distance.

Top 100 hotels

Rank 2007	Hotel	City	Score 2006
1	The Ritz-Carlton New York, Battery Park	New York	95.9
2	Four Seasons Hotel	San Francisco	95.4
3	Hotel Adlon Kempinski	Berlin	93.8
4	Four Seasons Hotel	Hong Kong	93.5
5	Four Seasons Hotel	New York	93.2
6	Çırağan Palace Kempinski	Istanbul	93
7	Baur au Lac	Zurich	92.9
8	The Sukhothai	Bangkok	92.8
9	Hotel Arts	Barcelona	92.4
10	Hôtel Le Bristol	Paris	92.3
11	The Ritz-Carlton (Four Seasons)	Chicago	92.2
12	Hotel Bel-Air	Los Angeles	92.1
13	Four Seasons Hotel	Bangkok	91.5
14	The Landmark Mandarin Oriental	Hong Kong	91.5
15	Four Seasons Hotel	Washington, DC	91.3
16	Peninsula	Bangkok	91.1
17	Alvear Palace	Buenos Aires	91
17	Phoenician	Phoenix	91
19*	Peninsula	Chicago	90.9
20*	Claridge's	London	90.9
21	Four Seasons Hotel George V	Paris	90.2
22	Taj Boston**	Boston	90
23*	Four Seasons Hotel	Boston	89.8
24*	Kämp	Helsinki	89.8
25	Four Seasons Hotel	Los Angeles	89.6
26	Mandarin Oriental	Hong Kong	89.2
27	Mandarin Oriental	New York	89
28	Four Seasons Hotel	Istanbul	88.8
29*	Park Hyatt	Chicago	88.6
30*	The Ritz-Carlton	Hong Kong	88.6
31*	Mandarin Oriental	San Francisco	88.5
32*	Park Hyatt Paris–Vendôme	Paris	88.5

The Four Seasons Hotel New York exudes quiet glamour.

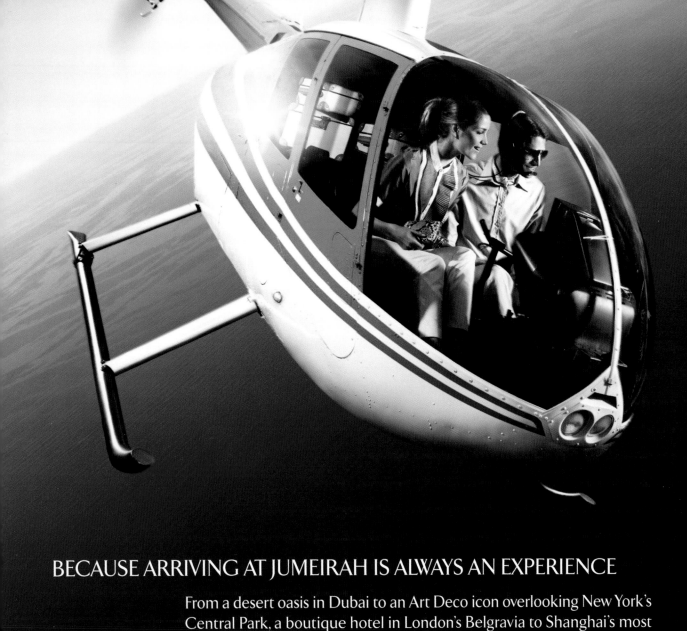

BECAUSE ARRIVING AT JUMEIRAH IS ALWAYS AN EXPERIENCE

From a desert oasis in Dubai to an Art Deco icon overlooking New York's Central Park, a boutique hotel in London's Belgravia to Shanghai's most anticipated new opening in Xintiandi. And if you want to arrive at the Burj Al Arab – the world's most luxurious hotel – in your own style, we'll prepare the helipad. STAY DIFFERENT™

jumeirah.com

DUBAI LONDON NEW YORK SHANGHAI OPENING 2008

Rank	Hotel	City	Score
68*	Mandarin Oriental	Washington, DC	84.7
69*	Conrad	Brussels	84.7
70	Jumeirah Beach Hotel	Dubai	84.5
71	Grand Hyatt	Beijing	84.1
72	Mandarin Oriental Hyde Park	London	83.9
73	The Ritz-Carlton, Marina Del Rey	Los Angeles	83.8
74	Makati Shangri-La	Manila	83.3
75	Conrad	Hong Kong	83
76	The Ritz-Carlton	Atlanta	82.8
77	The Berkeley	London	82.7
78	Grand Hyatt	Dubai	82.3
79	The Dorchester	London	82.2
80	The Westin Chosun	Seoul	82
81	The New York Palace Hotel	New York	81.9
82	Beverly Wilshire (Four Seasons) (formerly Regent Beverly Wilshire)	Los Angeles	81.7
83	The Taj Mahal Palace and Tower	Mumbai	81.6
84	Arizona Biltmore	Phoenix	81.4
85	Grand Hôtel	Stockholm	81.1
86	The Pierre	New York	81
87	Dukes	London	80.9
88	Grand Hyatt	Seoul	80.7
89	Grand Hyatt	Mumbai	80.5
90	Boston Harbor	Boston	80
91	InterContinental Amstel	Amsterdam	80
92	Marriott Royal Aurora	Moscow	80
93	Hilton Paddington	London	79.5
94	D'Angleterre	Copenhagen	79.3
95	Steigenberger Frankfurter Hof	Frankfurt	79.1
96	Four Seasons	London	78.7
97	The Imperial	Tokyo	78.4
98	The Fairmont	San Francisco	78.1
99	New Otani	Tokyo	76.3
100	Sheraton	Kuwait	75.3

* Order determined by actual scores before rounding.

** Formerly *The Ritz-Carlton, Boston*

A scarlet-and-gold colour scheme creates a striking effect in this suite at Steigenberger Frankfurter Hof.

The imposing façade of The Hay-Adams is appropriate to a hotel of its reputation.

Rank	Hotel	City	Score
33	Four Seasons Hotel	Dublin	88.3
34*	The Shangri-La	Singapore	88.2
35	Beverly Hills	Los Angeles	88.2
36	Island Shangri-La	Hong Kong	88.2
37	Raffles Hotel	Singapore	88.1
38	Four Seasons Hotel	Atlanta	87.9
39	Mandarin Oriental	Singapore	87.8
40	The Oriental	Bangkok	87.7
41*	Bellagio	Las Vegas	87.6
42*	Grand Hyatt	Hong Kong	87.6
43	Ararat Park Hyatt	Moscow	87.5
44	Four Seasons Hotel	Chicago	87.5
45	Millenium Hilton	New York	87.4
46*	Grand Hyatt	Tokyo	87.3
47*	Four Seasons Hotel	Miami	87.3
48*	Four Seasons Hotel Chinzan-So	Tokyo	87.2
49*	The Hay-Adams	Washington, DC	87.2
50*	The Oberoi Mumbai	Mumbai	87.1
51*	The Ritz-Carlton, Millenia Singapore	Singapore	87.1
52*	Le Meurice	Paris	87
53*	Peninsula	New York	87
54*	The Shilla	Seoul	86.9
55*	Willard InterContinental	Washington, DC	86.9
56	Peninsula	Hong Kong	86.8
57	InterContinental Le Grand	Paris	86.6
58	The Fullerton Hotel	Singapore	86.5
59*	Jumeirah Emirates Towers	Dubai	86.4
60*	Savoy	London	86.4
61	The Ritz-Carlton, Central Park	New York	86.1
62	The Ritz-Carlton	San Francisco	85.9
63	Shutters on the Beach	Los Angeles	85.5
64	The Ritz-Carlton, Boston Common	Boston	85.4
65	The Ritz	London	85.3
66	Okura	Tokyo	84.9
67	The St Regis	New York	84.8

Wrought-iron balustrades create a strong counterpoint to the cream carpet and white marble.

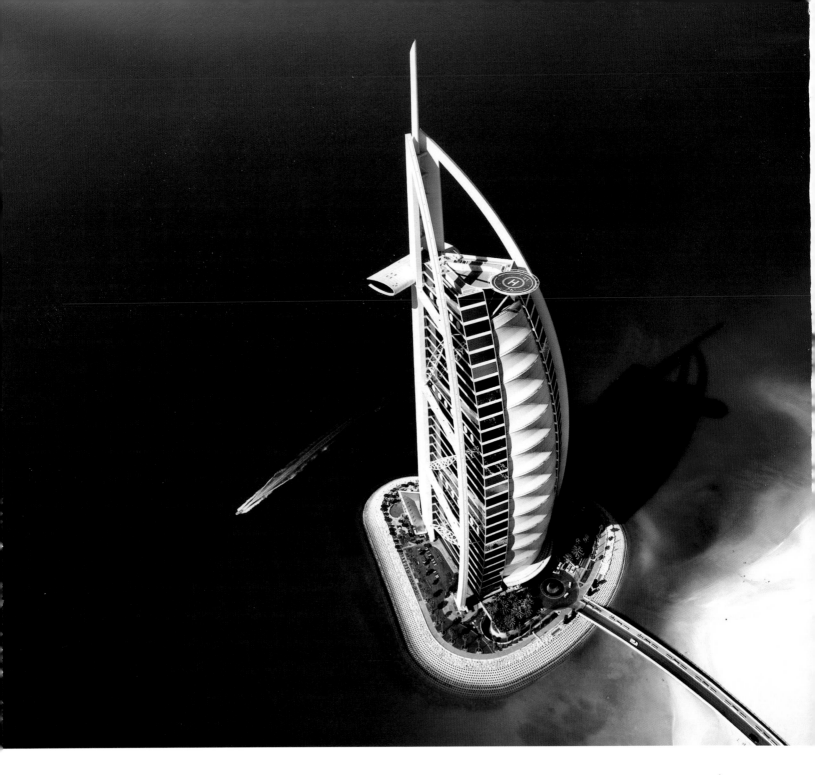

Top 5 hotels by region

2008	Hotel	City
THE TOP FIVE: THE AMERICAS		
1	The Ritz-Carlton, Battery Park	New York
2	Four Seasons Hotel	San Francisco
3	Four Seasons Hotel	New York
4	The Ritz-Carlton (Four Seasons)	Chicago
5	Hotel Bel-Air	Los Angeles
THE TOP FIVE: ASIA		
1	Four Seasons Hotel	Hong Kong
2	The Sukhothai	Bangkok
3	Four Seasons Hotel	Bangkok
4	The Landmark Mandarin Oriental	Hong Kong
5	Peninsula	Bangkok
THE TOP FIVE: EUROPE		
1	Hotel Adlon Kempinski	Berlin
2	Çırağan Palace Kempinski	Istanbul
3	Baur au Lac	Zürich
4	Arts	Barcelona
5	Le Bristol	Paris

The mark of a world's best hotel is its enduring presence in the minds of people, and in this respect the majestic InterContinental Amstel Amsterdam succeeds brilliantly.

Luxury doesn't always have to be fussy or complicated, as shown by this exquisite dish from Mandarin Oriental, Hong Kong's Man Wah.

Best hotels by city

WHERE TO STAY IN 60 CITIES AROUND THE WORLD

BEST HOTELS BY CITY 2008

AMERICAS

Atlanta*: Four Seasons
Boston*: Taj Boston**
Buenos Aires*: Alvear Palace
Chicago*: Ritz-Carlton (Four Seasons)
Dallas: Rosewood Mansion on
   Turtle Creek
Honolulu: Halekulani
Las Vegas*: Bellagio
Los Angeles*: Hotel Bel-Air
Mexico City: Four Seasons
Miami*: Four Seasons
New York*: The Ritz-Carlton, Battery Park
Philadelphia: Four Seasons
Phoenix*: Phoenician
Rio de Janeiro: Copacabana Palace
San Francisco*: Four Seasons
Seattle: Grand Hyatt
Toronto: Four Seasons
Vancouver: Pan Pacific
Washington, DC*: Four Seasons

ASIA

Bangkok*: The Sukhothai
Beijing*: Grand Hyatt

Hanoi: Sofitel Metropole
Hong Kong*: Four Seasons
Kuala Lumpur: Mandarin Oriental
Manila*: Makati Shangri-La
Melbourne: Grand Hyatt
Mumbai*: Oberoi Mumbai
New Delhi: Oberoi
Osaka: Ritz-Carlton
Seoul*: The Shilla
Shanghai: Portman Ritz-Carlton
Singapore*: The Shangri-La Hotel
Sydney: Four Seasons
Taipei: Grand Hyatt
Tokyo*: Grand Hyatt

EUROPE

Amsterdam*: InterContinental Amstel
Barcelona*: Arts
Berlin*: Adlon Kempinski
Brussels*: Conrad
Copenhagen*: D'Angleterre
Dublin*: Four Seasons
Dusseldorf: Steigenberger Parkhotel
Frankfurt*: Steigenberger
   Frankfurter Hof

Geneva: Mandarin Oriental
Helsinki*: Kämp
Istanbul*: Çırağan Palace Kempinski
London*: Claridge's
Luxembourg: Royal
Milan: Four Seasons
Moscow*: Ararat Park Hyatt
Munich: Bayerischer Hof
Oslo: Grand
Paris*: Le Bristol
Prague: Four Seasons
Stockholm*: Grand Hôtel
Vienna: Imperial
Zurich*: Baur au Lac

MIDDLE EAST/AFRICA

Abu Dhabi: Emirates Palace
Cairo: Four Seasons Cairo at Nile Plaza
Cape Town: Mount Nelson
Dubai*: Jumeirah Emirates Towers
   (formerly Emirates Towers)
Kuwait*: Sheraton
Muscat: Al Bustan Palace
   InterContinental
Riyadh: Four Seasons

*Also appeared in November's World's Best Hotels survey.
** Formerly *The Ritz-Carlton, Boston*

A buffet spread awaits guests in the morning at Four Seasons Hotel, Hong Kong.

thechiccollection

The Seychelles epitomise the very
concept of an island escape—
scenic and ineffably relaxing.

A year of great escapes

It's one of those immutable laws of travel. Every great destination has a great hotel. The best offer the essence of a place, gift-wrapped and just waiting to be opened. In spite of globalisation creating a 'McTravel' experience, sophisticated travellers increasingly opt for the unique and original. If you've ever dreamt about taking a year off to explore the world's best destinations, make sure the hotels you choose fit right in. Embark on a great escape, and indulge in a year of life-enriching journeys.

Brazil

Start the New Year off in style with the ultimate party on the beach in Rio de Janeiro, Brazil. Although Rio is justly famed for its riotous Carnival each year, it can be too crowded and chaotic for a relaxed visit. The New Year's celebration, called Reveillon, is less touristy. On December 31, over a million Cariocas, (as Rio's lively locals are called) throng Copacabana Beach for fireworks at midnight, white-clad and bearing offerings to lemanja, goddess of the sea. Bands play on the beach till dawn, and all Rio comes together.

Stay at the heart of the action, in the Copacabana Palace Hotel. Since it opened in 1923, it has reigned supreme at the epicentre of Rio's social life. Its VIP guestbook reads like a cross between *Debrett's* and *Hello!*. The Copa, as it is known, rises above the centre of Copacabana Beach in aristocratic white splendour. Just stroll across the street and you are on the sand.

The famed Copacabana Beach Hotel overlooks the equally legendary waterfront.

Seychelles

After all that late night partying, head for a restorative retreat in the secluded, seductive Seychelles. Even the most jaded island-hopper will be charmed by this laid-back archipelago cradled jewel-like in the warm waters of the Indian Ocean, with its spectacular scenery, lush tropical eco-system, unspoilt beaches, and an exotic blend of French, Indian and African cultures.

In February the colourful Hindu Kavadi Festival is celebrated at the beautiful temple in Victoria, capital of the main island, Mahé. Music, dancing, and the Seychellois joie de vivre make this one of the most popular festivals on the island. A 25-minute scenic drive from Victoria to the crescent-moon beach at Anse Louis brings you to Maia, a fabulous new resort tucked away in peace and privacy.

Maia is so beautifully designed, inside and out, that it feels as if it has always been part of the scene. It is an exquisitely crafted masterpiece of understated Seychelles elegance, with only 30 exceptional villas, each with sweeping views of the surrounding ocean, a private walled garden and a private infinity-edge pool perfect for moonlit dips. Service at the resort reflects the genuine warmth and hospitality of the Seychelles. Maia's La Prairie Spa is a serene retreat comprising outdoor pavilions set in a private garden. You can relax or enjoy water sports and sightseeing, as well as take in morning sessions of yoga and *qi gong*.

Indulge in an unlikely spa location—the desert wellness resort of Al Maha awaits.

Dubai

From the Seychelles it's a quick hop across the Indian Ocean to all the excitement of Dubai on the Arabian Gulf. March is the height of the sporting and social season, with glitterati jetting in for the Polo, the PGA Dubai Desert Classic, the Dubai Tennis Championships and the world's richest horse race, the Dubai World Cup. All year round, there are fashion shows, art exhibitions and gallery openings. Nightlife is booming, with places such as Madinat Jumeirah and Bastakiya attracting Dubai's affluent international set.

For an escape into the breathtaking desert dunes, stay at Al Maha, a luxurious eco-resort, where you can relax in your own private tented villa with every comfort, including your own private pool, while seeing the desert in all its timeless beauty. Gazelles, Oryx, camels and falcons are all part of the scene. Dedicated guides take guests on a variety of safaris, from horse riding at dawn to desert camel rides and champagne at sunset.

Thailand

In April, the lush green hills of Chiang Mai, Northern Thailand provide a complete contrast to Dubai's desert. The Mandarin Oriental Dhara Dhevi captures the spirit of this ancient city, once the heart of the Lanna Kingdom that ruled for centuries. The 24-hectare (60-acre) resort is an architectural gem, a sensitive recreation of a Thai walled village, with a backdrop of misty mountains and verdant rice paddies. You can visit 14th-century temples, shop for exquisite Thai crafts and textiles at the famous night markets, go for upcountry elephant safaris or just

Mandarin Oriental Dhara Dhevi is a fitting palatial resort in the ancient Siamese capital.

relax at the resort's breathtaking spa. You'll also find a Thai cooking school and great children's activities. At night there are dance and drama entertainments, revealing Thai culture at its most refined.

South Africa

If seeing the elephants in Thailand is inspiring, imagine a safari in Africa. In the heart of Big Five country, in the famed Kruger National Park, lies Royal Malewane, one of South Africa's most exclusive safari camps. Visit in May, when vegetation is sparse, providing better opportunity for spotting game. Temperatures during the day are high, but the star-filled nights are pleasantly cool.

With only 16 guests at maximum, Royal Malewane provides exceptional levels of privacy, pampering and personal service. The elegant, freestanding suites are a far cry from roughing it in the bush, with antiques, fine linens, fireplaces, plunge pools, and plenty of space. Each suite has a game-viewing deck, all the better to watch monkeys scampering up trees as you enjoy a pot of tea with freshly baked scones. There's a spa, a gym, library and gourmet dining. Expert rangers and trackers escort guests on game drives or on foot. The reserve has over 250 species of birds as well as lions, leopards, elephants and rhinos—to name a few of the many species making this one of Africa's most exciting safari destinations.

England

If the colonial British style of Royal Malewane has you feeling sentimental about England, visit in June. This is England's quintessential month. The countryside is

Nothing quite describes the magnificence of a South African sunset—just sit back and enjoy.

bursting with blossom, the strawberries have ripened in time for Royal Ascot, village greens echo to the thwack of cricket balls, and the evenings stay golden and warm until late. One of the most beautiful places to be in June is in Devon. With its thatched cottages covered in roses, winding lanes flanked by tall hedges, and the dramatic setting of Dartmoor abloom with yellow gorse, Devon is England at its most bucolic.

Gidleigh Park sets new standards in the tradition of British country house hotels. This historic property of just 24 rooms is nestled amongst acres of magnificent gardens and woodland by the River Teign in Dartmoor

National Park. The hotel's Restaurant has earned two Michelin stars, there's an 18-hole putting course, and a tennis court. The gardens provide an ideal setting for guided walks across the moor and through local villages. Gidleigh Park is redolent of 1920s aristocratic Britain, when leisure was a way of life.

Los Angeles

In July the beach beckons, with thoughts of white sand, blue waters, surfers riding the waves, and bikini-clad beauties. Malibu, in Los Angeles, California, is one of the great beaches for summer fun. Celebrate the 4th of July in true American style and stay at the Hotel Bel-Air. The hotel has its annual July 4th celebration barbecue, and among the many summer activities the Concierge staff will arrange are picnic concerts at the Hollywood Bowl, guided tours of the Getty Museum, a VIP day at Universal Studios or even a baseball game at Dodger Stadium.

The Bel-Air is in a class of its own, and has been one of *Institutional Investor*'s Top 25 Hotels in the World for more than 25 years. Impeccable service, a keen eye for details, luxury without ostentation, and the genuine desire to please—all these qualities make a visit to the Bel-Air something special. Its bungalows have hosted legends from Grace Kelly to Marilyn Monroe. The setting is considered the prettiest in LA, with a lake of swans and rambling gardens. Guests may run into Lauren Bacall walking her dog, Oprah Winfrey popping in for lunch, or Tom Cruise at the bar.

Hotel Bel-Air, Los Angeles exemplifies the glamour and luxury of the Californian city.

Italy

August, the most mellow of the summer months, is perfect for lazing in an idyllic spot perched high above the sea in the breathtaking village of Ravello, on Italy's Amalfi Coast. In the summer, Ravello plays host to a series of world-class music festivals. At these open air performances, enjoy a *passeggiata*—a gentle wander round at sunset—before a concert under the stars.

Stay at the Caruso Belvedere Hotel, which over the years has captivated the likes of Greta Garbo, Jackie Kennedy, Humphrey Bogart, and Peter O'Toole. The Caruso Belvedere also served as a favourite haunt of the Bloomsbury Group, with Virginia Woolf and Lord Keynes holding court in the garden.

The hotel was originally the property of a noble Englishman, Lord Bercket, who lavished his fortune on the gardens and villa. It recently had a multi-million-dollar makeover, and retains all its historic Italian charm but with every modern amenity.

France

Savour the last warm days of the season with a scenic drive across Italy to France and arrive in Champagne just in time for the grape harvest. The vines are heavy-laden with grapes glistening in the sun, as workers labour among the rows of vines in a tradition going back centuries. The heart of Champagne is the town of Reims. For close upon a thousand years the French monarchy was crowned in its magnificent cathedral.

Château Les Crayères is the former manor house of the aristocratic Polignac family, legendary for their Pommery Champagne. It is now an elegant Relais & Chateaux hotel, set in a 7-hectare (17-acre) park. On a large sunny terrace, guests can dine on the Michelin-starred gourmet cuisine and delight in a wine list that boasts more than 300 champagnes. For more than a century, Château Les Crayères has been at the hub of society life in Reims.

The hotel interiors, by the great Parisian designer Pierre-Yves Rochon are exquisite. Fine art, antiques, gilt mirrors, flowers and sumptuous fabrics reveal that flair for *calme, luxe et volupte* that is the essence of French style. If you can bear to leave the comforts of the hotel, enjoy a leisurely drive along the 'Routes du Champagne' that wind around the vineyards and

Italy's Amalfi coast is breathtakingly beautiful, with the impossible blues of the Mediterranean seas and skies.

Château Les Crayères is the former manor house of the aristocratic Polignac family, carrying with it generations of French nobility and elegance in Champagne.

Exquisite landscaped gardens with meticulously pruned greenery are a treat for the eyes.

hamlets of the region. The nearby town of Eperney is home to Moët & Chandon and is well worth a visit. Champagne is very much gourmet country, and visitors can indulge in mouthwatering foie gras, pungent cheese, fluffy soufflés, freshly baked breads, and good wine, even at the most basic brasserie.

India

With October's crisp arrival, India beckons. Autumn is an ideal time to visit this kaleidoscopic country. It's not yet high season and the weather is warm and sunny. Best of all you can experience Diwali, the Hindu festival of light usually held in October. At this traditional New Year, India is lit by millions of candles.

Nothing symbolises India like her most eloquent monument, the Taj Mahal. It was built by the Moghul Emperor and patron of the arts, Shah Jehan, in 1648,

as a memorial for his favourite wife, Mumtaz, who died giving birth to his 14th child. Court chronicles of the time reveal Shah Jehan's inconsolable grief when she passed away. The Taj Mahal in the ancient Moghul capital of Agra is just a few hours' drive away from the dynamism of New Delhi. In Agra you'll find the Oberoi Amarvilas, a stunning resort complex that perfectly complements the spirit of the Taj.

It is spread over 3.6 hectares (9 acres) of elaborate gardens, terraced lawns, fountains, reflection pools and pavilions, Rated the 10th best hotel in the world by the readers of *Travel & Leisure* magazine, the resort has earned many top awards since its grand opening in 2001. The spectacular Koh I Noor suite is very often ranked as one of the world's best. The hotel is only 600 m (2,000 ft) from the Taj Mahal and guests have Taj views from their rooms as well as throughout the hotel. Like the Taj itself, the Oberoi Amarvilas is a celebration of Indian craftsmanship. Drawing on the heritage and expertise of a wide range of master artisans, the hotel's interiors, with their intricate filigree and marble inlay work, hand-carved marble jaali screens, gold thread and bead embroidery, and hand-woven tapestries, showcase the rich artistic tradition of the region.

During Diwali, the resort becomes a fairytale palace, as thousands of tiny clay lamps are lit, music flows from the pavilions and bedrooms are adorned with flower petals and gifts of Indian sweets. In the distance, the illuminated Taj Mahal casts its radiant glow over the festivities.

New Zealand

Far from India's fabled palaces, in November New Zealand's summer is just getting into full swing. Yachts dot the coastline like white confetti, mountains rise majestically from the sea, miles of white beaches stretch into the hazy distance, and golden fields of farmland lie in sleepy contentment. New Zealand is delightfully removed from the modern world. Sheep still outnumber people by a large majority, and the pace is set by Nature rather than BlackBerry.

Huka Lodge is located on North Island, surrounded by magnificent natural beauty. The crystalline waters of nearby Lake Taupo are fed by mountain streams and are home to some of the most prized rainbow trout in the world. The spectacular cascades of water forming the Huka Falls are just a short stroll from the Lodge, along the banks of the Waikato River. Considered one of the world's top retreats, Huka Lodge attracts a fascinating mix of guests, from Pink Floyd to Queen Elizabeth II. You'll find captains of industry such as Bill Gates swapping fishing stories with the likes of actor Michael Douglas. The best way to arrive is by direct helicopter, just over an hour's flight from Auckland or Wellington across awesome landscapes right out of The Lord of The Rings film trilogy.

The Lodge began as a fishing retreat in the 1920s, and in the 22 years since it became New Zealand's very first luxury lodge, it has acquired a mellow patina that is part of its charm. Traditional yet far from stuffy, Huka Lodge reflects the best of New Zealand. It blends beautifully into its pristine environment, and gives its

guests a chance to explore all the pleasures of its special location: fly-fishing, boat trips, white water rafting, picnics, treks, heli-tours, kayaking, riding, tennis, golf, and more. Each of Huka Lodge's 20 guestrooms is set in its own garden, with doors opening out to views of the swiftly flowing river and ducks waddling past on their way to bathe. The bedrooms have an English country house feel, with tartan throws, landscape pictures, and fine furniture. There is also a secluded four-bedroom Owner's Cottage, ideal for friends or family travelling together who want their own space.

After cocktails by the fire in the Main Lodge, you can choose where to dine—perhaps a candlelit supper by the river? The five-course set menu shows off New

Huka Lodge is a showcase of New Zealand at its stylish best.

Snowy slopes beckon in December—enjoy a meal of freshly baked bread and good red wine before heading out to the ski runs.

generations of the Pfefferkorn family take pleasure in looking after their guests who come puffing in after a day's skiing, red cheeked and exhilarated. Many of the Goldener Berg's guests return year after year and there is a warm and friendly feel to the place. The award-winning cuisine features Austrian specialities such as Wienershnitzel and freshly baked Apple Strudel. The handsome wood-panelled restaurant dates from the 1500s. The family have been collecting fine wine for the last 50 years and the result is a wine cellar with an impressive treasure trove of vintages. For those post-piste aching muscles, there is a large and innovative spa with a swimming pool, an outdoor hot tub, steam room, sauna, massage and authentic Austrian beauty treatments such as the Edelweiss Wrap.

Off the slopes, there are lots of holiday happenings. Lech is a traditional Austrian ski resort, happily free from pretension. It has a lively après ski scene, good shopping, and lots of things to do, such as riding in a horse-drawn sleigh, night tobogganing, ice-skating, or snowshoe trekking. There are Christmas fairs, markets, concerts and festive events throughout the holidays. Goldener Berg has a brilliant kids programme with indoor and outdoor fun (including meals) organised for toddlers and older kids. There are family suites as well. Wake up Christmas morning knowing you have the best present of all—the perfect family holiday.

A year of dream getaways is an appealing idea, and surprisingly attainable. Create your ideal itinerary and enjoy matching your perfect holiday destination with the perfect hotel. When the day comes for you to take off in style, you'll have only the best to look forward to.

Zealand's superb fish and game, along with a select wine list. In an increasingly complex and technological world, a visit to Huka Lodge is a chance to reconnect with the simple pleasures of life—whether it's the thrill of a trout rising to snap up your dry fly, or lazing under a tree with a good book.

Austria

In December go someplace you're sure to have a white Christmas, with all the traditional activities of the season. Tucked up in the Austrian Alps, above the picture-postcard ski resort of Lech, the Hotel Goldener Berg is a classic Austrian chalet where the staff seem to have waltzed straight out of *The Sound of Music*, wearing Austrian dirndls and cheery smiles. Various

A new travel generation

The biggest new players in the luxury travel market are only about 4 feet tall. Bigger than toddlers, but not yet fully grown teenagers, these pint-sized power brokers command a multi-billion-dollar industry—luxury family travel. Their level of influence is all out of proportion to their size, age or experience, but they can make the most hardened hotelier tremble. Meet the VIKs, the Very Important Kids, who rule when it comes to where mummy and daddy will be spending the money each time a holiday rolls around.

And these days holidays are rolling around more than ever before. In the United Kingdom there are term breaks every five weeks. Easter and Christmas holidays now average about three weeks each for independent schools. In the United States, the three-month-long summer break is the biggest vacation hurdle of the year. The private school adage, "the more you pay, the less they stay" has never been truer. Parents are now constantly challenged to find the most fun, trendy, exciting and kid-friendly breaks on the planet.

One reason why the number of family holidays is soaring is the fact that many more women than before are keeping their careers after having children. Dual-income families have more money to spend on their children, and a lot more guilt about not being home as much as their own parents were. Juggling kids and careers is one of the biggest challenges that is facing parents of this generation. Parents are

working harder. Holidays are seen as the best way to get quality time with the family, a way of making up for the all late nights at work, the missed football matches, the microwave dinners—so parents will do everything they can to make holidays as perfect as possible for their children. It goes without saying that spending whatever it takes is part of the deal.

As strange as it sounds, rising divorce statistics can also be a factor contributing to this trend. If the kids go with dad for a holiday and he gives them a suitably "Wow!" experience, the bar is raised just that little bit higher when it's mum's turn to take the kids away. Children are very clever at getting the best deal for themselves. Kid's clubs at five-star hotels around the world are full of bratlets gleefully guilt-tripping their high-income single parents.

Holidays abroad, once seen as special treats, are now viewed as an unalienable right by children who have earned more air miles by their 5th birthday than their grandparents have in an entire lifetime. In one short generation, holidays have changed out of all recognition. Exotic destinations are taken for granted. Families still like a bucket and spade holiday, but now the beaches are in far-flung locales such as Thailand, the Maldives or Australia.

Long haul specialist travel company Kuoni sees luxury family travel as one of the fastest growing sections of the market. According to Product Director

A young boy takes a spectacular jump on the slopes—savvy kids are getting more and more out of holiday travel.

Ideal for bringing the family together, self-contained villas make it possible to kick back and enjoy the company.

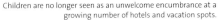

Children are no longer seen as an unwelcome encumbrance at a growing number of hotels and vacation spots.

Mark Robson, "It is an area that we predict will grow over the coming years. Our clients, who have grown used to travelling long haul before they started families, are now taking their families to all these wonderful five-star destinations, which have excellent family facilities. Where villas are part of the hotel—an increasing trend at the top end of the market—these are ideal for families, offering more space and privacy. More generically, the world of long-haul travel is hugely inspiring for all the family. There is history: the temples and tombs of Egypt, the jungle pyramids of Mexico, and Caribbean tales of smugglers and pirates. There are geographical wonders, abundant animal life and teeming coral reefs within easy access of many resorts. To respond to this demand, we are introducing a number of new initiatives for family travellers over the coming year."

Holiday one-upmanship is also accelerating the trend towards ever more elite family holidays. At smart dinner parties everywhere from Mayfair to Manhattan, when the conversation inevitably turns to the Christmas/Easter/Summer break, woe betide the couple who risk instant social death by admitting to staying home rather than schussing down the slopes of Courcheval 1850 or embarking on an elephant safari in Rajasthan with the family in tow, bag and baggage. Certain destinations bestow immediate status, and a whole new breed of upmarket travel consultants such as Quintessentially and Concierge are literally falling over themselves to make sure they secure the top villa/suite/island/private jet for their globetrotting

Junior golf sessions are a popular feature at Gleneagles in Scotland.

clients. Magazines such as *Condé Nast Traveller* are travel lifestyle bibles for affluent parents looking for the next hip destination, while upmarket parenting glossies such as *Junior* feature page upon page of deluxe holidays along with designer babywear and tips on how to keep the nanny happy.

The ongoing competition to have the best holiday ever (the mantra of the die-hard Alpha Parent) means that simplicity is out (you can't just lie by the pool, you need to Do Something) and creativity is in. This desire for the truly exceptional is creating a powerful and profitable niche within the overall field of the luxury family travel market. According to Lucy Clark, PR and Marketing Manager at the luxury independent travel experts Exsus, they have been observing "a marked increase in family travel over the last three years, with more and more people open to taking their children on adventurous luxury holidays, be it a Galapagos cruise or bicycling in Bhutan."

The Disney Corporation, never known to miss an opportunity when it comes to marketing to families, has launched its own luxury adventure family travel service. Adventures by Disney is a lavish series of kid-friendly holidays all over the world. A 12-day trip to China features Beijing, Hong Kong, Shanghai, Guilin and giant Pandas in Chengdu. The vividly illustrated brochure exhorts its young guests to "expect unique mementos, captivating local characters and delightful departures that celebrate the unexpected magic along the way". For a family of two adults and two kids under 12, the magic has a price—just over US$20,000,

not including flights. A 5-day trip to the Disneyland Resort in LA offers perks not available to the general public, such as guided tours of Walt Disney Studios and VIP fast track status at the theme park. A family of four will spend over US$11,000 for the fun of having breakfast with Mickey Mouse or jumping the queue for Space Mountain.

In the race for the hearts and wallets of family travellers, hotels make extraordinary efforts. At London's posh Lanesborough Hotel, the Head Butler, Sean Davoren, personally shops for gifts to please young guests: "If the family are booked in to see Mary Poppins, they might find a special souvenir CD or T-shirt from the show waiting for them when they return. If we keep the kids happy, the parents will love us forever." In Cyprus, the fashionable Anassa resort not only welcomes babies, but will also hand-pick

At Villa San Michele, kids can take up an enriching cookery course with top chefs.

veggies from the organic garden and puree them specially, so chic eco-mums are spared the horror of having to deal with anything so common as store-bought baby food from a jar. Up in the Highlands of Scotland, at plush Gleneagles, girls too young for the spa are offered age-appropriate treats such as "Little Miss Touch of Colour," a basic manicure and make-up lesson. Alternatively, kids can enjoy junior off-road driving around the estate in mini-Land Rovers, as well as falconry and golf lessons.

At Florence's famous Villa San Michele in the gorgeous Italian countryside, aspiring junior chefs travelling with their parents can take up a 3-day children's cookery course for €4,725. That's about as much as an adult Cordon Bleu course in the UK, but what's money when little Henry looks so happy making spaghetti alla vongole?

In tropical Hawaii, The Fairmont Orchid offers kids private surfing lessons with local beach boys, while in the Seychelles, luxury retreat Maia provides children with their very own personal butler. VIKs are spoiled for choice—or just spoiled rotten. It all depends on your point of view.

For international five-star hotel groups such as Jumeirah Group, Four Seasons, One&Only and The Ritz-Carlton, the solution to the VIK challenge has been the creation of award-winning, exemplary kids' clubs that offer a remarkable array of activities and options. The "Ritz Kids" programme has been hugely successful. Babies in Hong Kong can enjoy a butler-drawn bath, while families vacationing in Cancun can request quiet suites with phones that light up instead of ringing. Not to be outdone, Four Seasons has its own "Kids For All Seasons" youth programme, which provides supervised complimentary activities. Most resorts have children's swimming pools and play areas. Cribs, rollaway beds and amenities such as baby soap are complimentary. Four Seasons also launched an innovative "Teen Concierge" service, where specially recruited local teens give expert advice on everything from cool shops to hip hangouts.

Jumeirah put Dubai firmly on the map as a family destination by creating resorts that provide a whole range of experiences tailored to youngsters, from camel riding in the desert at Bab Al Shams, learning to sail at Jumeirah Beach Hotel, or plunging down the water slides at Wild Wadi Water Park. Their children's activities are so popular, it's virtually impossible to get a room at a Jumeirah property in Dubai during the school holidays. One&Only hotels and resorts offer a "KidsOnly" programme, which has earned a solid reputation for giving kids what they really want on holiday, whether it's pre-programmed iPod music players for poolside lounging, a dedicated arts and crafts room, outings and adventures, or gadgets such as Wii, XBox, GameCube and PlayStation video game consoles, Nintendo DS, portable DVD players—just about everything for today's high-tech tots. At times it all seems way over the top—it's not just milk and cookies at snack time; children are invited to create their own gourmet treats with the hotel's chefs, preparing everything from chocolate truffles to pizzas.

Providing these state-of-the-art facilities and the highly trained staff to run them doesn't come cheap. Are the kids' clubs worth the premium? Undoubtedly so. According to Debi Green, founder of popular online resource BabyGoes2, "there's been a big increase in the demand for luxury resorts that genuinely welcome young children. A lot of resorts have spent a fortune upgrading their kids' club facilities in the last five years to keep up." She carries on to say, "These days, parents are much more demanding. They will ask questions about everything, ranging from how warm the pool is to what food their kids will be served. Our clients choose the resorts that have the best kids' activities, and they are willing to pay for quality. An average family of four on a holiday in the Caribbean for a week spends about £8,000, while wealthy families spend much more".

Despite extensive programmes dedicated purely to children's needs, sometimes the simple pleasures of kite-flying will suffice to put a smile on young ones' faces.

There are more options than ever available to families on holiday—sand boarding in the Dubaian desert is only one scintillating example.

Location makes or breaks a vacation, and the Maldives takes the concept of tropical getaway to another level.

Even cruising, once a virtually kid-free zone populated by well-heeled retirees enjoying the good life, has had a makeover. According to Which?Holiday, the number of Britons taking ocean cruise holidays has doubled in a decade, with more than 1.2 million passengers coming aboard last year. Many of the new cruisers are families, lured by kid-friendly superships, such as Royal Caribbean's 'Freedom of the Seas', which boasts a water park, various pools, a variety of kids' clubs for all ages, a surf rider wave machine, a rock-climbing wall and specially tailored family shore excursions. They also have a fleet of "Voyager Family Ships", which promise fun and educational activities for babies of just six months to the most jaded teenager. There's ice-skating, mini-golf, roller-blading, teens-only discos, high-tech gaming arcades, art, drama—you name it. Increasingly, cruising is seen as a multi-generational holiday option. Grandparents don't necessarily have to compromise their bridge parties, shuffleboard or black-tie dinners, while their young relatives can run free in a safe, supervised environment.

Where will it all end? There's no let up in sight. Kids have become sophisticated travellers, searching out holiday options on the Internet from all corners of the planet. Parents used to having it all are just as enthusiastic as their offspring in going for the gold standard. The days when a swimming pool was all a child wanted from a holiday hotel are a dim memory. In the not-too-distant future, when kids ask for the moon, they'll probably be booked on the next flight (in First Class, of course).

Suntec Singapore International
Convention & Exhibition Centre,
set in the heart of downtown
Singapore, highlights the rising
profile of the Meetings Industry
in the Southeast Asian hub.

Of MICE and men

It used to be considered the fatally unglamorous and utilitarian extension of business travel, to be avoided if not strictly necessary. What a difference a decade makes. Gone are the days when the sight of flimsy aluminium-and-plastic booths, unimaginative brochure displays and safety-pinned name tags written in thick black marker evoked a morbid fear in jetsetting executives. Towards the turn of the millennium, event organisers became more attuned to the value-add ethos of luxury travel purveyors, starting a worldwide shift in the market and embracing a snappy new acronymous identity. Today, the MICE (Meetings, Incentive travel, Conferences and Exhibitions) sector favours the more streamlined term Meetings Industry, but for all those concerned, meetings are only the very tip of an extremely big, fat cheese.

One measure of how the industry has grown in recent years is the number of hotel groups that have launched specialised event programmes to cater to the various groups of travellers in this particular sector. This is no isolated policy; Fairmont Hotels & Resorts, Hilton Hotels, The Ritz-Carlton Hotels & Resorts and Mandarin Oriental Hotel Group are a few of the big names that implement MICE programmes in their properties, with dedicated in-house events teams and strategists purely for this purpose. Meetings by Mandarin Oriental is one such worldwide effort. In Singapore, where an estimated 3 million visitors came as MICE travellers in 2006 alone, generating US$2.9 billion in receipts, Mandarin Oriental

From small-scale executive meeting sessions to exhibtions catering for thousands, the industry is heating up.

has gamely taken up the challenge to meet the needs of this market. Scale is not a problem—boardroom brainstorming sessions for 10 are catered to with the same ease as week-long conferences culminating in a banquet for up to 460. Standards of personal service are immaculately maintained, and light massages for seminar-glazed participants are offered alongside cups of aromatic coffee. The interior of each business room reflects the smart, clean focus of working successfully out of the Southeast Asian hub, and the views reinforce this with inspiring panoramas of the city skyline or the tranquil resilience of bamboo gardens.

World Before You

Despite Beijing being the capital of the Asian behemoth that is China, Shanghai has traditionally reigned as the centre of commercial activity and the progressive face of the country. With Beijing stepping up its game in recent years, however, Shanghai faces new challenges to its financial hegemony, never more so than now, with all eyes on Beijing for the 2008 Olympic Games. One robust reaction to this call for bigger, faster, better and stronger is the Shanghai World Financial Centre (SWFC), otherwise known as the Vertical Complex City. The SWFC is reckoned among the tallest buildings in the world, and, situated right in the very heart of Pudong's Lujiazui business district, is uniquely situated to inject a fresh burst of vitality into Shanghai's financial scene.

Trade shows have moved up from the dismal, hectic events they were before—glittering venues are now *de rigueur*.

Filling in the obvious demand created by this new addition to the market is Park Hyatt Shanghai, located between the 79th and 93rd floor of the SWFC, making it the highest hotel in the world. Those with a head for heights will have a fine appreciation of Park Hyatt Shanghai's facilities. The Residence on the 86th floor has eight private rooms that provide full business and catering facilities for anywhere between eight and 100 guests, while the 93rd floor's Sky Residence is an exclusive set of rooms for up to 228 delegates. Such is the rarefied atmosphere for those paying top dollar to meet and mingle with like-minded associates. With Shanghai spread out glittering at its feet, the Park Hyatt will be one of the superlatives of the Meeting Industry.

MICE HQ

Standard event packages have long left the bare bones basic duo of venue and accommodation far behind, bundling treats such as golf on nearby championship courses and sightseeing tours into itineraries to give event participants a full complement of activities beyond the meeting room/conference hall. Across the world, luxury hotels and resorts are staking their claim on a piece of the action, courting organisers with bigger ballrooms, the very latest in technologically advanced audio-visual equipment, sophisticated dining and entertainment features—options running the full gamut of professional hospitality. In this competitive market, any edge over the rest is exploited to the full, and this frequently boils down to the old real estate adage of "Location, location, location".

Shanghai has an irresistible allure in the evening light.

Exotic locales are a draw, as are scenic surrounds—such places are popular with groups on incentive and team-building trips. When in the heart of a bustling capital city, proximity to the main commercial districts always helps, as do insane levels of luxury. In this, the larger hotel groups have the upper hand, capitalising on their reputations and ability to provide what is an oft-underestimated commodity in the life of a frequent business traveller—familiarity. A Grand Hyatt stay does not deviate much from Hong Kong to Hawaii, something desired by a dislocated, jet-lagged executive who has spent his (diurnally inverted) day being powerpointed, business-carded and sales-pitched ad infinitum.

In the international field of the Meetings Industry, conferences and exhibitions are held in cities scattered across the globe, in a variety of venues. But where do these purveyors of niche travel gather when the time comes for their own meeting of the minds? Leaving the metaphysics of lofty aims and shared goals aside, the answer is more prosaic and fabulously apt than one might think—Barcelona. The Global Meetings and Incentives Exhibition is held in this Mediterranean city, fittingly at the crosshairs of the Eastern/Western and Northern/Southern hemispheres ("Mediterranean" derives from the Latin for "middle of the earth") for an international trade meeting.

One hotel that caters to the exacting standards of this exhibition, organised by European Incentive, Business Travel and Meetings (EIBTM) is Hotel Claris. Apart from its own meeting facilities, one of Hotel Claris' outstanding features is its art collection, a meticulously curated body of Egyptian art, engravings commissioned by Napoleon Bonaparte and 2nd-and 3rd-century Roman sculptures and mosaics. It would be a shame to come to Barcelona for an intense three-day exhibition—as the Global Meetings and Incentives Exhibitions is—and leave without taking in the city's vibrant arts scene, and Hotel Claris brings it right to you.

Can Bonastre, nestled at the foot of the beautiful Monserrat range, is out beyond the hectic trade show atmosphere of Barcelona, but still attracts more than its fair share of boardroom events, with its scenic views and intimate villa setting, not to mention the prospect of helicopter tours of the estate and wine tastings at the adjoining vineyard. Can Bonastre is an alternative view of the Meetings Industry, one that brings guests closer to nature, away from the cacophonous city life that continually douses the harried executive's senses.

More and more people come together every year for exhibitions ranging from car expos to technology fairs.

CSR and Going Green

The prefix of the moment in the travel sector is "eco"—part of a worldwide business and lifestyle paradigm shift, some would say—and the Meetings Industry is no exception to this phenomenon. Going green may be seen as a cynical way to win over the rapidly burgeoning demographic of ecologically aware consumers, but one need only look at how equal gender opportunities in the workplace went from being pseudo-progressive PR spin to indispensable HR consideration in order to see the very real potential of the green movement. Corporate Social Responsibility, or CSR, is a big deal in the modern-day marketplace, and hotels are scrambling to colour their operations and brand with that elusive verdant shade—eco-credibility without the unattractive spectre of strident activism. After all, when World Earth Day delegates come marching in, with their high-profile speakers and international media coverage, host hotels will be proud to declare their card-carrying full membership in the green league without sacrificing an inch in hospitality standards.

Following in this vein, several hotels are offering energy-efficient event venues, environment-friendly housekeeping, serving up eco-cuisine, even pledging to emission-offsetting programmes to ameliorate the carbon footprints of their jet-setting guests. Activities outside the meetings proper that are aimed at raising social and environmental awareness are also popular, and range from a few hours of volunteer work with local communities to wilderness hikes in eco-reserves.

The fallacy that going green means taking a step backward is also being debunked—CSR is now seen as the path to maintaining competitive advantage. It's hard to argue with the fact that conserving resources translates into long-term cost savings, or that adopting socially responsible policies leads to a strong public relations position. For those who need solid figures to bolster their convictions, however, a study conducted by US-based Green Meetings Industry Council showed a US$12,000 overhead cost reduction from something as basic as supplying pitchers of water in lieu of bottled water to attendees. Day-lighting trade floor shows with plenty of natural illumination increased sales by 40 per cent as compared to relying solely on artificial lighting. Most tellingly as an industry indicator, a survey by the Travel Industry Association of America revealed that 83 per cent of US businesses and travellers are willing to spend 6.5 per cent more for services and products provided by environmentally responsible companies. Clearly, the eco-players in the Meetings Industry are on to something—the only thing left in question is how long the rest of the world will take to catch up.

Forging Ahead

One thing that has helped bring the Meetings Industry into greater prominence is the gutsy innovations of hoteliers and organisers worldwide that have resulted in the variety of options available to event planners and participants today. Each new frontier broached—team-building on safari, cruise ship conventions, spa

The Meetings Industry takes on a
major role in this era of networking
and communications.

The imposing steel, glass and stone façade of the Dubai International Financial Centre dominates the view from one
of Jumeirah Emirates Towers' meeting rooms.

idle boast. Five minutes away is the Dubai International Financial Centre, home to the bullish DIFX, a superb advantage that is certainly not let down by lacklustre meetings and event facilities. With the distinction of all these accomplishments in one place, Jumeirah Emirates Towers has tenaciously clung to its crown as the host with the most since its opening.

This being Dubai, however, one-upmanship is part of the natural order of things, and the up-and-coming Dubai Festival City looks set to draw some of the action away from downtown Dubai. Newly launched in January 2008, the InterContinental Festival City claims to have the most well-equipped event centre in the region, and has as its trump cards the setting of one of the city's most exciting new development projects and proximity to the cultural heartland of Bastakiya and creekside Deira. It may be too soon to tell if the InterContinental Festival City will go on to conquer the lion's share of the market with its slew of aces, but one would be wise to keep an open mind in Dubai, where the incredible often has a disconcerting habit of translating itself into grounded reality.

The future of Meetings Industry is anything but set in stone—it is as fluid and flexible as an industry in its first flush. If the current situation gives us any indicators to go by, it is that exciting times lie ahead, both for those on the demand and those on the supply ends—and even for the spectators watching on the sidelines. As the travel and business sectors consummate their symbiotic relationship, the Meetings Industry goes prime time.

resort seminars—opens up new markets and creates demand for higher standards and greater novelties. The industry is organically self-sustaining, flourishing in the systole and diastole of supply and demand.

In Dubai, where limits are seen as challenges and records set only to be broken, the soaring twin blades of Jumeirah Emirates Towers on Sheikh Zayed Road epitomise the emirate's cloud-piercing race to the top. Marketing itself as a meetings and events destination rather than simply a venue, Jumeirah Emirates Towers powers miles beyond the banal interchangeability of the glittering gamut of five-star hotels that dots the urban landscape of downtown Dubai. Besides housing a hotel in the epicentre of Dubai's financial square mile, Jumeirah Emirates Towers is also a vertiginous ascent of exclusive office space and shopping complex—its claim of being an all-encompassing destination is no

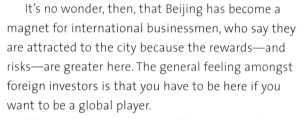

Eye on Beijing

With the Chinese economy booming and the 2008 Summer Olympics just around the corner, Beijing is embarking on one of the most ambitious remakes the world has ever seen, redrawing the map of a city that has essentially remained unchanged since its imperial days. In the short space of a few years, the city's face has changed radically as spectacular new Olympic venues spring up and a parade of shiny skyscrapers, glitzy malls and minimalist hotels and restaurants appear almost overnight.

The once staid capital of China is fast becoming one of the most influential economic and cultural capitals of the world, a magnet for financial whiz kids and daring entrepreneurs as well as innovative artists and designers from around China and the world. They are all attracted here by the raw energy and limitless potential that is increasingly synonymous with the essence of today's edgier China.

A street calligrapher represents the essential dichotomy of Beijing—ancient capital overlaid with a modern metropolis.

China has the fastest growing economy in the world, an economy which has been zipping along at a pace of around 9 per cent per annum for the past two decades. GDP growth is expected to hit 11.6 per cent this year, well above the government target of 10 per cent, making this likely the fifth consecutive year of double-digit growth. At the end of 2007, foreign exchange reserves stood at US$1.4 trillion and Chinese bank savings had exceeded US$2.2 trillion in total, which means banks were flush with cash.

It's no wonder, then, that Beijing has become a magnet for international businessmen, who say they are attracted to the city because the rewards—and risks—are greater here. The general feeling amongst foreign investors is that you have to be here if you want to be a global player.

"If you're doing business in China, you must have a significant presence in Beijing," says James McGregor, a long-time businessman in Beijing and the succesful author of *One Billion Customers*, a book describing how to avoid the pitfalls of doing business in China. "The regulators are here, and with the concentration of large universities, Beijing is also a gathering place for the best brains in China."

Finance Street, or Jinrong Jie, made up of gleaming steel-and-glass high-rise office buildings and swanky hotels is located on the western side of the city, just minutes from the Forbidden City. The purpose of the area was to create a Wall Street East, and while it is so new that Beijing cabbies still often can't find buildings here, Financial Street seems on the road to achieving this goal. It's already home to most of China's biggest banking and insurance firms, several of which have invested billions in setting up headquarters in the new marble floored corporate office buildings. According to *Asiamoney*, the local financial firms in this area control US$1.5 trillion in assets, more than 90 per cent of China's credit funds, and 65 per cent of its insurance premiums.

On the heels of the big domestic banks were the leading international banks and financial institutions, such as Goldman Sachs, JPMorgan, the Royal Bank of Canada, UBS and various top international law firms, consultants and accountants, all of which have long-term leases in prime office buildings.

The Central Business District, otherwise knows as the CBD, encompasses the China World Trade Center, which is adding a new phase of office and commercial space. Quite a few of the other creative (and sometimes controversial) architectural projects in the district are the work of some of the world's best-known architects. One example that attracted a good deal of public debate is the CCTV Tower, a 230-m (755-ft) structure that comprises two inverted L-shaped towers that are joined high above the ground. The impressive

The gorgeously fractured texture of the National Aquatics Center's exterior is visible through a fish-eye view of swimmers cleaving their way to the finish line.

complex, designed by Dutch architect Rem Koolhaas, one of the hottest international designers today, has shaken up the former look of the city.

The upcoming Summer Olympic Games have no doubt played a key role in these far-reaching changes. The vast majority of Chinese are exceedingly proud to host the Games, which will be a coming-out party for the world's fastest growing economy when more than 2 million visitors and 20,000 foreign journalists make their way to the Chinese capital.

China has invested some US$40 billion in 14 new Olympic venues and another dozen or so upgrades—more than double the US$16 billion Greece spent on the 2004 Summer Games. The total investment could shoot up to as high as $70 billion when the city's other infrastructure projects are figured in.

The highlight of these new additions to the city skyline is the US$386 million National Stadium. This modernistic 90,000-seat structure, made of twig-like intertwining strips of grey steel, has been nicknamed the "Bird's Nest". Also eye-catching is the impressive National Aquatics Center. The shiny translucent swimming venue, wrapped in a skin not unlike bubble wrap, is better known as the "water cube." The US$125 million venue is built of state-of-the-art polymers and other advanced plastic material designed to react to light, creating an amazing visual effect.

In December 2007, the space-age Grand National Theater, made of glass and titanium, opened with much fanfare. In the evening, the semi-transparent skin gives passers-by a view of the performances

The Grand National Theater glows incandescent in the evening light, its translucent skin giving intriguing half-glimpses of the performances taking place within.

going on in one of three auditoriums. The modernistic silver dome, which appears to float on water, was the source of a great deal of controversy because critics said it clashed with the ancient imperial structures in the neighbourhood, such as the Forbidden City and Zhongnanhai. The building was designed by French architect Paul Andreu, famous for his non-traditional approach to design, as shown in his work on Terminal 1 of Paris' Charles de Gaulle Airport.

New facilities are being added to smoothly whisk Olympic visitors around to the places they'll need to go to, including six spanking new subway lines that crisscross the city and a 43 km (7-mile) light-rail system. In addition, a bevy of flyovers and roads have been built to accommodate the rapidly increasing number of cars that are now clogging city streets, and a third airport terminal and runway have been built to handle the increase in visitors, from businessmen to tourists.

The rapid transformation of Beijing has also been accompanied by a corresponding culinary upheaval. The city has made a great leap forward from the early 1990s, when eating out here was confined to either Cantonese or Sichuan eateries, dull venues with bad fluorescent lighting and thin plastic tablecloths that stuck to your forearms in the summer. Today, Beijing offers a growing variety of cuisines from around China and the world in classy new venues, making the city a gastronomic capital on top of everything else.

Lan is the inspired creation of design heavyweight Philippe Starck.

One of the newest arrivals is Le Pré Lenôtre, cousin of the 3-Michelin-starred Le Pré Catelan in France. The restaurant, located within the stunning Sofitel Wanda Hotel on Jianguo Road, brings an exclusive Parisian touch to Beijing, with its plush black chairs, Baccarat chandeliers and crisp white tablecloths. The food does not disappoint. Exotic dishes here include crab with acidulated apple and avocado flavored with coriander and citrus, goose liver with spices, and an amazing fruit chutney. For a main dish, try their grilled lamb with thyme or cod studded with smoked salmon and served with eggplant marmalade.

Lan serves excellent Sichuan cuisine, albeit a bit on the nouveau side—but the real draw is its eclectic décor, the creation of daring French designer Philippe Starck. Reproductions of European Renaissance art hang from the ceiling and numerous furnishings are placed around the dining area, providing a sort of chaotic but orderly artistic sense. Lan has one of the best bars in town, offering a wide selection of New World and European wines and well-made cocktails, alongside an Oyster Bar and cigar divan.

My Humble House is anything but modest. This upscale restaurant has soft leather furnishings and a flower-strewn pool in the middle of the dining room, which sits beneath a sleek bar. The restaurant is one of the few that successfully taps Western ingredients while holding on to the Asian flavour. The fried crispy prawn with wasabi mayonnaise sauce is excellent. For dessert try the lemongrass jelly infused with delicate pandan flavour and served with sweet red wolfberries.

Beijing is slowly gaining a solid reputation as a playground for the gastronomically adventurous.

Din Tai Fung, the Taipei restaurant considered by some to be one of the best Chinese dining venues in the world, opened its first branch in Beijing in 2004, and has established itself as a firm favourite in the city's dining scene. The restaurant interior has a clean contemporary look and the menu is especially famous for its juicy cairou zhengjiao (mini vegetable dumplings in bamboo steamers). In the meantime, the very trendy Bellagio is where Beijing's beautiful people come to grab a bite at the beginning or end of a night out on the town. In addition to offering a range of typical Sichuanese dishes with a Taiwanese accent, Bellagio also serves specialities such as migao—glutinous rice with dried mushrooms and dried shrimp, stir-fried rice noodles, and meatball soup. Polish off your meal with a Taiwanese crushed ice topped with sweet red beans, green beans, mango slices, strawberries or peanuts—a dish particularly popular in the warmer months.

Those looking for something to do after dinner won't be disappointed. Beijing is fast becoming one of the hottest nightlife centres in Asia. The city has an estimated 400 rock bands, much more than any other city in China, and is home to a bustling music scene, encompassing genres as disparate as live rock, jazz, hip-hop, and metal. The number of clubs and bars is exploding with the growing sophistication of local music fans and arrival of expats moving to the city. This also explains the large number of international rock bands that have been touching down in Beijing. In 2007, Chinese packed concert venues to see such big names as The Roots (lyrical hip-hop), Sonic Youth (seminal alternative rock band), and Ziggy Marley, son of the reggae legend Bob Marley, all of whom played in sold-out venues to ecstatic hordes of young Chinese and Westerners in Beijing in 2007.

As Beijing's increasingly affluent toss aside their undifferentiated factory outlet brands for designer labels such as Marc Jacobs and Louis Vuitton, all the world's top designers are now fighting for shop space in the city's impressive new megamalls. And whereas putting even a little colour on your cheeks would have resulted in a slew of political denunciations in the 50s, 60s and 70s, Chanel, Christian Dior and Elizabeth Arden counters are now crowding the main floors of every department store in the city as the city's reborn fashion-conscious dig into their pockets for imported make-up that costs the equivalent of a month's salary for a typical Beijing office worker, and without batting a perfectly mascara-ed eyelash.

Hotel Côté Cour SL provides a boutique experience in a vivid colour palette that highlights the use of traditional Chinese furnishing elements.

The strong economy and the Olympics have also drawn many new hotels to Beijing. Most impressive is the sleek Park Hyatt, a 63-storey, 237-room boutique hotel, penthouse and condo residence, and retail complex flanked by two office buildings. The hotel's rooftop bar, designed to resemble a Chinese lantern, offers wonderful views of the city. Check-in takes place on the 63rd floor. "We want guests to have the beautiful sense of arrival," says PR manager Jeannie Mak. The rooms are very contemporary with clean lines, and with state-of-the art hotel technology, from Internet connections to one-touch room controls.

One of a handful of boutique hotels in city, Hotel Kapok is the creation of Pei Zhu, a well-known Beijing architect. The design encompasses a bit of Japanese style, with a tiny bamboo and pebble garden dividing the rooms. Beijing has a number of average-looking courtyard hotels that have failed to adequately capture the feel of old Peking. Hotel Côté Cour SL has changed all that. The hotel's 14 rooms face a courtyard with a lily pond, and are decorated with Chinese furniture, silk bed covers, and antique brick floors.

Beijing is the cultural capital of China, with every type of artist drawn to the city, a trend that goes back to imperial days. Despite the belief that Beijing is culturally stilted, this is the place to make it in China. Many creatively inclined Chinese—musicians, actors, writers, painters, and designers—feel there's a synergy here that can't be found anywhere else in China.

"Beijing is very fertile ground for the germination of new art," says Jan Leaming, owner of the beautiful Full Moon Gallery, located in a restored Ming dynasty hall in Ditan Park. "Visually, it is filled with new things, architecture, billboards, bright lights, night life, and all kinds of goods and services. These things, juxtaposed with the old, provide artists with rich material to document their insights and feelings."

While art long focused on Socialist Realism and serving politics, in recent years the cultural czars have been nudged aside and creative art has made a vigorous comeback, thanks largely to the power of the market. As a result, the works of many relatively unknown artists have become hot commodities in the global art world, making several artists millionaires overnight.

While many artists could not be exhibited in their own country for years, today their works are shown in galleries around the world, and they're fetching record prices. The UK's famous Saatchi Gallery kicked off its latest venture into China's booming art world in 2007 with the launch of its Chinese-language website, which will give local artists a chance to display their work online and globally.

Art galleries are springing up all over the city—in hotels, courtyard houses, old factories and even in an ancient watchtower, catering to the growing demand for art in China. The number of galleries in Beijing has increased stratospherically from about a dozen five years ago to close to 100 now, including many foreign galleries, says Ms Leaming, whose very own gallery is dedicated "to locating and promoting artists whose work stretches the mind and the soul to profound and original dimensions, thereby enriching the capacity for human thought and understanding."

Red Gate Gallery, run by Australian Brian Wallace, features the works of well-known contemporary Chinese artists. This gallery is especially interesting as it's located in the looming Dongbianmen Watchtower, the last remaining Ming watchtower in the city, which is worth a trip on its own.

Meanwhile, the trendy Danshanzi art district of Beijing, located in interesting old Bauhaus factories now turned into cool galleries, cafes and restaurants, attracts art lovers from around the world. With its interesting exhibitions and venues, Dashanzi is a great place to while away an afternoon.

All of this progress does not mean that Beijing has buried its past in a cloak of modernity. Beijingers continue to savour the historical remnants of this capital city and its rich culture. The city government

The Beijing art scene is benefitting from the country's heightened cultural awareness.

Red Gate Gallery is one of the crop of art museums and galleries springing up around the city.

Peking opera is experiencing a revival in the new culture-conscious Beijing.

has sought to salvage disappearing sections of the crumbling old city walls, recreating them along their former routes, as well as reviving the old folk arts of the people, such as Peking opera.

Meanwhile, enterprising entrepreneurs have been keeping busy bringing some much-missed authenticity back to Beijing. Nan Luogu Xiang, a 700 year old street with wonderful old architecture, has just recently been reincarnated and has come back to life as a fascinating collection of interesting cafés, modern restaurants and hip boutiques; Nanxincang, a collection of rare and unique Ming-era structures, has dusted itself off and reopened as a row of art galleries, restaurants and shops. Around the city, once-damaged courtyard houses are being renovated and turned into boutique hotels and dining venues where people of today can relive a small part of the city's past.

Take for example, property developer Handel Lee, an American-Chinese entrepreneur who had a hand in Shanghai's popular Three on The Bund complex, and who has launched Legation Quarter, a project that has turned the Qing Dynasty American Embassy compound into a stylish cultural centre. The complex will feature a Daniel Boulud restaurant, a theatre, contemporary art center and a branch of the chic London nightclub Boujis. "I think Legation Quarter is going to blow things open," Mr Lee told the *New York Times*. "Up to now, you could have had the Beijing experience [of hutongs and other historic attractions]," he added, "but there wasn't much excitement."

Beijing has certainly come an extremely long way over the past decade or so. Take a look around this city today and you'll see elegant high-rise apartment buildings, posh commercial centres, grand world-class hotels, space-age theatres, hip restaurants and clubs, impressive Olympic athletic venues, and a growing trend of historical preservation that keeps the past alive and continually relevant to the present. Add to this the diverse community of innovative talents who have been drawn here from all over the world by this boundless energy and potential, and who are each making their own small contribution to the building of a new Beijing. Who would have even come close to imagining this just a few years ago?

And it seems there's no end in sight for Beijing— the next decade will prove even more exciting as the Chinese capital continues its long march towards becoming a city like none other in the world.

Europe & The Middle East

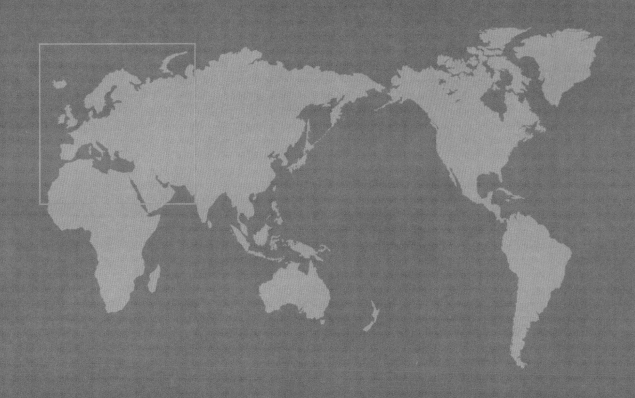

Conrad Hotels & Resorts

These days, global travel has become commonplace, whether for the reasons of business or leisure. Exotic locations are no longer as inaccessible as they once used to be, but with the impersonal chain hotels that have sprung up as a result, travellers find that they are rarely afforded the chance to enjoy the full range of experiences offered by these far-off destinations.

Designed in direct response to this trend, properties of Conrad Hotels & Resorts celebrate the individuality and exoticism inherent in their vibrant locations, reintroducing to both business and leisure travel the excitement and lifestyle pleasures that were in danger of becoming the exclusive domain of pure luxury holidays. Founded in 1982, the Conrad Hotels & Resorts brand currently represents the Hilton Group's most globally integrated chain of contemporary luxury hotels. This standing affords it the best of both worlds—freedom to reflect the culture, architecture, and flavour of local cities, as well as quality standards based on the group's core values: exclusive luxury offerings, service defined by warm and attentive staff, and an unmatched approach to hospitality.

Believing it no longer sufficient to offer guests purely material comforts, Conrad Hotels & Resorts continually challenges itself to redefine luxury in the personal terms of its guests, a fact embodied in its daring brand line, "The luxury of being yourself". From Asia to Australia, Europe to America and the Middle East, Conrad Hotels offer their guests rare glimpses of every region's individuality.

The Presidential Suite at the Conrad Istanbul features an outdoor terrace offering breathtaking views over the city.

Opposite: All suites at Conrad Miami are appointed to the highest standards.

Left: Private rooms are also available for intimate dining and meeting events at Conrad Hong Kong.

Enjoy a meal at Conrad Tokyo's China Blue, a Michelin-starred restaurant with stunning views of the Hamarikyu Gardens.

At the Conrad Bali, which took the top spot in *Condé Nast Traveller*'s 2004 'Hot List', the elegant Infinity wedding venue ensures that couples experience an unforgettably romantic wedding. The secluded resort draws inspiration from other facets of Balinese life, with a Jiwa Spa utilising Asian massage techniques, works of local art throughout the hotel's public areas, and special 'Meditation Platforms' for private yoga sessions overlooking tranquil water features or the resort's beach.

In the ultra-modern capital of Japan, the Conrad Tokyo offers some of the largest rooms in Tokyo, no mean feat considering the scarcity of horizontal real estate. Reflecting the unique aesthetic sensibilities of the Japanese, the Conrad Tokyo's pool is the first in the world to be created in a 'Sumi-e' style derived from the classic painting technique. Other touches include green tea bath amenities by Shiseido, and Hinoki soaking tubs at the Mizuki spa and fitness centre. Critically acclaimed British chef Gordon Ramsay's first restaurant in Asia can also be found here, bringing together one of the Western world's great culinary masters and one of the East's most enigmatic cities for an unprecedented dining collaboration.

Further westward, first-time visitors to Turkey may be overwhelmed by the energy of Istanbul upon arrival, but the Conrad Istanbul will have them speaking local phrases with confidence by check-out, with the help of its friendly staff and the provision of handy conversational phrasebooks. With all of the city's major shopping and sightseeing

The beautiful sunrise over Conrad Bali is a sight to be remembered.

destinations located close to the hotel, a few words go a long way toward a more fruitful trip. A stay at the Conrad Istanbul establishes a connection with the country's rich history, as design motifs from the Byzantine and Ottoman eras feature prominently throughout the lobby and all guestrooms.

These examples represent only a handful of the experiences that await guests of the Conrad's 18 diverse properties worldwide. By 2010, that number will swell to 25 with the launch of distinctive new hotel concepts in Shanghai, Koh Samui, Abu Dhabi, Dubai, the Bahamas, Beijing, and the Portuguese Algarve. When the Conrad Shanghai is completed in December 2008, it will feature an exciting modern exterior inspired by traditional Chinese designs that is unlike anything else on the city's skyline. Set in the lively entertainment district of Xintiandi, the hotel will boast 362 rooms, an urban spa, and advanced meeting facilities, as well as two standalone lifestyle annexes with a multitude of trendy boutiques and eateries.

Where others are content to merely acknowledge individuality, Conrad Hotels & Resorts embraces it. The increasing stream of accolades in recent years bears out the fact that its unique approach to business and leisure has won the hotel group devotees amongst some of the industry's biggest names. From awards like 'The World's Leading Luxury Hotel Brand' (World Travel Awards 2006) to 'The Best Hotel Chain in Europe' (*Global Traveler* 2007), the Conrad name has become one of certain distinction.

A unique dining experience is offered at the Conrad Maldives Rangali Island—the Ithaa restaurant is fully underwater.

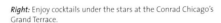

Right: Enjoy cocktails under the stars at the Conrad Chicago's Grand Terrace.

Below: A soothing massage is the perfect end to a long day at Conrad Bangkok.

Tel: +800.00.266 723
Website: www.conradhotels.com

The warm and inviting Living Room greets guests as they enter the hotel.

Andaz Liverpool Street, London

An entirely new luxury concept by the Hyatt Group, the Andaz brand was created in response to the shifting demands of hotel guests, and delivers all the familiarity and comforts of home. Andaz succeeds exceptionally at something many hotels only claim to do: placing the customer at the centre of the entire experience. As the first hotel to bear the Andaz name, the Liverpool Street property in London has certainly made a fine start.

For one thing, its location is guaranteed to draw appreciative bookings from travellers who know just how difficult it can be to get about in London. Situated on the eastern edge, between the city's major financial institutions and its creative centres of Shoreditch, Spitalfields and contemporary tourist attractions such as Tate Modern and Tower Bridge, the Andaz Liverpool Street London enjoys a vibrant location that is just a short taxi ride from central London and the city's major airports.

As an example of the care taken to provide highly personal service, an open living room takes the place of the usual reception desk. Guests are received by staff called 'Andaz Hosts' who personally oversee every aspect of their stays. Advanced wireless systems allow check-ins to be processed from anywhere in the hotel, so guests may begin their stay with a cocktail, or head right to their rooms from the start.

All of the hotel's 267 rooms and suites are fitted for both comfort and utility, with contemporary colour schemes and designer fittings alongside all the tools for modern business. In addition, the hotel is eco-conscious, using systems which save water and power wherever possible and sourcing for local suppliers of food and drinks. Wireless Internet access is provided throughout the hotel, and the workspaces in every room feature oversized desks, Eames chairs, and Jacobson lamps. A first for luxury hotels of this kind, room rates are inclusive of in-room amenities, including the 'healthy minibar', in-room premier movies, laundry, local calls and breakfast. Entertainment comes in the form of large LCD televisions with satellite channels, while iPods and PSP game consoles are available on loan.

One thing the hotel learned early is about what business travellers want: unpretentious, yet pleasurable environments. The result is a philosophy of casual luxury. All five restaurants and four bars serve world-class food and drink, but without posturing or staid rituals. The hotel's approach to meetings and conventions is similarly simple: things will get done. Over 14 fully equipped dining and function rooms, many of them offering beautiful views of the city, an efficient events team manages anything from a small board meeting to an all-out cocktail party without skipping a beat.

It is easy to forget that the Andaz Liverpool Street London accommodates quite as many people as it does. The feeling throughout is akin to that of staying at a hotel small enough for every guest's name to be remembered. One never has to look too far for a smiling face ready to help, and in an age of anonymous business stays, it's good to be recognised.

Suites are designed with light and open space in mind.

Right: Catch restaurant serves seafood and crustacea.
Below: John Barry, architect of the original building, also designed the UK Houses of Parliament.

Rooms and amenities
- 244 guestrooms
- 23 suites

Restaurants and bars
- 1901: modern fine dining and bar
- Miyako: Japanese
- Catch: seafood and crustacea
- Eastway: all-day dining
- George Pub: traditional English pub
- Champagne Bar: bar with live music

Facilities
- Business centre
- Wireless Internet access
- Health Club
- Limousine service
- Andaz Studio: private dining
- Masonic Temple: opulent event room

40 Liverpool Street, London EC2M 7QN, United Kingdom
Tel: +44.0.20.7961 1234 • Fax: +44.0.20.7961 1235
Email: info.londonliv@andaz.com
Website: www.andaz.com

The Artesian is the very epitome of Orientalist chic, keeping customers coming back for more of its exclusive house specialty rum cocktails.

The Langham, London

The Langham, London has been a landmark establishment in this glittering world capital since 1865. It was built in the style of the great Florentine palaces, with seven storeys of arched windows, soaring columns and ornate friezes.

Throughout its long and illustrious history, The Langham, London has hosted countless luminaries, including Oscar Wilde, Mark Twain, Richard Burton, Antonin Dvorak, Noel Coward, Prime Minister Gladstone and Napoleon III. As immortalised in the books of Sir Arthur Conan Doyle, The Langham, London set the scene for many a Sherlock Holmes mystery. The grand hotel also soldiered through two World Wars, surviving the London Blitz that destroyed the West Wing and damaged the rooftop water tank, flooding the entire building.

Located just off Regent Street, the hotel is an ideal base from which to explore all of the tourist attractions and the financial areas in the city. Here, guests can relax in utter peace in the spacious, traditionally styled guest rooms, which offer luxury amenities as well as high-tech facilities and high-speed Internet access.

For extra comfort, The Langham Hotel Club provides guests with superior accommodations, private check-in services, the complimentary pressing of one item upon check-in, and the use of two exclusive Club Lounges, which allows guests to enjoy complimentary breakfasts every morning, snacks and drinks throughout the day, as well as unlimited cocktails and canapés in the evening. Furthermore, the extended check-out time of 3.00 pm allows guests to proceed at their own leisurely pace.

Their superb luxury suites are individually furnished and decorated, offering a wealth of indulgent luxuries. For the ultimate escape, there is the Infinity Suite: 236-sq-m (2,540-sq-ft) of shameless extravagance with a mahogany four poster bed and a chandelier in the drawing room. The grand suite also boasts an infinity bath—a decadently oversized tub-within-a-tub of circulating water that constantly cascades over its sides.

The hotel's health club comes complete with a 16-m (52-ft) indoor swimming pool, fully equipped gym, men and women's saunas and steam rooms, jacuzzi and solarium.

Under celebrity designer David Collins and his team, the hotel's original ballroom has been reborn as one of London's top dining concepts. The Landau combines style and glamour with stunning interiors, including an atmospheric vaulted wine corridor, where the restaurant's extensive collection of world-class fine wines are displayed. Under Head Chef Andrew Turner, the restaurant offers a contemporary European menu, using only the best British ingredients coupled with a few surprising twists.

Also designed by David Collins Studio is the hotel's chic and deeply glamorous cocktail bar, Artesian. The bar combines exotic Orientalism with the romance of new nostalgia and contemporary touches. Artesian specialises in rum, offering over 50 different varieties on its menu, as well as a fantastic selection of cocktails, spirits and champagnes.

Above: Sophistication meets comfort in the tastefully decorated bedrooms.

Right: Built in 1865, The Langham, London has played host to countless names in history.

Redesigned by David Collins Studio, The Landau allows guests to dine in style.

Rooms and amenities
- 382 guestrooms and suites

Restaurants and bars
- The Landau: contemporary European
- Postillion: Private dining
- Artesian: drinks and light meals

Facilities
- 1 boardroom
- Health club and pool

1C Portland Place, Regent Street, London W1B 1JA, UK
Tel: +44.20.7636 1000 • Fax: +44.20.7323 2340
Email: lon.resv@langhamhotels.com
Website: www.langhamhotels.com

Like the rest of the renowned chain, Mandarin Oriental Hyde Park, London prides itself on its impeccable standards of service.

Mandarin Oriental Hyde Park, London

When Mandarin Oriental Hotel Group initially purchased the distinguished Hyde Park Hotel back in 1996, there was an immediate buzz of anticipation as people wondered what one of the world's great hotel groups would do with one of London's most prime locations. Four years later, after a £57 million refurbishment, they had their answer—and its results so far have greatly exceeded everyone's expectations.

Originally an 1880s gentlemen's club, the building the current Mandarin Oriental Hyde Park inhabits is a magnificent Victorian edifice built on one of the most prized pieces of real estate to be found in London, with the world-famous park on the one side and the shopper's paradise of Knightsbridge on the other.

But location is not the only reason for this hotel's record of continual success and acclaim. In many ways Mandarin Oriental Hyde Park sets the standard by which all London's other hotels can be judged. All 198 of the rooms and suites, for example, are the epitome of refined elegance and five-star luxury, combining the spacious dimensions of the Victorian age and traditional décor with high-tech gadgetry and every modern convenience. Suites come with clear views of the nearby park and a dedicated Floor Manager is always on hand for assistance if guests run into any unexpected difficulties.

Dining is yet another domain in which Mandarin Oriental Hyde Park reigns supreme. Foliage, the hotel's renowned main restaurant, has maintained its prestigious Michelin star for no less than seven consecutive years. Today it continues to wow diners with exquisite dishes that blend the freshest ingredients from fastidiously selected sources with modern European recipes, all under the expert guidance of their Executive Chef, Chris Tombling, and set within the unique interiors created by globally-renowned designer Adam Tihany.

The Park, by contrast, serves meals in a more casual ambience throughout the day, and boasts spectacular views of London's finest Royal Park from each table. Next door, exotic nibbles including tempura soft shell crab with wasabi dip, tandoori chicken winglets, and dim sum are all served in the hotel's wonderfully atmospheric Mandarin Bar, another Tihany creation, and much admired for its high chic factor.

Then there's The Spa at Mandarin Oriental, regularly rated as one of the best in the world. With its exclusive Sanarium, Vitality Pool and a large variety of other facilities, The Spa deftly combines harmonious design elements with the very latest in a wide range of restorative treatments, massages and therapies, creating a haven of tranquillity and harmony in the heart of the city. Together with a dedicated staff and a state-of-the-art gymnasium, a guest's relaxation and recuperation is almost a foregone conclusion. All in all, Mandarin Oriental Hyde Park is not just a London hotel—it is, without a doubt, the quintessential London hotel.

Above: The Presidential Suite at Mandarin Oriental Hyde Park, London is one of the most luxurious in the city.

Right: Relax at Mandarin Bar with a perfectly-chilled cocktail.

An aerial view of the hotel shows off its prime location by the lush greenery of London's most famous park.

Rooms and amenities
- 173 guestrooms
- 25 suites

Restaurants and bars
- Foliage: modern European
- The Park: Asian and international
- Mandarin Bar: cocktails and canapés

Facilities
- The Spa at Mandarin Oriental
- Gym
- Business centre
- Meeting rooms

66 Knightsbridge, London SW1X 7LA, UK
Tel: +44.20.7235 2000 • Fax:+44.20.7235 2001
Email: molon-info@mohg.com
Website: www.mandarinoriental.com/london/

The hotel's grand exterior makes it one of the most famous landmarks in London.

Renaissance Chancery Court, London

A truly unique hotel, Renaissance Chancery Court occupies one of the British capital's most stunning landmarks—a building so picturesque that, for the guests who stay here, sightseeing in London continues even after they check in.

The hotel's massive, stately building was constructed in 1914 in the Edwardian architectural style—similar to its Victorian roots, with highly ornate Corinthian columns that support elaborate stucco details and delicate domed cupolas along the rooftop. Originally built to house the headquarters of Pearl Assurance, Britain's second largest insurance company, its grand halls have been converted to awe-inspiring public spaces that feature high-arched ceilings and marble that covers almost every surface, including a magnificent seven-storey staircase crafted out of very rare Pavonazzo marble. In fact, many types of marble used in the hotel are so rare that they are either extremely expensive or altogether unavailable for use as materials in contemporary construction.

With such an old-world elegance, it is no wonder that the hotel has been chosen as the backdrop for many international film productions, such as the 1970s classic *The Three Musketeers*. It was shot in the courtyard, which stood in for a French royal palace.

Renaissance Chancery Court also enjoys a convenient location, a mere stroll away from Covent Garden, the British Museum and the London Eye. After a day of shopping and sightseeing, guests can return to reviving cocktails in the CC Bar followed by dinner in the famous Pearl Restaurant & Bar. A showpiece not to be missed, Pearl is considered one of London's most splendid dining venues for its cuisine and décor. Located in the old Pearl Assurance banking hall, over a million hand-strung pearls adorn the restaurant and its adjoining bar.

Because the building was originally used for commercial purposes, guestrooms are larger than most London rooms and are uniquely configured; no two are exactly alike. Dressed in rich red, green and gold tones, rooms are outfitted with warm wood furnishings, upholstered armchairs and lounges, brass lamps and framed prints. Luxurious bathrooms surround guests with glossy black- and gold-coloured marble, and are spacious enough to accommodate a long bath and separate glass shower stall.

For extra pampering, the hotel's award-winning spa transports guests to another world where East meets West in décor and therapeutic treatments. Choose from the exotic hot stone therapy, chocolate wraps, traditional Indian Ayurvedic or detoxifying marine treatments.

An oasis of historical charm and contemporary luxury, the award-winning Renaissance Chancery Court is one of the capital's most impressive places to stay for business travellers. The hotel provides a welcome respite for the stressed and jet-lagged, and is also a window to the past for visitors who want to soak up London's charm.

The hotel has been appointed to t he finest standards, with Old World aesthetic touches.

Below: The famous Pearl is well-known for its splendid cuisine and interior design.

Right: With columns wrapped in gold leaf, wood-veneered walls and soft lighting, the spa's Relaxation Room is truly a luxurious place where one can completely unwind.

Rooms and amenities
- 356 guestrooms
- 13 suites

Restaurants and bars
- Pearl Restaurant & Bar: modern French
- The Lounge: English afternoon tea and refreshments
- The CC Bar: cocktails and drinks

Facilities
- Business centre
- 13 meeting rooms
- Fitness centre
- Spa

252 High Holborn, London WC1V 7EN, UK
Tel: +44.20.7829 9888 • Fax: +44.20.7829 9889
Website: www.renaissancechancerycourt.co.uk

Hotel Claris, Barcelona

The Hotel Claris is a bastion of style and elegance in Barcelona.

The ultra-chic Hotel Claris is the brainchild of art collector Jordi Clos, who generously exhibits his private collection of impressive art pieces in the hotel's public and private spaces as well as its dedicated museum. The Indian sculptures, Napoleonic etchings and artefacts from ancient Egypt are strikingly set against the steel, glass and rare timbers that make up the Hotel Claris' unique avant-garde interior.

The elegant Renaissance-style façade of the Claris belies the newer, taller and narrower frame of the exclusive boutique hotel within. The refined lobby, adorned with 5th-century Roman mosaics, delivers its guests onto the lively streets of Barcelona, from which passers-by can glimpse the hotel's intriguing interior through solid glass walls.

Back within the captivating confines of the hotel, the suites are said to be bona fide attractions in their own right for the discerning cultural guest. The contemporary structure is overlaid with carefully placed antique pieces and *objets d'art*, such as Egyptian carvings, multi-hued Turkish kilims and genuine Burmese and Hindu sculptures, some dating back to the 5th century. Each air-conditioned and sound-proofed room has its own unique identity and colour scheme, and every suite is a spacious and lush testimonial to the hotel's admirable desire to integrate form with function, and practicality with beauty wherever possible.

In addition to its stunning visuals and cultural impact, the hotel tickles other fancies too. Gourmet appetites will be whetted by the creative Mediterranean cuisine served in the hotel's hip restaurant, East 47. The fusion food contains Catalonian specialities and delicacies such as sushi, game and fresh caviar. Sip on a perfectly-made Manhattan to the soothing accompaniment of a laid-back soundtrack and Andy Warhol lithographs in the fashionable ambience of East 47's cocktail bar.

To experience the real high life, ascend to the roof terrace of the Hotel Claris, La Terraza del Claris. The terrace's star attraction is the sleek rooftop pool, with a view encompassing the tangled maze of Barcelona's signature skyline. Modern dining options from light lunches to moonlit dinners can be enjoyed at the white-bedecked La Terraza del Claris. Its coolly decked floors and retractable roof help to maintain a harmonious balance between sun and shade. For the active and energetic, the Hotel Claris has fully equipped gymnasium, solarium and sauna facilities, and provides courtesy Mercedes Smart cars so guests may explore the myriad architectural marvels and other offerings of Barcelona at their own leisure.

Business travellers will find nothing lacking. The hotel's seven meeting and conference rooms are equipped with high-tech features, and the accommodating nature of the hotel means that the private Egyptian museum or terrace can also be utilised for corporate events. This provides a truly exceptional and unique experience for clients and delegates.

A luxurious five-star boutique hotel that is superbly located in a stylish and vibrant city, the Hotel Claris is truly a multi-faceted gem that adds to the beauty and shine of Barcelona.

The spacious suites are tastefully designed with contemporary furnishings and antique art pieces.

Right: Wine and dine under the stars at La Terraza del Claris.

Below: Soak in the warm afternoon sun by the pool and lull yourself to partake in the quintessential Spanish activity—the siesta.

Rooms and amenities
- 124 guestrooms and suites

Restaurants and bars
- East 47: Mediterranean
- La Terraza del Claris: light fare and cocktails

Facilities
- Business centre with ADSL Internet connection
- 7 high-tech meeting rooms
- Sauna, gymnasium, pool and solarium
- Ancient Egyptian Museum
- Wireless Internet access

Pau Claris 150, Barcelona 08009, Spain
Tel: +34.93.487 6262 • Fax: +34.93.215 7970
Email: claris@derbyhotels.com
Website: www.hotelclaris.com

Hotel Villa Real, Madrid

Centred around Plaza de Canovas and Plaza de Las Cortes are some of the best museums in Spain: the Prado, the Reina Sofía Museum, the Thyssen-Bornemisza Museum, and the famed historic Villahermosa Palace. Madrid's financial and commercial district shares the same space, and a mere stone's throw away from the Plaza de Las Cortes is the magnificent Hotel Villa Real.

Opened in 1989, this relatively youthful establishment has been designed with a rare sensitivity to and respect in mind for the surrounding historical landmarks and buildings, and blends in effortlessly with the other grand edifices in the vicinity. The 19th-century style borne by its façade is extended to the hotel's interior, which benefits from the use of the choicest materials and is adorned with fine artwork from Roman and Greek history.

Referred to at times as 'the balcony over Retiro Park', this fitting epithet is testament to the hotel's expansive view of the verdant gardens from its rooms. Bedrooms here are a cosy haven of creature comforts, complete with polished wooden floors, mahogany furniture, bathrooms lined with elegant Carrara marble and luxurious sitting areas. Other little touches such as piped music and sound-proofing point to Hotel Villa Real's unfailing attention to detail. Guests in Junior Suites enjoy spacious interiors and original artworks on the walls. Luxury Suites feature separate bedrooms and lounge areas, while Duplex Luxury Suites are completed by a bubbling jacuzzi, which makes for the perfect end to a busy day of work or sightseeing. A fairly recent refurbishment has resulted in

Each room in Hotel Villa Real is an example of the ingenious use of space.

East 47 presents the finest ingredients in a fresh and innovative contemporary style.

brand new furniture, floors and walls for each of the 115 rooms and suites, all of which proudly display contemporary Spanish lithographs.

Business travellers visiting Madrid will find the hotel's four meeting rooms fully equipped with the very latest in cutting-edge communications technology needed for conferences and meetings. For large-scale events, consider the spacious Cibeles Lounge or the vast Principe de Asturias.

The theme of fine art as décor is even extended to the hotel's restaurants. East 47, Hotel Villa Real's cocktail bar and restaurant, is a slick, contemporary venue which displays Andy Warhol's prints of Marilyn Monroe. At East 47, ingredients like fresh caviar, cod and game are innovatively transformed into a tempting series of delectable offerings. Contemporary in atmosphere and spirit, the fusion dishes on the menu of East 47 are ingenious flashes of culinary inspiration, and are perfectly complemented by the restaurant's selection of fine European wines.

Part of the Derby Hotels Collection, a group which prides itself on the singularity of each hotel under its umbrella, Hotel Villa Real has fulfilled what the group has set out to achieve in all its hotels. An expert focus on fine art and genuine antiques coupled with an unwavering attention to detail are the hallmarks of a Derby Hotel, and Hotel Villa Real, with its unparalleled collection of exquisite originals and exceptional service, has become widely known as a luxurious home away from home for its guests.

The outdoor terrace allows guests to dine to a view of the striking historical architecture that surrounds them.

Right: Andy Warhol's portraits of Marilyn Monroe cast their glance over diners at East 47.

Below: Style and comfort were paramount considerations for the interiors of Hotel Villa Real.

Rooms and amenities
- 115 guestrooms
- 5 Junior Suites
- 10 Duplex rooms
- 2 Duplex Superior rooms
- 2 Suites

Restaurants and bars
- East 47: Mediterranean, fusion, cocktails and drinks

Facilities
- Business centre
- 4 meeting rooms
- Wireless Internet access
- Ancient art collection

10 Plaza de Las Cortes, Madrid 28014, Spain
Tel: +34.91.420 3767 • Fax: +34.91.420 2547
Email: villareal@derbyhotels.com
Website: www.derbyhotels.com

All suites and rooms at Hotel Urban are elegantly modern, and feature their own unique piece of art.

Hotel Urban, Madrid

In a city with as much history as Madrid, it's no mean feat to make a splash on the architectural and entertainment scene the way the two-year-old Hotel Urban has. Not many hotels can boast a museum filled with Egyptian antiques dating back up to the 12th century BCE, not to mention Asian and African artworks displayed throughout the hotel. From the Papua New Guinean totems in the lobby to the Hindu statuettes attending each guestroom entrance, Hotel Urban is an art experience nonpareil.

The Art Deco exterior sets Hotel Urban apart from its surroundings, situated as it is between the Puerta del Sol and the museum district. The portico at the hotel's entrance, dramatically shaded by a spiral steel canopy, sets the stage for the imaginative interior.

Inside, there is a definite industrial feel, with stainless steel girders and glass lifts delineating the six-storey high atrium, while a 'golden chimney' (actually a staircase) ascends from the basement museum to the rooftop terrace. For contrast, a backlit alabaster column runs the full height of the building, complementing the skylight's natural illumination.

This air of elegant modernity also infuses the guestrooms. Dark wood furniture, leather fittings, carefully calibrated mood lighting and the very latest in technological conveniences come together to create a signature look of contemporary chic. The various rooms and suites reflect unique designs and different characters; to distinguish them further, every room has its own showpiece of ancient Asian art, complete with curatorial notes.

The hotel is also well wired for the modern traveller. Each room has wireless Internet access, testament to Hotel Urban's commitment to fulfilling all guests' modern-day requirements. It may be tempting to stay in, but that would certainly be a waste, considering the dining and entertainment opportunities offered by the hotel. The GlassBar serves cocktails, oysters and other light Japanese-inspired appetisers, and is stunningly designed, with a glass wall and floor cleverly underlit to set off the bar's luminous furnishing and chandelier.

The hotel's Europa Decó has taken Madrid by storm with its brand of Mediterranean cuisine, being named Best Restaurant during the Fifth Madrid fusion Gastronomic Meeting in 2007. The restaurant seats just 45, so that intimate air is always preserved. After dinner, head to the rooftop, where La Terraza del Urban awaits. A placid pool by day, it becomes a lively nightspot at sundown, serving exquisite cocktails in an open-air setting.

The latest addition to Hotel Urban's gastronomic offerings is El Cielo del Urban. Located on the roof terrace of the hotel, the intimate restaurant reminds one of Versailles in the 18th century, and serves fine hot and cold dishes in an exclusive setting by the pool.

With all this, it's little wonder that Hotel Urban was awarded Most Excellent Hotel in Europe and the Mediterranean from *Condé Nast Johansens* in 2006. A microcosm of what Madrid has to offer, Hotel Urban whets a visitor's appetite for the rich art and culture lying just minutes from its doorstep.

The hotel is committed to keeping every guest comfortable while still maintaining its unique style.

Below: La Terraza del Urban overlooks the city and is frequented by the city's chic crowd.
Below: Unique and strikingly designed, GlassBar is the perfect venue for a people-watching.

Rooms and amenities
· 84 guestrooms
· 14 suites

Restaurants and bars
· Europa Decó: Mediterranean and fusion
· GlassBar: oyster and cocktail bar, snack menu
· La Terraza del Urban: cocktails and snack menu
· El Cielo del Urban: international fine dining

Facilities
· Business centre
· 4 meeting rooms
· Limousine service
· Gym
· Solarium
· Egyptian museum and collection of ancient art
· Wireless Internet access

Carrera de San Jerónimo 34, Madrid 28014, Spain
Tel: +34.91.787 7770 • Fax: +34.91.787 7799
Email: urban@derbyhotels.com
Website: www.derbyhotels.com

Four Seasons Hotel George V, Paris

The most fashionable address in Paris, Four Seasons Hotel George V, Paris takes its name from avenue George V. A stone's throw away from the city's most fabulous landmarks: the Arc de Triomphe, Place de la Concorde and the Eiffel Tower, the hotel is located just off the Champs-Elysées.

Opened in 1928 as simply The George V, the hotel shot to international acclaim as the pinnacle of European hospitality. The word 'hotel' was deliberately omitted from its original name to announce a new standard of accommodation, that of a gracious private residence. Through the decades, noble heads of state, wealthy financiers and legendary glitterati have called the hotel home.

In 1997, Four Seasons Hotels and Resorts assumed management and started a two-year, US$125-million renovation. A most striking figure along avenue George V, the white stone Art Deco façade has been restored to its original minimalist grandeur, while the interiors were preserved to bring out the lavish splendour they once exuded. Also refurbished were countless works of art, which include 18th-century tapestries from Flanders, and a 47-sq-m (500-sq-ft) Savonnerie carpet. From the higher floors, panoramic views of the city make for a romantic respite.

The renovation also transformed the hotel's original 320 guestrooms into 245 of the most spacious rooms and suites in the city. Decorated to resemble small French apartments, the guestrooms are resplendent with Parisian flair, some with furniture in the

The epitome of Parisian opulence, the Presidential Suite is luxuriously appointed and plush.

Warm, rich wood tones add a cozy atmosphere to Le Bar.

style of Louis XVI, all with modern bathrooms of polished marble, and with separate showers and tubs. Each room also features the most cutting-edge telecommunications and entertainment technology.

Four Seasons Hotel George V, Paris is also renowned for its fine dining. Its centrepiece restaurant, Le Cinq, has been awarded two Michelin stars. Executive Chef Philippe Legendre has created an authentic French menu, executed by a staff of 70 cooks and delivered to tables in a sophisticated and intimate dining room.

The wine cellar is also a fascinating feature of the restaurant. It lies 14 m (46 ft) below ground level, and was built into a stone quarry directly under the hotel; guests can also book it as a dining space. With over 50,000 bottles, the cellar has a diverse range of tasteful labels to match every occasion or meal.

Classic French style is also ever-present in the spa, where beauty and relaxation treatments are carried out with expert care surrounded by rich Louis XVI décor and with vistas reminiscent of the gardens of Versailles.

For the casual traveller, Four Seasons Hotel George V, Paris is a destination in its own right; for the demanding business traveller it is the address for success.

Above: Opened in 1928, the hotel has since won several international accolades and has played host to various dignitaries and celebrities.
Left: Beautiful blooms add a soft touch to the hotel's interiors.

Exquisite murals depicting the gardens of Versailles surround the pool and whirlpool.

Rooms and amenities
- 186 guestrooms
- 33 one-bedroom suites
- 6 two-bedroom suites
- 11 Executive Suites
- 4 speciality suites
- 3 Presidential Suites
- 2 Royal Suites
- Bulgari toiletries

Restaurants and bars
- Le Cinq: haute French
- La Galerie: breakfast, afternoon tea, light fare, dinner
- Marble Courtyard: light fare (May–October)
- Le Bar: lunch, drinks and snacks

Facilities
- Business centre
- Boardroom
- 8 conference rooms
- Ballroom
- Spa
- Pool
- Fitness centre

31, avenue George V, Paris 75008, France
Tel: +33.1.4952 7000 • Fax: +33.1.4952 7010
Email: reservation.paris@fourseasons.com
Website: www.fourseasons.com/paris

The regal feel of the suites is extended to the bathrooms, which are lavishly appointed with the finest Carrara marble.

Hôtel de Crillon, Paris

A bona fide Parisian institution in its own right, the Hôtel de Crillon has retained all its turn-of-the-century charm in its décor. While it was only opened as a fully-fledged hotel in 1909, the history of this luxury guest house dates right back to the 18th century, when it served as the private residence of the Count de Crillon, friend and comrade of King Louis XV and his wife Marie-Charlotte de Corbon, subsequently passing through several illustrious generations of Crillons until the early 20th century.

While the impeccably restored fittings and interiors mean the Hôtel de Crillon bears little to no sign of its true age, its Louis XV style is a testament to its rich history and heritage. For want of a more suitable phrase, the Hôtel de Crillon has often been described as being the very epitome of *art de vivre*, bringing the art of living to new heights of luxury.

All guestrooms include trappings such as Carrara marble bathrooms with telephones, satellite flat-screen televisions and a full valet service; the suites are decorated with only the finest Aubusson carpets, Baccarat chandeliers and exquisite Wedgwood medallions.

Guests who are looking out for top-of-the-range Parisian accommodation will appreciate the opulent feel of the hotel's choicest suites. The Duc de Crillon Suite, with its oak-panelled floors and air of old-world refinement, has been entirely replicated in the Metropolitan Museum of New York. The Leonard Bernstein Suite, which is named after the world-famous composer and conductor, is a contemporary apartment comprising three bedrooms, two living rooms, a sauna, jacuzzi, and a Turkish bath. Each of the hotel's three Presidential Suites measure up to 344 sq m (3,700 sq ft), and have been recently redecorated with the finest materials, with the utmost care given to design and décor.

While its prime location on the Place de la Concorde means one has easy walking access to the best cafés and eateries in the city, it is hard to resist the bars and restaurants of Hôtel de Crillon. One may savour master chef Jean-François Piège's elegant and contemporary French cuisine served at the gourmet restaurant Les Ambassadeurs. Also not to be missed is L'Obélisque, where the same masterful touch shows itself in a selection of traditional yet creative light French dishes. The elegant bistro surroundings are relaxing and well-suited for an informal lunch or dinner. During the summer months, tables are set up outside in The Patio, allowing guests to enjoy the fine weather in a courtyard surrounded by the hotel's grand architecture. Warmed by sunshine, it's a perfect venue for drinks and light meals.

On a wintry day, little is more appealing than afternoon tea at the cosy and intimate Winter Garden, where refreshments and delicate teas are served in comfort and style. In the quintessentially Parisian Crillon Bar, designed by sculptor César and decorated by the famous Sonia Rykiel, one may enjoy a large selection of classic and trendy cocktails, all exclusive creations of the Head bartender. Sit back in one of the bar's comfortable chairs and enjoy the quiet piano—the perfect end to a day in the world's most romantic city.

Designer Sybille de Margerie combined 18th-century style with contemporary comfort in the Bernstein Suite.

Right: At The Patio, guests may enjoy casual drinks and meals in the open-air courtyard.

Below: A former ballroom now houses Les Ambassadeurs, which serves fine French gourmet cuisine.

Rooms and amenities
- 103 guestrooms
- 44 suites
- Annick Goutal toiletries

Restaurants and bars
- Les Ambassadeurs: gourmet French
- L'Obélisque: traditional French
- Winter Garden Tea Room: coffee, champagne, cocktails and afternoon tea
- Crillon Bar: drinks and bar snacks
- The Patio: light lunches

Facilities
- 24-hour business centre
- 8 banquet/meeting rooms
- 24-hour fitness centre
- Crillon boutique
- 24-hour room service
- Laundry and dry-cleaning services
- Baby-sitting services
- Personalised guest programmes

10 place de la Concorde, Paris 75008, France
Tel: +33.1.4471 1500 • Fax: +33.1.4471 1502
Email: crillon@crillon.com
Website: www.crillon.com

Hôtel Le Bristol, Paris

From the day Hôtel Le Bristol opened its doors in 1925, first and foremost in its owners' minds was providing guests with the best a hotel stay could offer while recreating the warm, intimate ambience of an opulent home. The rooms and suites house precious objects such as original engravings and Old Masters, crystal chandeliers, antique furniture and Persian carpets. Chintz curtains in lapis lazuli, emerald and raspberry impart freshness to the elaborate luxury.

Even the hotel's bathrooms have earned a reputation rivalling that of its rooms. Renowned for being one of the best and most spacious in Paris, much care has been taken with the décor, each of which features interiors of white Carrara marble, luxuriously large bathtubs, double wash basins and exquisite Anne Sémonin toiletries.

The rest of Hôtel Le Bristol bears the same touch. The white marble flooring and Île-de-France stone walls of the regal lobby are set off by 10 Baccarat crystal chandeliers, pink marble pillars, the finest tapestries from Gobelins and Louis XVI sofas upholstered in rare fabrics. The space is further graced by an imposing portrait of Marie Antoinette, set by the double line of pink marble columns flanking the path that leads up to the beautiful hotel garden. Many other 18th- and 19th-century art pieces, which were acquired via auction at the famed Louvre museum in the 1930s, decorate the hotel.

Hôtel Le Bristol is the only hotel in Paris with a restaurant that shifts with the seasons. From October to April, the restaurant occupies what was the private theatre of 19th-century owner Jules de Castellane, where much of the original

The luxurious restaurant is the only one of its kind in Paris that offers seasonal menus.

The bar at Hôtel Le Bristol, with its impressive portrait of Marie Antoinette to the side.

décor has been conserved. In summer, it moves outdoors to the Summer Restaurant Room in the largest hotel garden in Paris.

On Saturdays, Fashion High Teas make a fine accompaniment to afternoon tea, when guests can take in fashion shows whilst enjoying Chef Laurent Jeannin's array of fine pastry creations and special desserts inspired by the collection of the day. Other exciting new hotel developments include the acquisition of the adjacent building on the corner of avenue Matignon which means that the hotel will, by 2009, have 22 more rooms and 4 more suites, as well as a new grill restaurant accessible from the street. Some of the hotel's new facilities include the new concierge and reception desks, redecorated rooms, enlarged fitness room and kitchen, as well as children's VIP facilities.

Service at Le Bristol can lay claim to a long, illustrious tradition. Left your favourite novel behind after checking out? Housekeepers see to it that it will be just as you last left the next time you check in. The secret to this feat of memory is a photo of the room taken after each guest's departure. Such attention to fine detail ensure that a stay at Le Bristol will be marked only by complete peace of mind.

Sit back and relax with a drink at the Bar and Lounge, where light meals and refreshments are served too.

Top: The lavishly designed Suite Saint Honoré is characterised throughout by soft hues and elegant furnishings.

Left: The indoor pool at Hôtel Le Bristol offers relaxation sheltered from the vagaries of the changeable weather.

Right: The open air garden terrace is perfect for afternoon tea and refreshments.

Rooms and amenities
- 161 guestrooms including 73 suites (187 guestrooms including 77 suites by 2009)
- Anne Sémonin toiletries

Restaurants and bars
- restaurant: French gastronomy
- Bar and Lounge: light meals and drinks
- new grill restaurant by 2009

Facilities
- Business centre
- 5 function rooms
- Spa
- Fitness centre
- Hair salon
- On-site Mercedes smart cars
- Children's VIP facilities

112 rue du Faubourg Saint-Honoré, Paris 75008, France
Tel: +33.1.5343 4300 • Fax: + 33.1.5343 4301
Email: resa@lebristolparis.com
Website: www.lebristolparis.com

Natural light flooding in from the tall windows shows up the living room of the Imperial Suite in all its glorious space.

Park Hyatt
Paris–Vendôme

The prestigious Rue de la Paix is home to the luxurious Park Hyatt Paris–Vendôme. Its spotless 19th-century façade dominates the chic Parisian boulevards beneath, and it is a listed example of classical French architecture. Resplendent with high ceilings, colonnades and interior courtyards, the building attains an aesthetic symmetry, and the hotel's reverence for art is evident throughout. Famed architect and interior designer, Ed Tuttle, assimilated these classical influences when conceptualising this impressive contemporary creation.

The 168 custom-designed guestrooms and suites marry contemporary design with classic building materials such as rich mahogany and sleek limestone. Furnishings are understated and elegant, and the stylish fabrics exclusively commissioned from Jim Thompson.

Five years after its opening, Park Hyatt Paris–Vendôme has invested in revamping the hotel. Two new Presidential Suites have been added, both of them designed to integrate the 'In-Suite Spa' concept, unique in Paris, and the existing Presidential Suite has been similarly refurbished. Five prestigious Suites have also been newly renovated, as has the hotel's Spa.

Imagine a 250-sq-m (2,700-sq-ft) Suite featuring a 85-sq-m (915-sq-ft) high-ceiling living room, a bathroom that includes a steam room shower and a whirlpool bath, an area dedicated to soothing massages or a 60-sq-m (650-sq-ft) terrace overlooking Rue de la Paix and Place Vendôme. This is the stuff of which dreams are made: Park Hyatt Paris–Vendôme's Presidential Suites. Located on the 2nd and 5th floors, these suites are charming Parisian apartments that combine a private and homely feel with a warm atmosphere and design environment.

Park Hyatt Paris–Vendôme guests are invited to indulge in 250-sq-m (2,700-sq-ft) of Le Spa, dedicated to the ultimate sensory experiences. A mixed whirlpool bath, sauna and steam bath, and additional treatment rooms, including a special duo treatment room with a private whirlpool bath, make the spa a true sanctuary.

The crème de la crème of French cuisine is featured at Park Hyatt Paris–Vendôme's three restaurants. Executive Chef Jean-François Rouquette continually comes up with menus created around seasonal specialities. Sample breakfast or lunch in the lovely Les Orchidées restaurant-lounge, where the walls are hung with vibrant scenes of Parisian life, created by Christiane Durand. In the summer, guests may also dine al fresco amidst the olive trees and creamy parasols of La Terrasse. For evening dining options, the contemporary gastronomic Pur'Grill is an obvious choice. Honoured with one Michelin star, guests also enjoy a first-hand view of the chefs' mastery over their craft in the unveiled kitchen. For a post-dinner dram of whisky, try Le Bar, where over 70 varieties of the finest whiskies are offered in an elegant setting overlooking the interior courtyard.

Effortlessly combining classic opulence with contemporary hospitality and stellar levels of service, Park Hyatt Paris–Vendôme embodies a rare blend of tradition and luxury.

Tasteful furnishings and warm colour tones make the suites endlessly inviting after a long day.

Right: Park Hyatt Paris–Vendôme's classic architecture gives the hotel a distinct atmosphere of elegance.

Below: Enjoy an exquisite meal at the gastronomic Pur'Grill restaurant, and admire the culinary artistry that goes into each dish.

Rooms and amenities
- 132 guestrooms
- 36 suites
- Blaise Mautin toiletries

Restaurants and bars
- Les Orchidées: breakfast, lunch and afternoon teas
- Pur'Grill: Michelin-starred gastronomic restaurant, open for dinner
- Le Bar: drinks and cocktails
- La Terrasse: summer al fresco lunches and dinners

Facilities
- 24-hour business centre
- Wireless Internet in all public areas
- 2 boardrooms
- 5 function rooms
- Technology concierge and secretarial services
- Hyatt Pure Spa and fitness centre

5 rue de la Paix, Paris 75002, France
Tel: +33.1.5871 1234 • Fax: +33.1.5871 1235
Email: vendome@hyatt.com
Website: www.paris.vendome.hyatt.com

Enjoy a short break in the finely appointed lounge.

InterContinental Amstel Amsterdam

Amsterdam's first international-calibre hotel opened over 140 years ago, in 1867, as the Amstel Hotel. Since then, the waterfront establishment has maintained its status as the most renowned hotel in the Netherlands, and the de facto choice for the discerning traveller and visiting celebrities.

The story of the Amstel began with Dr Samuel Sarphati, a philanthropist with a vision for a grand hotel that would boost Amsterdam's standing in the travel world. Upon completion, it was a national icon of luxury, and over the years its history and fortunes have been deeply entwined with that of its city. In addition to being a cultural focal point and venue for countless parties and film shoots, the hotel has also enjoyed a long-standing relationship with Dutch nobility, hosting many royal weddings and banquets.

After an extensive two-year restoration that was completed in 1992, the InterContinental Amstel Amsterdam proudly displays its French Renaissance-inspired exterior and lavish interior in all of their original glory. Visitors have been known to stop on their way through the main entrance hall, overcome in admiration of its high ceilings and authentic 19th century details. Elaborate chandeliers, a classic winged staircase, and highlights of precious gold make for a stunning first impression before any rooms are even unlocked.

While the Amstel's 55 guest rooms and 24 suites all possess unique and varying designs, the one thing which remains consistent is their distinctly Dutch aesthetic. Traditional

The hotel location offers an exquisite waterfront view..

delftware porcelain work shows itself on lamps and ornamental vases, while sincere hospitality motivates the provision of the standard amenities on a more personal level. The customary in-room minibars come with their own touch of class, stocking exclusive snacks and beverages, and even full-sized bottles which would not seem out of place in any connoisseur's liquor cabinet. Some suites are also furnished with shelves carrying editions of the Encyclopædia Britannica.

Much of the Amstel's charm comes from its prominent location by the river. Evening brings with it spectacular views from the hotel's bedrooms as well as from its Michelin-starred restaurant, La Rive. Serving fine French Mediterranean cuisine just a few feet from the water's edge, it is unmatched in offering both mood and elegance. Wine aficionados will find hundreds of reasons to love the extensive cellar, much of its exquisite stock coming directly from France.

In the Amstel Bar & Brasserie, informal charm and clubhouse atmosphere come together in the best of ways. Unpretentious and understated, it's an obvious choice for a casual meal with friends, or for enjoying a chat accompanied by cocktails expertly poured at the solid wood-panelled bar. One could easily grow accustomed to this sort of cosiness. It takes a certain kind of temerity to provide so high a level of service with so casual an air, but the InterContinental Amstel Amsterdam has been doing it for close to a century and a half, and doing it right.

Above: Spacious yet cosy, the Executive Suite is a representation of both comfort and luxury.

Right: Tall windows and elegant pillars surround the hotel's swimming pool.
Below: An extensive selection of fine wines are available to complement your meal at La Rive.

Rooms and amenities
- 55 guestrooms
- 24 suites

Restaurants and bars
- La Rive: French Mediterranean fine dining
- Amstel Bar & Brasserie: cocktails and brasserie-style menu
- Glass Conservatory Lounge

Facilities
- Health Club & Fitness Centre
- 15 m heated indoor pool
- Spa with sauna, Turkish bath and jacuzzi
- Limousine service
- Business centre
- 6 meeting rooms
- High-speed wireless Internet access
- Three antique boats available for private canal cruises

Professor Tulpplein 1, Amsterdam 1018 GX, Netherlands
Tel: +31.20.622 6060 • Fax: +31.20.622 5808
Email: amstel@ihg.com
Website: amsterdam.intercontinental.com

Hotel Adlon Kempinski, Berlin

Old world charm meets new age luxury at the Hotel Adlon Kempinski, Berlin, a landmark in its own right beside Berlin's hallowed Brandenburg Gate. Fully restored to its century-old grandeur, the hotel continues to attract the luminaries and connoisseurs that bestow upon Berlin its cosmopolitan cachet.

Timeless elegance is a byword here—from the building's sweeping exterior, to its elegant lobby crowned by a stained glass dome, to the classical modern aesthetic that accents the interiors. Since 2003, the hotel has gradually expanded with new wings, presidential suites and conference facilities, offering the height of comfort and luxury to every guest.

The hotel's rooms and suites are impeccably appointed, and soothing shades of beige and gold predominate. The newest rooms all come equipped with state-of-the-art technological conveniences, such as built-in LCD screens which double as Internet terminals, and the ability to create private computer networks spanning several rooms, perfect for a group of business travellers. The entire hotel also has its own wireless Internet network. For those wanting a more personal brand of pampering, the newest private suites come with their own fitness room and sauna.

The very best in accommodation finds itself in the hotel's presidential suites. All three suites are appointed with the finest antiques and fittings from all over the world, and served by a butler round the clock. The newest presidential suite comes integrated with the security wing, offering cutting-edge

The Hotel Adlon Kempinski's interiors are marked by a recognisably classical modern aesthetic.

The hotel's relaxing spa is the perfect end to any long day of business or sight-seeing.

security technology, a direct lift, and rooms and suites to house accompanying members of the guest's party.

Adjacent to the hotel building, the Adlon Palais brings the sophisticated Adlon touch to modern conference facilities. The centrepiece of the building is the Palais ballroom, its lavish décor reminiscent of Versailles, Sanssouci and other castles. The smaller academy rooms are also opulently decorated, while tall rooms feature the latest presentation and communication technologies, such as high-power projectors and networked camera systems, which allow conferences to be transmitted live.

A highlight of any stay at the hotel would be a meal at the Michelin-starred Lorenz Adlon, which serves French haute cuisine in what used to be the reading room. Tables by the window enjoy a lovely view of the Brandenburg Gate. Alternatively, guests may choose to dine at the Restaurant Quarré. Featuring a patio that opens out directly to the Pariser Platz, the Restaurant Quarré uses regional produce to concoct new and exciting tastes, presenting exquisitely prepared cuisine with a modern flavour.

With a slew of national as well as international travel awards under its belt, the hotel is the hallmark of a true luxury stay in Berlin. Pairing an excellent location at the nexus of many historic sites with exquisite amenities and service, the Hotel Adlon Kempinski, Berlin will certainly leave even the most discerning guest well satisfied.

Window-side tables at the Lorenz Adlon overlook the famous Brandenburg Gate, allowing guests to enjoy the view along with fine French cuisine at the Michelin-starred restaurant.

Right: Situated next to the Brandenburg Gate, the majestic Hotel Adlon Kempinski, Berlin, is a landmark in its own right.
Below: The hotel's suites are all fitted with the finest in antiques and furnishings, and enjoy a butler's services around the clock.

Rooms and amenities
- 304 guestrooms
- 78 suites

Restaurants and bars
- Lorenz Adlon: French haute cuisine
- Restaurant Quarré: cuisine with a modern flavour
- Lobby Lounge & Bar: drinks and snacks

Facilities
- Conference facilities
- 2 ballrooms
- 13 conference rooms
- Adlon Day Spa
- Adlon Pool and Gym

Unter den Linden 77, 10117 Berlin, Germany
Tel: +49.30.2261 0 • Fax: +49.30.2261 2222
Email: hotel.adlon@kempinski.com
Website: www.hotel-adlon.de

The gorgeous, shimmering glass tiles and marble floors lend La Prairie Boutique Spa an otherworldly air.

The Ritz-Carlton, Berlin

Potsdamer Platz, one of the most bustling city squares of Europe, was razed during World War II and replaced by a section of the Berlin Wall. Today, after a reconstruction project of staggering proportions, Potsdamer Platz has been resurrected with an underground station, a shopping and entertainment centre, and several landmark towers, one of which houses The Ritz-Carlton, Berlin.

One of the exclusive hotel group's newer properties, The Ritz-Carlton, Berlin welcomes the well-heeled and worldly with a seamless combination of modern convenience and Old-World opulence. The hotel's exterior resembles the Art Deco styles glorified during the golden age of skyscrapers in New York City and Chicago. Inside, the hotel's clean, contemporary designs are accented with classical German imperial touches, crafted from only the finest marble, wood and bronze. The two-storey entrance features a massive central staircase and sturdy columns, invoking a sense of majesty.

Dining at The Ritz-Carlton, Berlin is more than just a gastronomic experience. Brasserie Desbrosses, discovered in Macon, France, was originally established in 1875. Hotel designers carefully dismantled the brasserie and moved it piece by piece to Berlin, restoring all of its authentic chairs, mirrors, panelling, Art Deco light fixtures and tile-work. Serving freshly baked confectionaries and simple French fare, plus a daily oyster and lobster buffet, guests are welcome to dine indoors or on the patio. Vitrum's fine cuisine is a blend of innovative, light gourmet fare, with special focus on the flavours from fresh herbs, spices, as well as vegetables, and their ideal combinations with fish and meat. The 54-seat restaurant, which has been honoured with one Michelin star, has a Venetian ambiance supported by inlaid Italian marble floors and old mirror-covered columns refreshed by the modern art of a Berlin art gallery. The handmade china, inspired by Murano & Burano, is created exclusively for the hotel.

Sumptuous rooms surround every guest with luxurious furnishing and cutting-edge technological conveniences at one's fingertips. Gold-coloured textiles drape over sofas and featherbeds, and polished inlaid cherry wood armoires glow alongside antique pieces and original artwork. The bathrooms have oversized tubs that can be filled to order by the bath butlers, with aromatherapy scents and essential oils, plus fresh flowers and delicious treats.

At the La Prairie Boutique Spa, escape to a secluded world of shimmering glass tiles, gold leaf, and glossy marble, where one can revitalise with treatments from La Prairie, swim in the indoor pool, or work out in the fitness area.

Distinguished Clefs d'Or concierges team with an army of butlers to deliver excellent service, a hallmark of the superior quality of Ritz-Carlton properties.

The rich, sumptuous fabrics and the refined décor make every suite fit for a king.

Above: The imperial staircase adds a sophisticated finishing touch to the lobby.
Left: The Grand Suite combines luxury with elegance.

Rooms and amenities

- 225 deluxe rooms
- 40 suites
- 37 club rooms

Restaurants and bars

- Vitrum: fine dining, one Michelin star
- Brasserie Desbrosses: brunch on sundays
- Terrace
- Tea Lounge: afternoon tea, cocktails and snacks
- The Curtain Club: drinks and snacks

Facilities

- Full-service business centre
- 8 meeting rooms; grand ballroom (divisible into three sections)
- La Prairie Boutique Spa
- Fitness area
- The Ritz-Carlton Boutique

Attention to details is what makes the hotel so distinctive.

Potsdamer Platz 3, Berlin 10785, Germany
Tel: +49.0.3033 7777 • Fax: +49.0.303 3777 5555
Email: berlin@ritzcarlton.com
Website: www.ritzcarlton.com

Bayerischer Hof, Munich

Situated on Promenadeplatz, in the heart of Munich, the Bayerischer Hof was built by the master architect Friedrich von Gärtner at the behest of King Ludwig I of Bavaria. With such illustrious beginnings, it is little wonder then that the hotel sets great store by its history. Almost completely obliterated during the Second World War, save for the Spiegelsaal (the Mirror Hall), it was restored by Falk Volkhardt, whose family has owned the hotel since 1897. The neighbouring Palais Montgelas, an equally famous building which saw the crowning of Maximilian III and the signing of the Bayerisches Konkordat, adds to the hotel's allure.

Continuing the family tradition, Volkhardt's daughter Innegrit now manages Bayerischer Hof, lavishing the same care and attention to detail, as well as the exquisite service that has been the hotel's hallmark for generations.

The hotel entered the 21st century with a strong sense of identity, reflected in the bold moves it has made in terms of interior design and refurbishment, all of which preserve the hotel's grand origins while keeping ahead of the latest trends in style and technology.

This is evident in its unique guestrooms and in the newly refurbished Panorama Floor. The elegantly timeless suites can be combined in any number of ways, including the option of a six bedroom suite. Bayerischer Hof offers six room styles: timeless classic Count Pilati style rooms and suites, chic Hans Minarik rooms, Colonial style rooms and suites in a luscious earth palette with exotic Afro-Asian details, cosy Country House style rooms, Grand Hotel

Wintergarten at the Blue Spa offers unmatched views over the city.

Above: The hotel's finely appointed bathrooms are indicative of their dedication to the comfort and enjoyment of their guests.
Left: falk's Bar proudly occupies the Spiegelsaal, which escaped the extensive bombings of World War Two.
Opposite: The stunning glass ceiling in the Atrium catches the eye as guests enter the lobby.

The sophisticated new Cosmopolitan R&B style rooms are designer chic and thoroughly comfortable.

style decorated with fresh and opulent fabrics from Laura Ashley, and the new, sophisticated Cosmopolitan R&B style rooms and suites with urban chic décor. Rooms and suites on the historical floors at the Palais Montgelas are large, regal affairs which can be combined for more space. For a truly lavish experience, the penthouse suites come with a fireplace and a whirlpool, and either an 80-sq-m (861-sq-ft) Mediterranean terrace, or an astonishing bedroom encased in glass for a breathtaking view over the rooftops of Munich.

The hotel's diversity extends to its many restaurants. International haute cuisine with Mediterranean and South-German influences is served at Garden-Restaurant, which boasts a rating of 16 Gault Millau points. Palais Keller, built in the 13th-century vaults which once hoarded the precious salt supplies of the city, offers hearty Bavarian fare, and its bakery is a source of fresh pastries, Bavarian pretzels and other delectable baked goods. For those with a taste for the exotic, Trader Vic's Polynesian and Pan-Asian menu and its Tiki style atmosphere will prove to be irresistible. The health-conscious guest will find a balanced choice of healthy meals that have Mediterranean and Oriental elements at the Wintergarten at the Blue Spa and at the Blue Spa barbecue on the panoramic terrace during the summer months.

For an award-winning spa experience, visit the hotel's Blue Spa. Designed by the famous French architect Andrée Putman, using only the finest of materials, the spa is a blend of elegance and timeless sophistication, well in

A colonial style room with sandy-coloured walls, adorned with exotic Afro-Asian artefacts.

touch with the contemporary vibe of Munich, but also seamlessly melding with the traditions of the hotel. Spanning over 1,200-sq-m (13,000-sq-ft) and set in rolling green vistas of landscaped gardens, it offers a myriad of ways to indulge and recharge. Guests may rejuvenate themselves with a traditional massage or take an invigorating swim in the crystalline pool, the natural light flooding in through the sliding glass roof illuminating its cobalt blue, silver and gold mosaic tiles. For relaxing after a hard day, the sauna has a range of soothing water therapies. Blue Spa also offers a makko ho and powernapping relaxation training programme, suited to the needs of business travellers.

When it's time for work, the hotel's well-equipped business centre offers full Internet and video-conferencing facilities, along with professional secretarial and translation services. Forty large, splendidly designed banquet rooms and a magnificent ballroom are also available to cater to events of all sizes, with capacities of up to 2,500 people.

For a night's entertainment, guests can try any of the hotel's six cosmopolitan bars, with *falk's* Bar and its original historical setting from 1831 as *primus inter pares*. Komödie im Bayerischen Hof features light theatrical-style entertainment performed by German stars of the stage and television. Night Club has become well known as a world-class contemporary jazz venue with a list of star performers. It is no wonder guests can always find something new and fascinating at the Bayerischer Hof.

The magnificent pool at the Blue Spa is a sight to behold with sunlight reflecting off the gorgeous mosaic tiles.

Right: An open air massage is the ideal way for any visitor to de-stress after an intensive morning of sightseeing or business meetings.
Below: The warm tones and luxurious fittings of the hotel suites give them an endlessly welcoming feel.

Rooms and amenities
- 313 guestrooms
- 60 suites

Restaurants and bars
- Garden-Restaurant: Mediterranean
- Trader Vic's: Polynesian
- Palais Keller: Bavarian
- Patio: breakfast
- Night Club: live jazz and drinks
- Piano Bar: live music, drinks and snacks
- *falk's* Bar: drinks and snacks
- Menehune Bar: drinks
- Blue Spa Bar & Lounge: drinks and light spa meals
- Wintergarten at the Blue Spa: international
- Kamin Lounge: drinks
- Empore: drinks
- Atrium: drinks
- Kömodie im Bayerischen Hof: theatrical performances and light entertainment

Facilities
- 40 function rooms
- Conference and banquet planning
- Spa and fitness centre
- A&T Hair salon with Hair Spa
- Beauty salon

2-6 Promenadeplatz, Munich 80333, Germany
Tel: +49.89.21200 • Fax: +49.89.2120 906
Email: info@bayerischerhof.de
Website: www.bayerischerhof.de

The magnificent grounds of the Çırağan Palace are just one aspect of the luxury that hotel guests enjoy.

Çırağan Palace Kempinski, Istanbul

When one of the world's great luxury hotel groups takes over one of the world's great palaces in one of the world's great cities, the results are bound to be as impressive as they are spectacular—and that is certainly the case with the Çırağan Palace Kempinski Istanbul.

Occupying prime position on the European bank of the Bosphorus, the Çırağan Palace (pronounced 'Chiraan') originally served as the main residence of the last of the magnificent Ottoman sultans, then subsequently as the country's parliament building. Today, having been wonderfully restored and expanded in size, it retains its palatial elements of Old World elegance and grandeur, skilfully combining them with first-class facilities and five-star levels of quality and customer service.

Indeed, everything here is on a grand scale. There are over 300 suites and bedrooms, 20 function rooms, a ballroom, two magnificent swimming pools, and a fully equipped health club and spa complex, all set within splendidly landscaped gardens—to name but a few of its features and facilities. All the hotel's features have undergone a recent renovation, ensuring that the uncompromisingly high standards and quality expected of a Kempinski hotel will be maintained for many years to come.

In addition, the hotel also houses its own shopping arcade and three of Istanbul's finest restaurants. Tuğra serves traditional Ottoman cuisine; while the acclaimed Laledan specialises in fish and seafood dishes; and Gazebo provides Turkish and international high tea as well as lighter meals and snacks. All of them enjoy extended beautiful views of the Bosphorus, and additionally, an extensive wine cellar and an attractive bar, the Çırağan, perfectly complement these dining arrangements.

Businessmen and event organisers will also find the Çırağan Palace ideally suited to their needs and requirements. State-of-the-art facilities and highly experienced staff ensure that their every conceivable need is smoothly anticipated and provided for with the utmost professionalism and consummate style for which the hotel is known. Of especial note are the Çırağan Weddings, highly sought after throughout the year, held on the beautiful grounds in the summer or in the ballroom overlooking the Bosphorus in the winter.

With so much the hotel has to offer, guests enjoy an attractive resort-like atmosphere that will tempt many to stay within its perimeters. For those wishing to explore the attractions in the surrounding city, however, quite a few of Istanbul's major shopping and entertainment districts are within convenient distance.

On one side of the hotel compound is the famed harbourside district of Ortakoy, which is renowned for its seafood restaurants, antique shops, mosque and a colourful street market. On the other side lies Besiktas, where small boats offering sightseeing tours of the several historical landmarks that line the Bosphorus can be found; and a short taxi ride away are the well-known shopping and entertainment districts of Akmerkez and Taksim.

Guests can dine in exquisite comfort in the newly renovated Tuğra restaurant.

Rooms and amenities
- 282 guestrooms
- 31 suites

Restaurants and bars
- Laledan: fish and seafood
- Gazebo: international and Turkish high tea
- Tuğra: traditional Ottoman and Turkish fine dining
- Çırağan Bar: cocktails and snacks

Facilities
- Health club
- Indoor and outdoor pools (heated during winter)
- Gardens
- Business centre
- Conference facilities

Right: An open air massage treatment is the perfect way to relax and unwind after a full day of sightseeing.

Below: The Çırağan Palace hosts elaborate open-air functions with consummate style and flourish.

Çırağan Caddesi. No: 32, Besiktas 34349, Turkey
Tel: +90.212.326 4646 • Fax: +90.212.259 6687
Website: www.kempinski-istanbul.com

The Ritz-Carlton, Istanbul

The pace of life in Istanbul increases by the day as countless traders, entertainers, and visitors come and go in the world's only city to straddle two continents. For the former capital of three landmark empires, that's saying a lot. But for every advancement made in the East Roman, Byzantine, and Ottoman eras, more are made every day in what is slated to be the European Capital of Culture in 2010.

Situated right in the middle of the famed Dolmabahçe quarter is the unrivalled Ritz-Carlton, Istanbul. In the same way that Istanbul naturally blends influences from Europe and Asia, the hotel smoothly juxtaposes the clean, sharp lines of a modern skyscraper with a distinctively relaxing and opulent interior. The main reception lobby is fitted with Turkish accents and designs inspired by Ottoman art. Everything, from the lush Turkish carpets and marble-inlaid floors to the artwork on the walls, commissioned from acclaimed artist Timur Kerim Incedayı, sharply contrasts the modern hotel format to wondrous effect.

From the guestrooms which overlook the Bosphorus Strait, the source of this productive commingling, the landscape is even clearer. Observe fleeting moments of Istanbul life—morning prayers at the mosque, the rush hour traffic between ancient monuments, and the fading lights of the financial district as lovers meander into Maçka Park—and the prospect of a personal adventure in the city becomes irresistible. Many major attractions lie within walking distance, including the popular meeting place, Taksim Square.

The elegant reception lobby is accented with Turkish designs and specially commissioned artwork.

Enjoy the sun's rays in comfort and luxury.

Tulips, the flowers celebrated by Ottoman sultans, subtly dominate the interiors in the form of fabric print motifs. The luxurious bathrooms are appointed in marble and cobalt blue Iznik tiles, and the soft, feather down beds and 300-thread count sheets are gold-leafed and fit for royalty. Housekeeping adds a delightful touch with a turndown service that places scented olive oil soap, a pumice stone, or lavender essence on every pillow in time for the evening.

At the Laveda Spa, guests may indulge in the therapies of the traditional Turkish Hamam, a relaxing total body wash. The spa also has nine treatment rooms, including two intimate couple suites, complete with private whirlpool. Their menu of signature massages and therapies promise to replenish even the most tired bodies.

Those looking to navigate the history of the world's first fusion cuisine would do well to start at the Çintemani restaurant, which serves Mediterranean food as well as a selection of Turkish wines and spirits, including traditional Raki aniseed liquor.

At night, sweet cocktails paired with grilled dishes on Güney Park Terrace complement the view of the nearby Princess Islands perfectly, while a warming glass of whisky at the RC Bar is an obvious choice during the winter months. Romantic, invigorating, and anything but still, Istanbul deserves a partner that can keep the pace. With its ability to set a few paces of its own, The Ritz-Carlton, Istanbul may just prove to be the most fitting candidate.

At The Ritz-Carlton, Istanbul, returning to your room is as comfortable as going home.

Right: Elegant furnishings accent the hotel with a touch of Ottoman splendor.
Below: Indulge in the full treatment offered at the Laveda Spa.

Rooms and amenities
- 164 guestrooms
- 21 Executive Suites
- 57 Club Level Rooms
- The Presidential Suite
- The Ritz-Carlton Suite

Restaurants and bars
- Çintemani: all-day dining, Mediterranean cuisine
- The Lobby Lounge: afternoon tea, evening cocktails
- Güney Park: outdoor terrace, Turkish grilled menu
- RC Bar: malt whiskies, cigars, live music

Facilities
- Laveda Spa
- 24-hour fitness centre
- Full-service business centre
- Gift and jewellery shop
- Beauty and hair salon
- Technology Butler
- High-speed wireless Internet access

Suzer Plaza, Elmadag, 34367 Sisli, Istanbul Turkey
Tel: +90 .212. 334 4444 • Fax: +90 .212. 334 4455
Email: rc.istrz.reservations@ritzcarlton.com
Website: www.ritzcarlton.com/en/properties/istanbul

The hotel terrace allows guests to dine in comfort while enjoying the exquisite views of Moscow.

Ararat Park Hyatt Moscow

Right in the heart of the old Moscow stands the Hyatt International's majestic contribution to the stunning architectural landscape of this city: the Ararat Park Hyatt Moscow. Bringing with it the outstanding quality and personalised service that is synonymous with this world-class hotel chain, the Ararat Park Hyatt Moscow deftly combines cutting edge technology and luxurious amenities with traditional homely comforts. Being within walking distance of the historical trio of Red Square, the Kremlin and the Duma—and also the Tverskaya Street shopping district— the age-old real estate adage of 'location, location, location' has most certainly been heeded to great advantage.

As a tribute to the Hotel Armenia—which once occupied the very site where the Ararat Park Hyatt Moscow currently stands—and in keeping with the historical landmarks that surround it, the hotel's outward appearance resembles an ancient Armenian building. The elaborately carved white stone façade features cornices and high reliefs, giving the building a gracious air of antiquity. The moment guests walk through the tall granite columns framing the entrance, however, they will see that everything else about the hotel is set firmly in the 21st century.

The vast atrium, eleven floors high, with glass lifts cruising between floors, is only a taste of what is to come. All guestrooms and suites are light and spacious, and some offer Moscow's best views over the iconic Bolshoi Theatre and the Kremlin. Plush bed linens

and luxurious feather duvets proffer a cosy respite against the biting cold weather outside, while lavish marble bathrooms that come with oversized tubs and heated floors are sanctuaries of indulgence.

Those on business can continue their work in comfort and convenience, sitting at a large desk, with wireless Internet access, while still enjoying the privacy of their own rooms.

If the morning's work has been grueling or sightseeing exhausting, the hotel's Quantum Club offers the perfect remedy. No ordinary hotel gym, the Quantum Club boasts a 17-m (55-ft) lap pool, with built-in resistance current to heighten the workout, and the latest range of next-generation 'smart' equipment. The choice of spa treatments is astoundingly wide; highly recommended is the Banya with besom in the roman baths, guaranteed to revive the weary.

The Ararat Park Hyatt Moscow is so named for the renowned Café Ararat, located in the old Hotel Armenia. Today, a complete and faithful replica of this exquisite café, serving up traditional Armenian fare, can be found within the Ararat Park Hyatt and it is undoubtedly the jewel in the hotel's crown. With a distinctly art nouveau feel, the atmospheric café is resplendent in carved stone and period wooden furnishings, with a sumptuous draped roof and, like the hotel itself, shouldn't be missed.

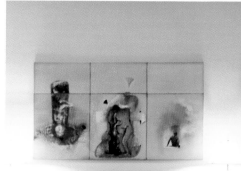

Sumptuous use of material and fabric in the interiors make Ararat Park Hyatt Moscow a sight to behold.

The Ararat Park Hyatt Moscow's indoor pool is a bastion of relaxation and also boasts the benefits of exercise.

Rooms and amenities
- 216 guestrooms and suites

Restaurants and bars
- Café Ararat: Armenian
- Enoki Sushi Bar: Japanese
- Park Restaurant: international
- Conservatory Lounge & Bar: drinks and snacks

Facilities
- Quantum Club: gym and spa
- Conference facilities
- Business centre

The Winter Garden Suite commands clear views of Moscow on a bright day.

4 Neglinnaya Street, Moscow 109012, Russia
Tel: +7.495.783 1234 • Fax: +7.495.783 1235
Email: moscow@hyatt.com
Website: moscow.park.hyatt.com

The Ritz-Carlton, Moscow

For more than two hundred years, Number 3 Tverskaya Street has remained a famed point of hospitality in the city of Moscow. Beginning as a popular tavern and lodge for travellers in the 18th century, it was also the site of the Hotel Paris until the 1930s—an establishment famous for its place in the hearts of many Russian writers and poets. From 1970 to 2002, the much-loved Intourist Hotel stood in its place, watching over the iconic Kremlin and Red Square as the former Soviet Union grew ever more affluent with the passing of time.

In 2007, the historic address was reborn as The Ritz-Carlton, Moscow, perhaps the most luxurious hotel that Russia has ever seen. Built at a cost of US$350 million, its dramatic exterior designed by architectural heavyweights Mosproject, the building calls to mind the palatial forms of imperial Russian classicism. Inside, every guestroom and public space is an opulent concoction of striking modernity and vintage elegance handcrafted by the famous interior designer, Peter Silling.

Home to three-star Michelin chef Heinz Winkler's newest restaurant, Jeroboam, The Ritz-Carlton, Moscow raises the bar for service and quality in the region, which may explain its popularity with government and social elites. Gourmands will also want to explore one gastronomical feature unique to the hotel: the Tsar's Breakfast. At a cost of US$700 per person, this extravagant morning meal features a bottle of Cristal champagne, Kobe beef, a cheese and truffle omelette, foie gras 'au torchon' and an assortment of other rich delights.

The hotel offers a view of famous landmarks from guests' very own bedrooms.

Enjoy fine dining with a local touch in Jeroboam.

Another five-star contribution The Ritz-Carlton, Moscow brings to the table is an entirely new breed of glamorous spa experience by ESPA. The stylish facility boasts a seemingly endless pool, created from gold-flecked black glass and hundreds of glittering Swarovski crystals. Occupying over 2,000 sq m (21,528 sq ft), the lavishly decorated ESPA offers 14 massage rooms, saunas, air-jet hot pools and showers, relaxation halls, and an ice fountain amidst atmospheric features such as a golden glass mosaic water wall. Treatments and skin therapies holistically bring together the timeless disciplines of hydrotherapy, aromatherapy, phytotherapy and thalassotherapy to help soothe tense muscles and rediscover the body's natural balance.

Famously beginning at rates of US$1,000 a night, all of the 334 guestrooms and suites in The Ritz-Carlton, Moscow boast a privileged view of the city centre. Guests on the exclusive Ritz-Carlton Club floors also enjoy a personal concierge service, private check-ins, and five indulgent food and beverage presentations, complete with champagne, throughout the day and in the evening.

The Red Square lies adjacent to the hotel, putting many famous landmarks such as the Lenin Mausoleum and St Basil's Cathedral within walking distance. With its impressive first year on historic Tverskaya Street, The Ritz-Carlton, Moscow is destined to become a part of Moscow's reinvention as a renaissance city.

The opulent hotel suites in The Ritz-Carlton, Moscow were all individually designed by acclaimed hotel interior designer Peter Silling.

Right: O2, the stylish rooftop lounge, turns into a trendy and upbeat nightspot when the sun goes down.
Below: Bold yet elegant, the hotel's interior is a striking combination of modern and classic elements.

Rooms and amenities

- 268 guestrooms
- 66 suites

Restaurants and bars

- Jeroboam: fine dining with a regional accent
- Caviarterra: Russian and Georgian
- O2 Lounge: rooftop lounge and terrace with Japanese food
- Ritz-Carlton Bar & Lobby Lounge: featuring a champagne and vodka selection

Facilities

- Health club and spa by ESPA
- Beauty salon
- Technology Butler service
- Bath Butler service
- Shoe Butler service
- Nightlife Butler service
- Multi-lingual staff
- Meeting and conference facilities

Tverskaya Ulitsa 3, Moscow 125009, Russia
Tel: +7.495.225 8888 • Fax: +7.495.225 8400
Email: moscow.inquiries@ritzcarlton.com
Website: www.ritzcarlton.com

Swissôtel Krasnye Holmy, Moscow

The city of Moscow probably has one of the most tumultuous and colourful histories of any capital in Europe. Witness to repeated sackings and uprisings, bloody revolutions, dictatorships, sieges and coup attempts, to name but a few of its travails, Moscow has finally emerged as a booming, sophisticated market economy. Testament to this radical evolution is the stunning new Swissôtel Krasnye Holmy, which at 34 floors, offers some of the most breathtaking views of Moscow, and an exclusive haven of comfort for the discerning business and leisure traveller.

Ideally located close to the historic Kremlin, residence of the Tsars—with its impressive multitude of palaces, armouries, churches and fortresses—the Swissôtel Krasnye Holmy is built in an elegant, contemporary style. The spacious rooms are decorated in light beiges, creams and taupes which, when combined with polished wood floors and subtle lighting, make for a warm, inviting retreat.

The luxurious bathrooms of chestnut wood and marble, with walk-in showers and deep bathtubs are nothing short of complete and utter indulgence. With guestrooms that boast nearly every single modern convenience imaginable and thoughtful extras such as espresso machines, flat screen televisions, and full-height windows overlooking Moscow's downtown, guests will be hard pressed to find a reason to leave the comforts of their rooms.

Business travellers will find that every detail has been considered in order to make their stay a productive one. Spacious work desks, wireless

The towering façade of the Swissôtel Krasnye Holmy affords guests matchless views of Moscow.

Internet access, data ports and dual phone lines are standard in all rooms, as well as the fully equipped Business Centre. The Executive Club Lounge offers breakfast, all-day refreshments and light snacks, and a boardroom for groups of up to eight people, while a total of 11 state-of-the-art conference rooms are available for large-scale and medium events.

As an antidote to the icy wind and snow, or simply to unwind and relax after a hectic day's sightseeing, guests can indulge at the Amrita Spa & Wellness Centre. The award-winning Amrita concept focuses on providing a haven of relaxation and wellbeing, through holistic and integrated care of the skin, body and soul. This sanctuary of tranquillity is well equipped with all the latest technology for aromatherapy and thalassotherapy, as well as sports, Thai and Swedish massages.

Dining has been elevated to a fine art at the Swissôtel Krasnye Holmy. Guests are spoilt for choice with several bars and restaurants to choose from, including the innovative Café Swiss which offers a different themed buffet every weeknight. Alternatively, those with a head for heights can enjoy bird's eye views of Moscow while sipping on a cool cocktail at the ultra-chic City Space Bar & Lounge on the 34th floor—a memorable addition to an ideal evening spent at the Swissôtel Krasnye Holmy.

The towering full-height windows afford marvellous views of Moscow, particularly impressive at night.

Above: Rooms are stylishly and tastefully furnished in order to maximise the highest levels of guest comfort and satisfaction.

Left: The fully equipped fitness centre is a welcome opportunity to compensate for the exquisitely indulgent meals served at the hotel restaurants.

Rooms and amenities
- 233 guestrooms and suites

Restaurants and bars
- Café Swiss: all-day meals, themed buffet dinners from Monday to Friday
- Concerto Bar: burgers and light meals
- City Space Bar & Lounge: contemporary Japanese and cocktails
- Lightbar: light snacks and desserts
- PURE: opening in September 2008

Facilities
- Amrita Spa & Wellness Centre
- Business Centre
- 11 conference rooms

Artistic flourishes make the Swissôtel Krasnye Holmy a stylish haven of luxury.

Kosmodamianskaya Nab 52
Building 6, Moscow 115054, Russia
Tel: +7.495.787 9800 • Fax: +7.495.787 9800
Email: moscow@swissotel.com
Webpage: www.moscow.swissotel.com

Grand Hyatt Dubai

Towering majestically by the edge of the creek that runs through Dubai, Grand Hyatt Dubai is the epitome of its home city—vast, lavish and exceedingly comfortable. With 674 rooms, it is the largest hotel in Dubai and boasts everything that a five-star status has come to mean.

Its immense lobby draws exclamations of awe from guests from the moment they enter. Outdoors, the city may not exactly be lush with greenery, but step into Grand Hyatt Dubai's lobby to witness Dubai's only rainforest—albeit a man-made one. More than an oasis, the hotel has brought the tropics into the desert.

While everything within these luxurious walls may seem incredibly modern, there really is plenty of Dubai's history captured within its design. Unbeknownst to most guests, on the ceiling are four dhows (traditional Arabic boats), embedded in the atrium. A nod to the pivotal role of such boats in Dubai's commercial history, these dhows—made of Ghulam timber from New Zealand—bear the weight of the roof.

The magnificent chandelier in the lobby's Al Nakheel Lounge is yet another extraordinary feature. In further tribute to Dubai's history, the chandelier comprises sparkling ropes of crystals fashioned to resemble a long string of shining pearls—a nod to Dubai's historic pearl fishing trade. The name of the lobby lounge, Al Nakheel, means 'palm trees', inspired by the date palms found all over the city to this day.

Additionally, specially commissioned art for the hotel abounds. In the lobby, two impressive light sculptures adorn the walls, each made of approximately 1,200 pieces of elegantly curved

The sparkling pool is a tempting way to spend an afternoon.

Above: The majestic Baniyas Grand Ballroom offers over 4,340 sq m (46,700 sq ft) of event space.

Right: The lobby of the hotel is unimaginably grand, and plays host to Dubai's only rainforest.

Opposite: The breathtaking view of Dubai out of the Grand King Room.

glass slivers from Andromeda, Italy. The glass is infused with gold, endowing the sculptures with a warm glow. The sculptures reflect Dubai's sea and desert. The piece that represents the sea is resplendent in shades of coral and aquamarine, while the desert piece is a calming work in sandy hues and oasis-bright touches.

On the hotel's walls are paintings created by three Arabic artists on commission by the hotel. Cairo-based Mohammed Youssef Hossen's work was inspired by Dubai's camels and horses, with village scenes featuring the old ways of Dubai. Zohra Moideen focuses on traditional Arabic jewellery, and Abdul Quadir Hassan Elmubarak's work is abstract with Afro-Islamic influences.

From the hotel's gorgeous rooms guests can gaze at Dubai's brilliant skyline. Room décor is contemporary meets classical Arabian, with amenities such as sumptuous king-size beds with Dorfmueller duvets, spacious work areas with high-speed Internet access, and stylish Italian marble baths. There are also 186 fully serviced apartments and 10 four-bedroom villas available for long-term lease.

Business travellers will appreciate Grand Hyatt Dubai's meeting space—all 4,340 sq m (46,700 sq ft) of it. It is easily the Middle East's largest, most sophisticated luxury conference facility, equipped with the latest ultra-modern digital technology. Suitable for everything from corporate meetings to global conferences, the hotel offers two ballrooms, each of which can be divided into three sound-proof sections and 11 further meeting rooms. A dedicated team ensures seamless operation of every event.

With 674 rooms, all of them luxuriously appointed, Grand Hyatt Dubai is the largest hotel in Dubai.

Naturally, the dining and entertainment options at Grand Hyatt Dubai are nothing less than exceptional. A grand total of 14 bars, fine restaurants and cafés are available throughout the hotel, offering a diverse range of world cuisines, including Lebanese, Italian, Singaporean, Japanese and American. For pre- and post-meal drinks, head to Vinoteca, which boasts a vast collection of the finest Italian wines, or Cooz jazz bar, with its large menu of premium champagnes, single-malt whiskies, cognacs and cocktails.

Jumeirah Beach may be just a 20-minute drive away, but this hardly seems to matter in the least when the hotel's massive pool area and opulent green gardens are so near at hand. A landscaped outdoor pool is perfect for a day of soaking up the sunshine, while a children's and toddler's wading pool comes with a special shaded area to protect delicate young ones from harmful UV rays. Inside, a sophisticated temperature-controlled lap pool is accompanied by a sub-aquatic sound system, making the crawl from one end of the pool to the other a soothing musical experience.

After a long workday, The Grand Spa offers treatments to help melt away any strain. Just be sure to indulge only after a hard day, not before, for it may be too tempting to forget all about business and relax in the pleasures that the spa (and hotel) have to offer.

Unmatched levels of luxury are what distinguish Grand Hyatt Dubai from other hotels.

Above: Enjoy smooth jazz and a cocktail at Cooz.
Below: At iZ, experience a taste of India with their selection of tandoori and other authentic dishes.

Rooms and amenities
- 632 guestrooms
- 42 suites
- 186 serviced apartments

Restaurants and bars
- Atwar: Lebanese
- Manhattan Grill
- Andiamo: Italian
- Market Café: international
- Peppercrab: Singaporean seafood
- iZ: Indian tandoori
- Sushi
- Vinoteca: Italian wine bar
- Al Nakheel Lounge: snacks and drinks
- Cooz: jazz bar
- Pool bar: salads and Asian specialities
- Mix: nightclub
- Panini: Italian café and deli

Facilities
- 2 conference pillarless ballrooms (divisible into three soundproof sections)
- 11 multi-use meeting rooms
- Events lawn for outdoor events
- VIP room with separate entrance to Convention Centre
- Technology Concierge
- Wireless Internet access throughout the hotel
- Business Centre
- Spa
- Gym
- Jogging track
- 4 tennis courts
- Kid's Club
- 2 squash courts

P.O. Box 7978, Dubai, UAE
Tel: +971.4.317 1234 • Fax: +971.4.317 1235
Email: reservations.grandhyattdubai@hyattintl.com
Website: dubai.grand.hyatt.com

The Palace –
The Old Town

In a city that has experienced one of the fastest evolutions in history, going from the development of downtown skyscrapers to becoming the home of the world's tallest building just years later, a new hotel takes the less-travelled road to five-star luxury. Part of The Old Town Island project, The Palace – The Old Town has an excellent view of the record-breaking Burj Dubai tower with which it shares a large man-made lake, yet the two experiences could not be more dissimilar.

Created as a modern re-imagining of ancient Arabian life, The Old Town Island emphasises the personal over the public and low-rises over the high-rise buildings which are so common today. Its array of winding streets and lively market squares stand in wonderfully marked contrast to the orderly, vertical arrangement found in most modern lifestyle complexes. In this spirit, The Palace – The Old Town possesses a commanding palatial presence truly worthy of its name.

Seamlessly blending past and present, the approximately 40,000-sq m (215,278-sq ft) property integrates symmetrical arches, high ceilings, open courtyards, and enchanting terraces, all fronted by a classically Middle-Eastern façade that belies the richly appointed interiors and wealth of modern conveniences within. Every one of the 242 rooms and suites offers a charming Arabian atmosphere and a level of comfort worthy of the world's most opulent city. Utilising fine materials such as silk, with furnishings and woodwork that embrace traditional lattices and motifs, the

The rich Arabian atmosphere extends to the hotel's palatial suites.

The hotel's exterior is designed in a typically Middle Eastern style.

rich, tactile environments communicate a sense of place that matches the view beyond their windows.

As an upgrade to the standard Deluxe rooms, Palace rooms come with a range of services suited to business travellers, including airport transfers, Executive Lounge access, a dedicated Guest Relations and Butler service, and the use of the hotel's LeSpa sanctuary. Consisting of two separate levels for male and female guests, LeSpa has a unique selection of massage therapies that make use of its relaxed treatment rooms, Vichy shower, and full Oriental bathhouse.

In addition to the typically Mediterranean and Middle-Eastern cuisine found at the Ewaan restaurant, the hotel also houses two exotic eateries: Asado, where an Argentinean style influences the grill cuisine, and Thiptara, Dubai's first Thai fine dining restaurant, with magnificent views of the Burj Dubai from its secluded location on the lake. For larger events, two of the hotel's four spacious meeting rooms are able to accommodate up to 250 people for corporate functions or banquets.

With such essential destinations as the Dubai World Trade Centre and Convention Centre nearby, one might be forgiven for imagining The Palace – The Old Town as little more than a downtown hotel with a fanciful name. Upon closer inspection, however, the hotel and its spot in Old Town Island present a far more colourful side of the Emirates.

The hotel rooms provide a range of modern amenities, all of which blend in seamlessly with the traditional décor.

Left: The outdoor pool is framed by palm trees, adding to the hotel's Middle-Eastern atmosphere.

Below: The hotel offers a range of cuisine from all over the world, from local fare to Argentinean grill and Thai fine dining.

Rooms and amenities
- 161 guestrooms
- 81 suites

Restaurants and bars
- Asado: Argentinean grill
- Ewaan: Mediterranean and Middle Eastern
- Thiptara: royal Thai

Facilities
- LeSpa: spa and Oriental bathhouse with hammam table
- Fitness centre
- Outdoor pool
- Four meeting rooms including a pre-function area
- Wireless Internet access
- Private beach access
- 24-hour dedicated butler service

The Old Town Island, Downtown Burj Dubai,
PO Box 9770 Dubai, UAR
Tel: +971.4.428 7888 • Fax: +971.4.428 7999
Email: h6230-re@accor.com
Website: www.sofitel.com

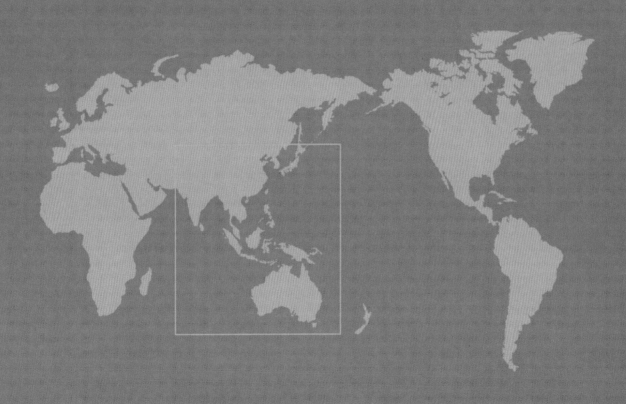

Asia & The Pacific

Grand Hyatt Beijing

Created to accommodate every conceivable need a business traveller might have while in Beijing, the Grand Hyatt Beijing in Oriental Plaza on East Chang An Avenue is easily one of the capital's greatest assets. Located a heartbeat away from such tourist attractions as the Forbidden City, Tiananmen Square, and the shopping street of Wangfujing, its central location makes it especially suitable for those travelling with partners or families.

The hotel's beautiful yet unobtrusive design scheme is the result of observing Chinese aesthetic traditions whilst endeavouring to create streamlined, modern configurations suited to international tastes. Each of the 825 rooms and suites come with such thoughtful provisions as enhanced work desks, dual-line phones with voicemail and high-speed Internet access. Club Rooms and select suites include access to the exclusive Grand Club Lounge, where guests enjoy complimentary breakfasts, evening cocktails, and beverages served all day.

For the ultimate in executive indulgence, the Grand Hyatt Beijing offers a series of newly renovated Diplomat Suites. With the luxury of overlooking the Forbidden City from the highest floors of the hotel, these suites of up to 91 sq m (980 sq ft) are an exceptional exercise in hospitality and comfort. Each suite is composed of a large living room, bar area, study area, and a spacious bedroom with soft down duvets and crisp linens. When the need to connect arises, the oversized working desks in study areas are equipped with fax machines and AV docks, while wireless Internet access

With the business amenities offered by the Diplomat Suite, even work can be a pleasure.

The pool has been designed to resemble a lush tropical resort.

turns any area into an impromptu workspace. Blurring the line between work and play are high-tech features such as twin 42-inch plasma TVs, iPod docking stations, and entertainment systems that play DVDs, VCDs, CDs, and MP3s.

Unique to the business experience at the Grand Hyatt Beijing is 'the residence'. Occupying over 1,142 sq m (12,292 sq ft), it is the first multi-function venue in the city to be presented as a luxury lifestyle space. The facility includes three meeting rooms, two coffee bars, a lounge area, and a private office that can be arranged to allow any event from a small board meeting to a presentation for 600. Displayed throughout are specially commissioned pieces of art—such as Tony Scott's Temple Series, comprised of 1,000 painted wood panels—meant to express the multiple facets of the fast-changing Chinese identity. The paintings and sculptures instill a sense of place and meaning in the area that is sure to enhance any assembly of international professionals held here in the capital city.

For more traditional events and meetings, there is a Grand Ballroom as well as several Grand Salons and Drawing Rooms for a total of 2,924 sq m (31,474 sq ft) of function facilities. A series of restaurants and bars provide the scene for entertainment, and a marvelous Hyatt Pure Spa and fitness centre take care of everything in between, making Grand Hyatt Beijing a perfect destination for both work and play.

Made in China serves delicacies from northern China, and the show kitchen allows one to watch chefs at work.

Right: The jacuzzi is another feature that guests will appreciate.
Below: The rooms have an appealing minimalist décor which blends modern and Chinese influences.

Rooms and amenities
- 825 guestrooms and suites

Restaurants and bars
- Made In China: contemporary Chinese
- Noble Court: Cantonese
- Da Giorgio: Italian
- Grand Café: all-day international dining and buffet
- Fountain Lounge: drinks and afternoon tea
- Redmoon: Japanese and drinks
- The Patisserie: freshly baked pastries

Facilities
- Hyatt Pure Spa and Club Oasis fitness centre
- Indoor pool
- Grand Club Lounge
- Business centre
- 2,924 sq m (31,474 sq ft) of function space
- Shopping arcade

Beijing Oriental Plaza, 1 East Chang An Avenue, Beijing 100738, China
Tel: +86.10.8518 1234 • Fax: +86.10.8518 0000
Email: grandhyattbeijing@hyattintl.com
Website: beijing.grand.hyatt.com

The Shangri-La Hotel, Beijing

With the intention of creating an iconic new landmark in China's capital city, one that would represent the leading edge of Asian hospitality at the crossroads of Beijing's most desirable avenues, the Shangri-La Hotel, Beijing was reborn. Located in the western half of the city, amidst vibrant financial and technological growth, the hotel enjoys a location that is convenient to both holidaymakers and business travellers. From Beijing Capital Airport, the restful charms of the hotel's 670 inviting rooms and suites are a scant 30 minutes away.

Originally occupying a single 24-storey, 528-room tower, the Shangri-La Hotel, Beijing has recently expanded in a lavish way with the construction of a brand new Valley Wing, named after the original, highly successful Shangri-La Valley Wing in Singapore. On top of adding another 142 rooms, of which 22 are some of the city's grandest suites, the Valley Wing brings several new aspects of luxury living to the property and to the city itself. The Valley Wing's opening in March 2007 marked the debut of CHI—the hotel group's signature spa brand—in Beijing.

Guestrooms at the Valley Wing were designed to exceed expectations. For starters, they are some of the largest in the city, with standard rooms beginning at no less than a staggering 50 sq m (538 sq ft). Measurements rise exponentially all the way up to the 245-sq-m (2,670-sq-ft) Presidential Suite. A butler service is available to all guests at the Valley Wing, as is access to an exclusive Valley Wing Lounge where days begin with complimentary buffet

Above: With its soothing waterfall feature and koi pond, The Garden Bar and Terrace is ideal for a relaxing cocktail.

Left: After just a year, CHI, The Spa at the Shangri-La Hotel, Beijing has been crowned the best spa in China by *Travel Weekly*.

Below: The heated indoor pool is large and sports a modern design.

Opposite: The luxuriously appointed and spacious Valley Wing Premier Rooms are some of the largest in Beijing.

The décor in the Valley Wing is a mixture of contemporary and Asian influences.

breakfasts and continue with champagne, wine, and canapés throughout the afternoons and evenings. Other complimentary services at the Lounge include the use of its meeting room and computers. The entire wing is also equipped with wireless Internet access.

The 120 spacious Valley Wing Premier Rooms all enjoy views of the Beijing skyline or the hotel's remarkable Chinese gardens. Their bedrooms are decorated in a style that is both contemporary and Asian, and have adjoined sitting areas, large en suite marble bathrooms with walk-in rainforest showers, soaking tubs, and even 15-inch LCD televisions to complement the larger 32-inch televisions outside. Other amenities include DVD players, digital in-room safes, and dual phone lines. Business-friendly technology means nothing without a place from which to work, so all rooms are furnished with generously sized executive writing desks.

In addition to the comforts of Premier rooms, Valley Wing suites provide iHomes and two-in-one fax and copy machines. With their enormous bay windows, guests can enjoy superb views all day. The 200-sq-m (2,173-sq-ft) Speciality Suite gives guests a chance to unwind in their own jacuzzi, while the Presidential Suite goes even further with a separate study that includes a private exercise area.

The original Shangri-La building has been named the Garden Wing, and with guestrooms sized at a minimum of 35 sq m (377 sq ft), they provide comfort and amenities to the highest standard. A number of Horizon Club Rooms offer access to the exclusive Horizon Club, where discerning business guests will find many benefits, including food and beverage presentations, purser service, and express check-in as well as check-out.

One of the most impressive features of the Shangri-La Hotel, Beijing is its new Grand Ballroom. A completely pillarless 1,350 sq m (14,531 sq ft) space, it seats 1,400 people under an 8-m (26-ft) high ceiling with crystal chandeliers. All events, whether in the Grand Ballroom or smaller function rooms, are served by a dedicated team of professionals.

For a taste of local fare, Shang Palace serves dim sum and other specialities from around the region. Savour fresh sashimi and fine sake at the newly renovated Nishimura, or try Café Cha, which offers international cuisine prepared at vibrant live cooking stations or open kitchens. Blu Lobster was rated one of the 'Top 50 Restaurants in China' by *Food & Wine*. With its décor reminiscent of a shimmering ocean, and cuisine combining the best of modern and classic elements, it's easy to see why.

The hotel itself is no stranger to awards, having won a spot on *Condé Nast*'s 2008 'Top 75 Hotels in Asia' list, as well the honour of being *National Geographic Traveler*'s 'Best Business Hotel in China' for 2007 and one of 'Asia's Best Hotels' in the 16th annual travel poll of *Asiamoney* magazine. An old Chinese saying advises that 'attitude decides everything', and so credit must also go to the earnest staff whose visible pride in discharging their duties is the one feature that elevates the Shangri-La Hotel, Beijing over simple material opulence.

Above: Blu Lobster serves innovative Western cuisine and chic cocktails in quiet and sophisticated surroundings.

Right: Guests can take a cool morning walk in the hotel gardens.

Bottom: At Nishimura, guests may enjoy Japanese food freshly prepared by the chefs at their very table.

Rooms and amenities
- 640 guestrooms
- 30 suites

Restaurants and bars
- Blu Lobster: contemporary Western
- Café Cha: international buffet and à la carte
- Nishimura: Japanese
- Shang Palace: Cantonese
- Cloud Nine Bar: cocktail bar
- Lobby Lounge: beverages and cocktails
- The Delicatessen: pastries and freshly baked breads
- The Garden Bar and Terrace: outdoor garden bar

Facilities
- CHI, The Spa
- Health Club with gym and indoor pool
- Business centre
- Valley Wing Lounge and Horizon Club
- 21 function and meeting rooms
- 2 Grand Ballrooms
- Exclusive River Dragon boat tours to Summer Palace

29 Zizhuyuan Road, Beijing 100089, China
Tel: +86.10.6841 2211 • Fax: +86.10.6841 8002
Email: slb@shangri-la.com
Website: www.shangri-la.com

The Westin Beijing, Financial Street

In preparation for the 2008 Summer Olympic Games, Beijing has undergone a programme of significant development and renewal, at a pace unusual even for this rapidly expanding republic. When The Westin Beijing, Financial Street opened a year ago, expectations were running at fever pitch for the latest international hotel to make an appearance in the capital.

Located in the highly desirable real estate region of Financial Street—a major commercial and business zone that still manages to be within striking distance of essential tourist destinations such as the Forbidden City and Tiananmen Square—industry watchers had every reason to believe in The Westin Beijing, Financial Street's success. And yet, none could have foreseen just how wide the margins of its success would eventually become.

Praise such as 'China's Best New City Hotel', 'Leading Business Hotel', and 'Best New Business Hotel' has come in from sources like *Forbes China*, *Business Traveller China*, and the *World Travel Awards*. Even the notoriously discerning readers of *Condé Nast Traveller* have ranked it 37th in a list of the top 75 hotels in Asia. Scooping up no less than eight major awards in merely twelve months, the hotel has moved far beyond proving itself worthy of its city.

To understand the reasons behind its meteoric rise, one must inevitably start with appearances. The Westin Beijing, Financial Street is an accomplishment of bold urban design with two sleek towers standing at 26 storeys each, fronted by intriguing asymmetrical faces. One tower

Above: Tasteful furnishings and soothing cream hues ensure that guests can truly relax upon returning to their hotel rooms.
Opposite: Guests are bathed in sunlight as they swim laps in the hotel's large indoor pool.

Right: Enjoy home-style Italian food with Prego's range of signature dishes.
Below: The Executive Suite is luxuriously appointed with leather sofas and other pieces of designer furniture.

The hotel's meeting rooms effortlessly match style and businesslike functionality.

is host to the hotel's 486 guestrooms, while the other houses 205 serviced apartments. The exterior was designed by Skidmore Owings & Merrill in a daring modern style, making every side of The Westin Beijing, Financial Street its best side. The interiors were carefully designed by Wilson & Associates Inc to produce a peaceful and soothing effect—white roses and orchids blend harmoniously with the cream-coloured shades used throughout, and the relaxing sound of flowing water features is never too far away.

In The Westin Beijing, Financial Street, the emphasis on total relaxation is evident in every corner. The hotel's greatest achievement lies in its ability to put anyone at ease, and to this end, a series of Personal Guest Experiences have been developed to ensure that guests leave with a greater sense of well-being than when they first arrived. One such program, Unwind®, delivers an evening ritual of rest and relaxation ideal for business travellers.

Drawing on the expertise of China's first in-house hotel bathologists, a customised menu of bath treatments is designed for every guest, creating a personal spa-like environment that features scented candles and music in their own bathrooms. Evenings at The Westin Beijing, Financial Street are filled with truly unique services that will leave guests wondering how they ever managed without them. Even those who are travelling with children can relax in luxury without worrying, as the Westin Kids Club® helps keep young ones safely entertained with professional babysitting services.

In the day, guests may continue their odyssey of indulgence at the newly completed Heavenly Spa by Westin®. A sanctuary of comfort in the city, the spa is the first to be opened in China by the global hospitality network and seems destined to remain one of the best. By fusing modern therapies with traditional Chinese methods, their treatments appeal to the five senses, calming mind and body alike. Those who prefer putting their bodies to work in a different way will find the hotel's fitness facilities more than ready to accommodate. The WestinWORKOUT® Powered by Reebok Gym combines the expertise of the renowned athletics company with state-of-the-art fitness equipment, and their large 25-m (80-ft) indoor swimming pool is great for doing laps. Finally, out by the pool or open-air terrace, guests can enjoy a variety of beverages and healthy, yet tasty snacks from Shui Bar, specially formulated to complement any fitness regime.

When in the mood for something a little more substantial, seven restaurants and bars offer a wide range of choices from around the world. For Italian food, few can beat Prego's authentic home-style cooking and signature recipes. Its open kitchen and central pizza oven offer a fun and lively dining atmosphere, while The Westin Beijing, Financial Street's own Cantonese restaurant, Jewel, is a paragon of fine Chinese dining. Combining contemporary design ideas and time-honoured Eastern preparation techniques, this is local flavour at its best.

Above: Fresh lilies elegantly decorate every table in the Treasury Ballroom.

Right: Modern and traditional methods mix harmoniously in the soothing treatments offered at the Heavenly Spa by Westin®.
Below: The stylish spa treatment rooms allow guests to enjoy a professional massage in the utmost of comfort.

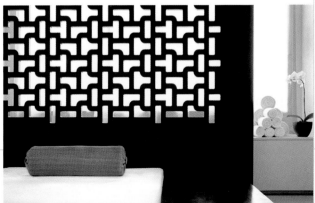

Rooms and amenities
- 486 guestrooms
- 205 serviced apartments

Restaurants and bars
- Senses: Asian and international buffet and à la carte
- Prego: modern Italian
- Jewel: Chinese fine dining
- Treats Bakery: freshly made cakes, pies and pastries
- Plush: lobby lounge with live entertainment
- Buzz: relaxed whisky, cognac, and wine bar
- Shui Bar: health drinks and light meals

Facilities
- Heavenly Spa by Westin®
- WestinWORKOUT® Powered by Reebok Gym
- Westin Kids Club®
- 7 elegant function rooms
- 24-hour business centre
- 24-hour valet parking
- 25-m heated indoor swimming pool
- Wireless Internet access
- Beauty salon
- Airport transfers

9B Financial Street, XiCheng District,
Beijing 100032, China
Tel: +86.10.6606 8866 • Fax: +86.10.6606 8899
Email: reservation.beijing@westin.com
Website: www.westin.com/beijingfinancial

As guests step off the elevator, they are greeted by the hotel's quietly elegant lobby.

JW Marriott Hotel Shanghai

Whether one visits Shanghai for business or pleasure, it makes sense to choose a hotel that keeps major attractions close, and city essentials closer. Located in a landmark mixed-use development known as Tomorrow Square, the JW Marriott Hotel Shanghai provides an ideal starting point for discovering the city in style. Iconic locations such as People's Square, the Shanghai Grand Theatre, the Bund, and Yu Yuan Garden are close by, and minutes away, Huaihai Road and Xin Tian Di provide a wealth of shopping and dining options.

The 60-storey Tomorrow Square tower also houses 255 units of the Marriott Executive Apartments and 20,000 sq m (215,278 sq ft) of commercial space. Designed by Richard Nixon of John Portman & Associates, the structure features a number of striking features. From the 38th floor upwards, the building appears to have been rotated at a 45° angle to its base, creating an unusual geometric form that changes in appearance depending on one's position. At its peak, a large 'Marriott Jewel' floats suspended between the tips of four outstretched projections. Envisioned as a work of modern architecture that would stand the test of time in one of Asia's fastest growing cities, the distinct Tomorrow Square is instantly recognisable in Shanghai's skyline.

Though the exterior may seem daunting, the hotel's 342 guestrooms and suites are anything but. Dressed in warm colours, dark woods, and luxurious materials, they convey the feeling of a slower, more relaxed pace of life. This stands in glorious contrast to the luminous metropolitan scene that stretches out beyond the walls. Every room enjoys a panoramic view of Shanghai, while in the Corner Rooms, the bathrooms feature ceiling-high windows. All of the 41 Studio Suites have bay windows that extend out into a vastness of view. For a truly above-it-all sensation, the exclusive 59th floor Executive Lounge provides the highest vantage point in the building, and is an excellent place to enjoy breakfast, evening cocktails, and other refreshments during the day.

From gourmet fare to casual drinking and dining, the hotel's three restaurants and two lounge bars cover a whole spectrum of gastronomical delights. One non-negotiable stop for the palate is the award-winning Wan Hao Chinese Restaurant. Contemporary, elegant and comfortable, the restaurant showcases fine traditional Cantonese cuisine with dim sum and Shanghainese highlights, and guests dine with magnificent views of the Shanghai skyline. JW's Lounge Bar also offers gorgeous views along with one of the most extensive champagne lists in Shanghai. After a long day, unwind with fine champagne and soothing music, played live at the bar.

Complete with a 24-hour health club, pools, Mandara Spa, and award-winning conference facilities, the JW Marriott Hotel Shanghai at Tomorrow Square raises the bar for five-star luxury hotels not only in the city, but the entire region.

The hotel's indoor pool is an inviting place to relax, working out tense muscles with a refreshing swim.

Right: Wth its menu of Cantonese and Shangainese specialities, the award-winning Wan Hao Chinese Restaurant is not to be missed.
Below: JW's Lounge Bar offers an extensive selection of champagne as well as excellent wines and cocktails.

Rooms and amenities
- 264 guestrooms
- 78 suites

Restaurants and bars
- 360 Gourmet Shop: deli items and light meals
- JW's California Grill: Californian-Asian and sushi
- Marriott Cafe: international casual dining and buffets
- Wan Hao Chinese Restaurant: fine Cantonese and Shanghainese
- JW's Lounge Bar: champagne bar overlooking the city
- Lobby Lounge: meeting place for cocktails, snacks, afternoon tea

Facilities
- Mandara Spa
- 24-hour Health Club
- Business Centre
- Executive Lounge
- 12 meeting rooms
- Two pools
- Wireless Internet access

399 Nanjing West Road, Shanghai, 200003 China
Tel: +86.21.5359 4969 • Fax: +86.21.6375 5565
Email: mhrs.shajw.reservations@marriotthotels.com
Website: www.marriotthotels.com/shajw

The hotel's understated and elegant Oriental décor was imagined by award-winning Tony Chi.

Park Hyatt Shanghai

Soaring past the 88-storey Jin Mao Tower and its Grand Hyatt Shanghai hotel, formerly the world's tallest, the newly completed Shanghai World Financial Center stands at an impressive 101 storeys in the heart of the Lujiazui business district. The tallest building in the People's Republic of China, it boosts the Park Hyatt Shanghai 93 storeys above ground, making it the highest hotel in the world and giving guests an alluring sense of detachment as they look out of the hotel windows.

From such great heights, the entire city of Shanghai lies open like a map, with views stretching out past the Pudong district and over the Huangpu River. In a move designed to establish a standard worthy of its privileged location, the hotel has created only 142 rooms and 32 suites, each of the highest quality. Occupying the 79th to the 93rd floors, the rooms were designed to reflect the tenets of contemporary Chinese residential luxury by award-winning New York-based interior designer, Tony Chi. Combining earth tones and understated Oriental touches, they are some of the most unique rooms in Shanghai, a fact demonstrated by their hitherto unheard-of dimensions: standard rooms measure 55–60 sq m (592–646 sq ft), with 3.2-m- (10.5-ft-) high ceilings that create a sense of limitless space.

Guests enter the hotel through express elevators that lead directly to the lobby on the 87th floor, where they will also find three dining venues simply called the Living Room, Dining Room, and The Bar. Between them, informal Chinese dining and all-day European cuisine, as well as Western and Chinese snacks, fresh pastries and classy cocktails are provided as fitting accompaniments to a majestic view unmatched anywhere in the city.

On the three uppermost floors, a 'mountain cottage' concept unites a selection of first-class dining destinations. From the 91st to 93rd floors, 100 Century Avenue offers the world on a platter, with Western, Japanese, and Chinese menus in a single establishment. Featuring fiery show kitchens and 25-m (82-ft) floor-to-ceiling windows, it is destined to bring a renewed sense of drama to Shanghai's dining scene. After dinner, retire to the 92nd floor for a relaxing drink at the Western-style bar with its live band and extensive collection of fine whisky, or lounge at the cosy Chinese-themed bar. For more intimate events, the restaurant caters to three private function rooms on the 93rd floor, which offer the world's most altitudinous dining experience.

The Shanghai World Financial Center has been dubbed 'The Vertical Complex City', and no city is without its quiet areas where the pace of life can wind down. On the 85th floor, Water's Edge offers an infinity-edge pool, a Tai Chi courtyard, and a wellness studio. True to the 'residential' vision of Park Hyatt Shanghai, a variety of spa treatments available from Water's Edge can be enjoyed at the facility's two treatment rooms, or even in the comfort of guests' own residences.

Elegant earth tones give the Park Hyatt Shanghai an atmosphere of contemporary class.

Left: Bowls of local fruit add a touch of colour to the rooms.
Below: The hotel bathrooms are spacious and modern, with invitingly large bathtubs.

Rooms and amenities

- 142 guestrooms
- 32 suites

Restaurants and bars

- Living Room: light Western and Chinese
- Dining Room: informal Chinese and European cuisine and classic pastries, desserts and light dishes in the casual area of the room
- The Bar: cocktails
- 100 Century Avenue: Western, Chinese, and Japanese cuisine on the 91st floor
  Western and Chinese-style bars on the 92nd floor

Facilities

- 24-hour butler and room service
- Technology concierge
- Spa and fitness studio
- Infinity-edge pool
- Whirlpool spa
- Tai Chi courtyard
- Meeting/dining rooms
- 86th and 93rd floors: private dining/event space
- Wireless Internet access

100 Century Avenue, Pudong New Area
Shanghai 200120, China
Tel: +86.21.6888 1234 • Fax: +86.21.6888 3400
Email: shanghai.park@hyatt.com
Website: www.parkhyattshanghai.com

The St Regis Shanghai

The history of Shanghai and its role in China's progress as a modern superpower is a well-storied one, and remnants of colonial influence are still visible today throughout the republic's largest city. Examples inevitably include such popular tourist destinations as Frenchtown, the Bund, and the many historical sights of Puxi. Not far from these, in the centrally located Pudong financial district, is the award-winning St Regis Shanghai, where another instantly recognisable symbol of European service and luxury still prevails: the butler.

Wholly dedicated to providing a superlative level of comfort, The St Regis Shanghai is the only hotel in Shanghai to provide all guests with the use of a 24-hour butler service. With yearly accolades from *Travel + Leisure* magazine and a place on the Condé Nast Gold List, the move has paid off. In a city where opulence and five-star titles have almost become a matter-of-course, the St Regis Butler is more than a mere convenience—it is a statement of service excellence. From reservations to check-in and all the way to check-out, a personal assistant remains on hand to see to every guest's needs, including unpacking, shopping, and making arrangements for personal trips. Thoughtful and resourceful, the hotel's butlers reflect the elegance of the establishment.

Continuing the hotel's atmosphere of absolute welcome are 328 guestrooms and suites of remarkable splendour, including the largest standard rooms in Shanghai. Guests in all rooms enjoy such top-level amenities as the ergonomic perfection that is the Herman

Choose the perfect vintage to complement your meal at Danieli's.

Miller Aeron chair, custom mattresses, audiophile-quality sound by Bose, and refreshing rainforest showers in every bathroom. Keeping in touch is made easy with wireless Internet access and fax machines, and the provision of large executive desks make work a distinctive pleasure. Ladies may elect to stay on one of the three female-only floors designed to pamper them with Bulgari beauty products, Evian atomisers, and a number of other tailored considerations.

All guests are welcome to unwind at the St Regis SPA and enjoy its signature La Stone Massage therapy. Using hot stones coated in essential oils, the sensuous massage eases tired muscles and refreshes the mind, making it a perfect relief for jet lag. Alternatively, yoga and aerobics classes are available at the gym and fitness centre. For professionals attending events at the hotel, having these stress-relieving services close at hand are an asset. With over 1,000 sq m (10,764 sq ft) of meeting and conference space equipped with the latest technology and managed by an experienced events team, The St Regis Shanghai easily plays host to groups of up to 400.

Dubbed the Pearl of Shanghai, itself known as the Pearl of the Orient, the hotel presents world-class hospitality amidst first-class surroundings. When no room for error exists, there are few teams better equipped to see things through than the one placed at The St Regis Shanghai.

The comfortable beds and large executive desks make both work and rest a pleasure.

Right: Displays of modern artwork add to the contemporary elegance of the lobby.

Below: The hotel's pool is illuminated by natural light during the day, perfect for a leisurely swim.

Rooms and amenities
- 281 guestrooms
- 47 suites

Restaurants and bars
- Danieli's: modern Italian
- Carrianna: Cantonese
- Saints International Restaurant: all-day dining and buffets
- Mezzanine Lounge: cocktails and snacks with live music
- Executive Lounge & Library: cocktails on the 40th floor

Facilities
- 24-hour St Regis Butler service
- Executive Lounge access to all guests
- St Regis SPA and Fitness Centre
- Indoor heated pool and whirlpool
- Limousine service
- Personalised art and shopping tours
- 24-hour Business Centre
- Complimentary wireless Internet access

889 Dong Fang Road, Pudong,
Shanghai 200122, China
Tel: +86.21.5050 4567 • Fax: +86.21.6875 6789
Email: stregis.shanghai@stregis.com
Website: www.stregis.com/shanghai

The Westin Bund Center, Shanghai

Located in China's most fashionable city, The Westin Bund Center, Shanghai is a triumph of Eastern style and grace. Mere minutes from the popular tourist destination known as The Bund, where a stretch of beautiful historic buildings once housed the trading headquarters and consulates that powered Shanghai's rise as a regional economic force, the hotel is also in close proximity to Shanghai's dynamic waterfront. From the illuminated peak of its 26-storey building, formed in the shape of a crown, the hotel enjoys some of the best views of Huangpu River by night.

Featuring two buildings, the original Crown Tower and the newly opened Grand Tower, The Westin Bund Center, Shanghai represents the only world-class modern luxury hotel in the vicinity. Created to the exacting standards of celebrated architect John Portman, the two towers visually embody the innovation in guest experience that the Westin name brought to China. Amongst other achievements, the towers were the first architectural concept in China to receive the FIABCI Prix d'Excellence award, and on the technological front, it was also the first hotel in Shanghai to introduce wireless Internet access throughout the building.

In just 2007 alone, the hotel received an impressive 15 international awards, including a place on the *Condé Nast Traveller*'s Reader's Choice list of Top 10 hotels in Asia, and the Top 100 in the world. To enter and behold the inside of its dramatic four storey-high atrium lobby, where towering palm trees reach up

The suites are elegantly appointed with a distinctly Oriental aesthetic.

Above: Rooms are all fitted with the Westin's trademark Heavenly Bed, considered the best in the industry.
Right: The modern amenities provided allow guests to enjoy entertainment at their own convenience.
Opposite: Guests are greeted by soothing, muted tones as they enter the hotel's Grand Tower Lobby.

The magnificent glass staircase is the highlight of the hotel's grand, four storey-high lobby.

towards a glass skylight, is to understand—at least in part—the praise that has been heaped on the hotel. A magnificent cantilevered glass staircase is the focal point of the entrance lobby. This marvel of engineering technology leads the eye to levels two and three, while lighting on the inside filters gently through rice paper laid into each step. Accompanied by soft music and the sweet scent of white tea, every guest is warmly received by a hostess in traditional Chinese dress offering moist towels and a cup of herbal refreshment.

With 269 guestrooms and suites in the new Grand Tower, the hotel now boasts a total of 570 luxury accommodations. Blending relaxation and refinement in a contemporary style, Grand Tower rooms are decorated with light earth tones and streamlined furnishing schemes. An establishment-wide focus on art sees every room enhanced with original pieces, so every display is different, and the hotel also arranges gallery exhibitions by request.

True to the theme of comfort and serenity, a series of ultramodern technologies like video-on-demand and a shared database of MP3 music allows guests to enjoy entertainment at their own convenience. With the addition of Westin mainstays such as high-speed Internet, multiple telephone lines, bathrooms with deep soaking tubs, and separate rainforest showers, every stay is comfortable and relaxing, free of any unnecessary complications. To that end, the hotel's revolutionary Service Express helpline allows guests just to dial just one number from their rooms for requests of any kind.

EEST—The Crystal Garden is set in a park-like environment, allowing for an unusual and enjoyable dining experience.

That convenience extends to an unusual form of room service, namely the hotel's new In-Room Spa Service, offered in conjunction with the in-house Banyan Tree Spa. Inclusive of music, room scents, and luxurious plant-based aromatherapy oils, the service creates a complete spa atmosphere in any guestroom. Guests can enjoy soothing treatments right in their own rooms, just as they might at the 1,000-sq-m (10,734-sq-ft) sanctuary below. Operated by Asia's premier name in spas, the Banyan Tree's facilities include 13 mesmerising treatment rooms designed to reflect the five Chinese elements of Earth, Wood, Gold, Water, and Fire. From the grand entranceway to the outstanding Yin Yang Deluxe Suite, distinctive Oriental touches such as the use of crane figures, red carpets and bonsai trees create a sensuous and exotic atmosphere.

The hotel's seven restaurants encompass a world of fine dining, from the Far East to the heart of Europe. EEST—The Crystal Garden serves a range of Asian delicacies from Chinese, Thai, and Japanese chefs in a park-like setting, with panoramic views of the surrounding area. Looking for authentic Italian food in Shanghai might be a tricky task, but Prego is famous for getting it right. From the wood-fired pizzas to its selection of grappas, the largest in Asia, this modern restaurant is an exquisite dining destination. With its eclectic mix of cultures under one dazzling, crown-shaped roof, it should come as no surprise that The Westin Bund Center, Shanghai offers best of class features in every regard.

Above: At Prego, guests may enjoy genuine Italian food with a modern touch.
Right: The hotel's décor is tastefully understated, and adds a warm and welcoming feeling.
Below: The distinct, crown-shaped roof makes The Westin Bund Center, Shanghai instantly recognisable.

Rooms and amenities
- 570 guestrooms and suites

Restaurants and bars
- Niche: bar with live band and canapés
- The Stage: international à la carte and buffet
- EEST—The Crystal Garden: Asian cuisine in a garden environment
- Prego: modern Italian
- Treats: Western-style deli with freshly baked items
- Bliss: health drinks, snacks and fresh juices
- Heavenlies: casual lobby lounge with live entertainment

Facilities
- Banyan Tree Spa with In-Room Spa Service
- Two-storey WestinWORKOUT® Powered by Reebok Gym
- Indoor pool
- Sauna and steam room
- Complimentary wireless Internet access
- Westin Kids Club (only available at Sunday brunch)
- 24-hour business centre
- Airport transfers
- 24-hour valet parking

88 Henan Central Road,
Shanghai 200002, China •
Tel: +86.21.6335 1888 • Fax: +86.21.6335 2888
Email: rsvns-shanghai@westin.com
Website: www.westin.com

Four Seasons Hotel Hong Kong

If Hong Kong is the Pearl of the Orient, then Four Seasons Hotel Hong Kong is the core at the nucleus of this gem. This five-star hotel is a haven of modern luxury and perceptive service at the very heart of the prestigious International Finance Centre, redefining new benchmarks of excellence in a city renowned for its already exceptional accommodations.

The building itself has rapidly become a waterfront landmark. It is exceptionally well placed for easy access to leisure, culture and commerce, boasting captivating vistas across the colourful bustle of Victoria Harbour. The Hong Kong International Airport is only half an hour away, and the ferry piers lie mere minutes from the hotel, granting guests convenient access to the Kowloon Peninsula and outlying islands, as well as Macau.

The Four Seasons' hallmarks of comfort and luxury are visible at every turn, with the hotel's 399 guest rooms and suites keeping pace with Hong Kong's new forward-looking philosophy. The interior design of the suites adopts different themes to highlight exotic Asian and modern styles, in recognition of the increasingly heterogeneous tastes of the modern-day traveller. For a contemporary feel, room décor includes wood- and silk-panelled walls and cool, marble-floored entry foyers. Some suites are fitted in a style inspired by traditional Chinese décor, while still managing to remain wholly modern.

From guestrooms to the expansive Deluxe Suites with their own separate living space, all accommodations feature both spacious work

Opposite: Set on the sixth floor, the pools on the rooftop offer swimmers and sunbathers a resort-like experience.

Left: Enjoy a relaxing massage after a full day spent in Hong Kong's key business, entertainment and shopping areas.

Below: The Four Seasons Executive Suites are spacious and well-appointed with modern amenities and stylish contemporary décor.

The hotel's elegant lobby features intriguing displays of art and sculpture.

and entertainment areas. High-speed Internet access, DVD players and astounding 42-inch plasma-screen televisions are at the disposal of guests. Built-in LCD television sets are also available so one can watch programmes from the relaxing depths of a steaming tub in the large, gleaming marble bathrooms.

The Premier and Presidential Suites each have oversized king bedrooms, a well-stocked pantry, guest powder rooms and also exclusive private dining facilities that enable all visiting luminaries and VIPs to maintain their privacy. Whichever style is preferred, the wall-to-wall windows will provide unsurpassed views of the sparkling city and Victoria Harbour, as well as Kowloon. Apart from the magnetic allure of the beautifully furnished rooms and suites, Four Seasons Hotel Hong Kong also dazzles with its array of facilities. Business travellers fresh out of teleconferences or meetings in the hotel's impressive, cutting-edge conference rooms can network closely alongside other corporate heavyweights as they relax in the light and airy Executive Club Lounge. Alternatively, there is also a state-of-the-art, 24-hour fitness centre, where expert in-house personal trainers will be delighted to tailor full programmes to fulfill all guests' individual gym needs.

The elegant, calming Spa is a 2,044-sq-m (22,000-sq-ft) tranquil urban sanctuary, with 16 treatment rooms, including two exclusive suites, Aqua and Crystal. Guests may choose a private therapy room, or perhaps indulge in the spa's vitality pool lounge, which offers Finnish saunas, a crystal steam room and myriad heat

experiences. Perhaps the hotel's *pièce de résistance* is its serene rooftop oasis. Exercise in the lap pool, cool down in the plunge pool, soak up the incredible harbour views from the whirlpool, and then reward these efforts with some fun in the free-form infinity-edge pool.

Hong Kong's cuisine is as much a fusion as its culture, and Four Seasons Hotel Hong Kong reflects this in its culinary provision. Caprice is the location for fine French dining, with a menu of light yet richly flavoured delicacies. Glittering chandeliers crown the whole experience, and the private dining rooms provide the ultimate in exclusive dining. This 100-seat restaurant offers spectacular harbour and Kowloon views as an appetiser. The open kitchen provides an almost theatrical nightly performance of the distinguished chefs at work, and also sets the mouth-watering aromas free to mingle with the chatter and anticipation of the patrons. Other dining experiences include the Lung King Heen Cantonese Restaurant, famous for its delectable dim sum. For drinks, try the Blue Bar, whose internally lit glass mosaic column radiates an almost palpable energy, reminiscent of the many towering skyscrapers nearby.

An exotic cultural mix and an iconic skyline merely touch the surface of what makes Hong Kong the premier tourist destination in Asia. These words, too, only scratch the surface of the contemporary luxury which marks every stay at Four Seasons Hotel Hong Kong.

Enjoy the panoramic views from the Executive Club Lounge at Four Seasons Hotel Hong Kong.

Right: Stylish and elegant, Caprice offers the best of contemporary French cuisine.
Below: The urban oasis that is the spa pampers guests with a variety of exquisite spa facilities and treatments.

Rooms and amenities
- 345 guestrooms
- 54 suites

Restaurants and bars
- Caprice: contemporary French
- The Lounge: light meals, afternoon tea and desserts
- Pool Terrace: light cuisine and refreshments
- Lung King Heen: Cantonese
- Blue Bar: cocktails and fine wine

Facilities
- Spa
- 24-hour Fitness Centre
- Oxygenated yoga studio
- Pilates and stretch studio
- Business centre
- 2 ballrooms
- 7 boardrooms
- Hair salon
- Executive Club

8 Finance Street, Central, Hong Kong, China
Tel: +852.3196 8888 · Fax: +852.3196 8899
Website: www.fourseasons.com/hongkong

Grand Hyatt Hong Kong

From the outside, Grand Hyatt Hong Kong is all polished marble and futuristic glass. Step inside and you'll be pleasantly surprised by its charming Art Deco interior. The lobby, with its marbled columns and statuettes, is strongly reminiscent of a vintage luxury liner.

Lush natural foliage and soothing water features create space and harmony within the majestic lobby. With such grandeur, it is little wonder that Grand Hyatt Hong Kong is the flagship hotel of Hyatt International.

One of the best features of the hotel is its panoramic views of Victoria Harbour. Over 70 per cent of the guestrooms have been cleverly laid out and oriented to take full advantage of this truly exceptional view.

The hotel's guestrooms were designed by renowned Hong Kong-based architect designer John Morford, and were built with business travellers in mind. The in-room writing desk comes with an adjacent ledge that maximises work space, while a nearby cabinet is almost a business centre in itself, complete with wired and wireless high-speed Internet connections.

Other features which can be found in Grand Hyatt Hong Kong's guestrooms include soft down duvets sheathed in Egyptian cotton and striking black and white photographs of traditional Chinese gardens by the famed architect, Chung Wah Nan. The subtle and natural colour scheme lends a comfortable, home-like feel to the guestrooms. Bathrooms retain the marble bath with separate shower and 14-carat gold-plated fixtures.

Above: Plateau Residential Spa offers a full range of result-oriented treatments.
Opposite: The outdoor heated swimming pool is the largest of its kind in Hong Kong.

Above: The Ambassador Suite is one of the 13 specialty suites in the hotel, served by a team of professional butlers.
Right: More than 70 per cent of the guestrooms enjoy a stunning view of Victoria Harbour.

Plateau Residential Spa offers luxurious accommodations as well as in-room massage treatments.

Those who take a room on the Grand Club Executive Floors will be spoiled even further. Aside from an hour's use per day of a private office, each of the 102 Grand Club rooms and suites come with luxurious amenities such as a DVD player and a wide selection of music CDs, in addition to the array of movie titles available in the Grand Club lounge. As a resident of the Grand Club, guests may enjoy a complimentary buffet breakfast in the morning, cocktails and light canapés in the evenings, coffee and tea throughout the day in the lounge, and stay connected through complimentary Internet access. For lazy afternoons indoors, the library offers a variety of reading material and games such as chess and backgammon.

The award-winning Plateau Residential Spa, situated on the 11th floor, provides fitness and beauty facilities in a luxurious and spacious setting. Results-oriented spa treatments, outdoor heated pool, jogging track and fitness and exercise studios aside, 23 rooms and suites are available if guests need to work out or release a day's tension with a relaxing massage.

Club JJ's, comprised of the Music Room and JJ's Thai & Grill, captivates the city with live music, authentic Thai cuisine, and grilled specialities. The highly fêted Music Room on the upper floor is an extension of the two-storey main bar. Extra lounge seating and an elegantly chic bar overlooking the restaurant below help set up the entire area for drinks and cocktails. At JJ's Thai & Grill, Chef Mum from Bangkok serves up 'home-style' cuisine as well as grilled, 100 per cent natural Angus beef.

The lower level also features two sleek exclusive private dining rooms and a wine room.

For the ultimate in elegant Cantonese dining, take a ride in the private glass-walled elevator from the lobby to One Harbour Road for stylishly prepared Cantonese cuisine, or host an extraordinary meal at Chef's Table inside the kitchen, which offers guests a rare deep glance into the workings of a Chinese kitchen while they remain in the privacy of a contemporary dining room.

Named after the quintessential Italian breadstick, Grissini is the place to go for fine Italian cuisine. Much like a sleek New York eatery, the air around is often filled with the delicious aroma of piping hot, freshly baked grissini wafting from the large oven at the entrance of the restaurant.

The simplicity and serenity of Japan is reflected in Kaetsu, whose menu features traditional Japanese favourites and seasonal specialities prepared with only the freshest of ingredients, flown directly in from Japan.

Amongst the exhaustive list of famous politicians, actors and celebrities who have stayed at Grand Hyatt Hong Kong are Bill and Hillary Clinton, George Bush, Prince Albert of Monaco, Karl Lagerfeld and Keanu Reeves. One might even be tempted to think that they arrived via the hotel's magnificent 46-m (150-ft) mega-yacht, *Grand Cru*, from Hong Kong International Airport, refreshed with a chilled glass of bubbly on board and adding their own special brand of sparkling glamour to the Grand Hyatt Hong Kong.

Above: Tiffin's famous dessert buffet is the perfect place to relax and enjoy a sweet treat with friends.
Right: Grissini offers authentic Italian cuisine with panoramic harbour views.
Bottom: The split-level One Harbour Road serves traditional Cantonese cuisine, lovingly prepared and graciously presented.

Rooms and amenities
- 549 guestrooms and suites
- 8 floors of Grand Club for lounge and speciality suites

Restaurants and bars
- One Harbour Road: award-winning Cantonese cuisine
- Grissini: authentic Italian cuisine
- JJ's Thai & Grill: home-style Thai cuisine and grilled specialities
- JJ's Music Room: bars and live music
- Kaetsu: exquisite and seasonal Japanese cuisine
- Tiffin: lunch, tea and dessert buffets
- Grand Café: international cuisine and dinner buffet
- The Grill: char-grilled specialities by the pool
- Champagne Bar: premium champagne and snacks

Facilities
- Business centre and 25 function rooms
- Residential spa and fitness centre
- 50-m (164-ft) outdoor heated pool
- Golf driving range
- 2 floodlit tennis courts and 2 squash courts
- 400-m (1,312-ft) jogging track
- Baby-sitting services
- Hairdresser
- Yacht

1 Harbour Road, Hong Kong, China
Tel: +852.2588 1234 • Fax: +852.2802 0677
Email: info.ghhk@hyatt.com
Website: www.hongkong.grand.hyatt.com

The Landmark's stunningly cool façade makes it an icon in Hong Kong.

The Landmark Mandarin Oriental, Hong Kong

The Landmark Mandarin Oriental stands out for many things, not least for the size of its rooms in a city where space is considered sheer luxury. With most rooms spreading over 50 sq m (540 sq ft), they are the largest hotel rooms Hong Kong has to offer. Its location in the heart of Central is also a winning point. Surrounded by temples of high fashion, from Louis Vuitton to Armani, the hotel exudes unabashed style, and in turn, attracts the city's hippest. By day, well-coiffed *tai tai*s take their afternoon tea after a languid session at The Oriental Spa; by night, the young jet-set take over at the achingly cool MO Bar.

Every element of the hotel is up-to-the-minute, hip and hot. To wit: up-to-the-minute—a technology butler, who sees to one's every networking and IT need; hip—entertainment systems complete with iPod docks; hot—the yoga and pilates studios operated by gurus in their field, and the newly-opened 18-m (59-ft) indoor heated pool.

Now add to that list 'connected'. As the gateway to Hong Kong's best, The Landmark Mandarin Oriental's concierge is the fixer every traveller covets. A private dining table in the city's most booked-out restaurant? The secret address to that spot you have heard of but never seen? The hotel's concierge is the person who can make it happen.

The Landmark Mandarin Oriental's lobby, appointed with rich wooden cabinets and stocked with art books and brass table lamps, sits above an angled staircase that hangs above an ethereal cloak of lush Italian marble. The stairs were designed to recall the junks that ply Victoria Harbour, while the wave-like marble sculpture conveys the gleaming waters.

In its 113 rooms designed by Hong Kong-born and Los Angeles-based Peter Remedios, light black African wood floors bestow a glamorous warmth, while dark cabinets are inlaid with the shine of silver. All rooms come with sumptuous 400-thread-count bed linen, wide-screen plasma televisions and incomparable services including personal shoppers from Harvey Nichols who can be summoned to your room. The devil, as the saying goes, is in the details—and in these rooms, they come in the form of phones that display guests' names digitally, full-sized bath products infused with lavender and ylang ylang, and yoga mats in every closet.

Like any five-star hotel worth its fleur de sel, The Landmark Mandarin Oriental's signature restaurant Amber boasts not just food worth waiting for, but also designer style, created by award-winning interior designer Adam Tihany, worth a mention in glossy magazines. Its polished mahogany walls are set off with a monumental hanging sculpture of over 4,200 copper rods—think of it as a conversational amuse-bouche to an exquisite meal with flavours from North Africa, Europe and Asia, by Dutch chef Richard Ekkebus.

For more sedate pleasures, the hotel's amazing Oriental Spa is a haven of serenity where guests can indulge in minted showers, hot mists and tropical saunas with ceilings that 'rain'.

The famous Amber is renowned for its outstanding cuisine and astoundingly stylish interior design.

Rooms and amenities
- 101 guestrooms
- 12 suites

Restaurants and bars
- Amber: modern European cuisine
- MO Bar: drinks and all day dining

Facilities
- 2,320 sq m (25,000 sq ft) premier spa with state-of-the-art gym and pilates and yoga studios
- 18-m (59-ft) heated indoor pool
- High-tech meeting and banqueting facilities for up to 110 guests

Right:Most of the guestrooms come with luxurious round spa bathtubs and ultra-sleek features.

Below The Landmark offers the largest room in the city, complete with the latest in technology and design.

15 Queen's Road Central, The Landmark
Central, Hong Kong, China
Tel: +852.2132 0188 • Fax: +852.2132 0199
Website: www.mandarinoriental.com/landmark

The hotel's minimalist aesthetic gives it an airy, open feeling.

Lanson Place Hotel, Hong Kong

In Hong Kong's heavily-developed Causeway Bay area, one of the most spirited shopping districts in the world with retail rent rivalling New York's Fifth Avenue, a 26-storey hotel of charismatic design offers a sanctum of calm and seclusion. With its stately façade of grey stone, modelled after neo-classical European designs, Lanson Place is a new boutique hotel that stands with a confidence which rivals that of any early 1900s building. Inside, the decorating scheme developed by Joseph Fung of SP2 and Simon Tong of LRF Designers subverts expectations with a mix of classical and retro-modernist fittings.

The unconventional interior design works not by way of being bold and quirky, but by its tasteful restraint. The minimalist aesthetic, which persists even in the smallest of spaces, serves to open up the hotel by a fair amount— an important consideration, as anybody familiar with the limitations of Hong Kong real estate would know.

Ranging between 35 to 56 sq m (380 to 600 sq ft) in area, all of Lanson Place's 188 guestrooms are unique in both their layout and appearance. Wherever possible, natural light floods the luxurious accommodations by way of floor-to-ceiling windows. In the middle of Causeway Bay, minutes from boisterous local teahouses and the flagship stores of famous international design houses, Lanson Place offers a remarkably different view of the city. Situated in a quiet enclave on one end of Leighton Road, its rooms overlook the nearby Victoria Park and distant mountain scenes. Every room is fitted with a kitchenette, microwave oven, crockery, and utensils, a touch of convenience that few short-term accommodations offer. Six penthouse serviced apartments are well-suited to longer stays and may be the most extraordinary addresses yet on the East Point.

True to its aim of creating a haven for discerning visitors and travellers who frequent Hong Kong, Lanson Place takes the unconventional step of limiting the use of all its facilities to hotel guests only. Without unnecessary interruptions, having a relaxed continental breakfast or end-of-day cocktail to live jazz music at the cosy 133 Lounge is transformed into an exclusive club experience. As they enjoy the full use of hotel facilities and undivided attention of the service staff, guests are free to work or relax as they please, especially with the provision of ubiquitous wireless Internet access.

Upon inspection, the rules which govern and differentiate Lanson Place are simple ones. Although the hotel staff are always happy to serve the needs of every guest, they also know the importance of remaining unobtrusive. Likewise, the hotel does not impose limits on how guests choose to schedule their time—the gymnasium and laundry facilities operate around the clock. Remaining a sanctuary of peace in bustling Hong Kong, Lanson Place invites accolades.

Lanson Place remains tranquil despite its location in one of Hong Kong's busiest shopping districts.

Rooms and amenities
- 188 guest suites
- 6 serviced penthouse apartments

Restaurants and bars
- 133 Lounge: Lobby bar with breakfast service and wireless Internet access

Facilities
- 24-hour gymnasium and launderette
- Business centre
- Boardroom with videoconferencing facilities
- Personal mobile phone for guests
- Murano Room: private dining room for events
- Wireless Internet access

Right: With comfortable furnishings and attentive staff, Lanson Place is dedicated to guests' well-being.

Below: Rooms are fitted with thoughtful amenities, making every stay in Lanson Place a smooth one.

133 Leighton Road, Causeway Bay, Hong Kong, China
Tel: +85.2.3477 6888 • Fax: +85.2.3477 6999
Email: enquiry.lphk@lansonplace.com
Website: www.lansonplace.com

Mandarin Oriental, Hong Kong

Built in place of the colonial Queen's Building in 1963, the Mandarin Oriental, Hong Kong has stood in Hong Kong's financial district for more than four decades, symbolising the city's pride and status as a world-class business centre. Its landmark architecture and lavish interiors, designed by art director Don Ashton, led to its 1967 ranking by *Fortune Magazine* as one of the world's 11 grandest hotels. With its popular restaurants, first-rate service, and romantic views of Victoria Harbour, Mandarin Oriental, Hong Kong was beloved as the heart of society for some of the colony's most distinguished residents.

Over nine months in 2005, that legendary glamour was updated in a US$150 million makeover which brought the hotel fully into the 21st century with a plethora of technological innovations. Redesigned by Jeffrey Wilkes, the new interior recreates the impact and grandeur of the original upon its launch 45 years ago, while carefully incorporating hallmarks of the style that made its name. The hotel's signature restaurant, Mandarin Grill, has been literally opened up by Sir Terence Conran's re-imagined layout, featuring windows wide open to the views of Statue Square.

All of the Mandarin Oriental, Hong Kong's rooms and suites have been reworked in the image of contemporary luxury. Guestrooms now come with enclosed balconies, allowing for larger interior spaces, which in turn are

The hotel lobby is richly furnished in the Mandarin Oriental, Hong Kong's hallmark style.

Above: Suites are decorated in a variety of styles, but all share the same comforts and amenities.

Right: The Macau Suite boasts a richly-appointed living room, with large windows overlooking the city.

Opposite: Comfortable and welcoming, returning to the hotel is a perfect end to a long day.

Pierre restaurant serves French food infused with a touch of the chef's unique style and energy.

individually furnished and detailed with rich materials and handcrafted finishes. The 68 suites each possess unique identities, but all rooms under the hotel's roof enjoy a unifying aesthetic that is distinctly Oriental, full of Asian charm that matches the spectacular views that stretch out beyond the windows.

Complementing the sensuality of the rooms' pure linen sheets, Black Forest Chinese marble, and authentic timber panelling is a wealth of modern business and entertainment technology. In addition to complimentary high-definition programming and Hollywood movies available on demand, one may also connect a laptop, iPod, or other media device to access personal entertainment content over the hotel network. Every room enjoys wireless Internet access, and the television may be used with a supplied wireless keyboard to access the web.

The Mandarin Oriental, Hong Kong is also fully equipped to accommodate parties of up to 600 delegates with four modular function rooms. For those wishing to conduct business in a more private setting, a boardroom that seats 14 is available. Enabled with advanced teleconferencing facilities, twin plasma displays, and an intelligent electronic whiteboard, it provides high-tech professional amenities in a distraction-free work environment, allowing focus to remain on the most important issues.

At the end of any long day, the comfort of the Mandarin Spa provides the ultimate in rejuvenation and relaxation. Built as part of the hotel's rebirth, the 2,100-sq-m (22,600-sq-ft) facility stretches over three floors and includes

an indoor pool, gymnasium with Kinesis equipment, spa, Mandarin Salon, and even a traditional Mandarin Barber for gentlemen. The spa itself offers a range of treatments centred on holistic Asian philosophies such as Traditional Chinese Medicine and Ayurveda, and is richly decorated in the style of 1930s Shanghai. Throughout the spa's eight treatment rooms and couple suites, guests are invited to enjoy specially customised programmes of relaxing massages and natural therapies tailored to their individual needs.

With a reputation for being the theatre of elite decision making in the city, Mandarin Grill is one business that has never sold itself short. Newly minted with an abundance of natural light, the Mandarin Grill now has an entertaining open kitchen and Crustacea Bar, serving fresh oysters and sashimi.

Joining the roster of ten stellar bars and restaurants is Pierre, a very personal project by Michelin-starred master chef, Pierre Gagnaire. At the heart of his ever-changing menu is a desire to produce emotional experiences through food, and the result is classic flavours fused with an air of excitement and energy. The same can be said of the Mandarin Oriental, Hong Kong—although it has mastered the art of service, it never rests. Whether that takes the form of a multi-million-dollar revitalisation, or the learning of a single guest's preferences, it sets a standard that will prove difficult for anyone else to match.

Top: M Bar is the perfect place to unwind with after-dinner cocktails and tapas.
Right: The Mandarin Spa offers treatment menus custom-designed for every guest.
Bottom: Simply yet elegantly decorated with wooden furniture and flooring, the spa guarantees relaxation.

Rooms and amenities
- 434 guestrooms
- 68 suites

Restaurants and bars
- Mandarin Grill: executive lunches and dinners with Crustacea Bar
- Pierre: French fine dining
- Café Causette: all-day dining with international cuisine
- Man Wah: Cantonese
- The Krug Room: private champagne dining experience for 10
- The Clipper Lounge: buffets and afternoon tea
- M Bar: contemporary cocktail bar
- The Chinnery: British food and single malt whiskies
- The Captain's Bar: cocktails and live entertainment
- The Mandarin Cake Shop: fresh pastries and coffees

Facilities
- Mandarin Spa
- Beauty Salon
- Fitness centre
- Penthouse pool
- Gentlemen's Barber
- High-tech meeting and business facilities
- Wireless and in-room television Internet access
- Mercedes Benz airport transfers
- IT butlers

5 Connaught Road, Central, Hong Kong
Tel: +85.2.2522 0111 • Fax: +85.2.2810 6190
Email: mohkg-reservations@mohg.com
Website: www.mandarinoriental.com

Grand Hyatt Tokyo

As one of Japan's largest urban redevelopment projects, the Roppongi Hills area of Tokyo is a nerve centre of culture and commerce in the city. Built on a 11-hectare (27-acre) site at a cost of over US$4 billion, the immense integrated complex is a city in its own right. Adjacent to the 54-storey centrepiece Mori Tower, which houses an art museum, cinema complex, a television station, and countless other shops, restaurants and businesses, lies the luxurious five-star hotel, Grand Hyatt Tokyo.

Designed and decorated by some of the most acclaimed international innovators and artists working in unison, from California's Remedios Siembieda Inc to New York-based Tony Chi, the Grand Hyatt Tokyo is the epitome of style and visual harmony. The warm lighting schemes created by Charles G Stone II of New York provide a conducive environment for relaxation and the enjoyment of Roppongi's luxurious pleasures. Joining a number of high-profile art installations in place throughout the property are two inspiring spaces by Takeshi Sugimoto: a traditional Shinto Shrine and a Grand Chapel with a ceiling 16 m (52 ft) high, allowing the hotel to accommodate wedding ceremonies of both the East and West.

Guestrooms and suites are decorated with a careful balance of light fabrics and natural woods such as mahogany to create a soothing residential ambience. Extra-high ceilings further the sense of space, while fine Italian furniture and linens, by B&B and Frette, respectively, assure discerning guests that comfort is far from being an afterthought. Hidden behind

Located on the top floor of the hotel, Presidential Suite offers modern décor and sweeping views.

Guests may enjoy fresh seasonal foods prepared teppanyaki-style at the Michelin-starred Keyakizaka.

sliding glass doors are large, well-appointed bathrooms that are a reflection of the bath's importance in Japanese culture. The philosophy of Japanese bathing is shown by such touches as the use of Rebecca beige limestone, deep soaking tubs designed to overflow into separate rainforest showers, and the bath products provided by REN and SUBTILIS. The end result is 389 contemporary living spaces that raise the bar of luxury in one of the world's most stylish cities.

Extending the concept of relaxation is the Nagomi Spa and Fitness facility. Guests may enjoy the use of a high-tech gymnasium and 20-m (66-ft) long swimming pool made from imported Chinese red granite for a stimulating workout, followed by a series of calming whirlpool baths, saunas, and spa treatment rooms.

The hotel completes its promise of being a 'lifestyle destination' with seven leading restaurants, including the Michelin-starred Keyakizaka, where fresh seasonal meat, seafood, and vegetables are prepared Teppanyaki style. The elegant live entertainment bar, Maduro, is an old favourite amongst connoisseurs for its extensive selection of boutique whiskies, rare and highly sought after in Japan. For the traveller who wants to be at the heart of it all, Grand Hyatt Tokyo in Roppongi Hills will prove itself to be a gateway to the very best that Tokyo has to offer.

After a brisk workout at the gymnasium, guests may wind down in the relaxing whirlpool baths offered by Nagomi Spa and Fitness.

Right: Roku Roku offers premium quality fresh sushi and sashimi, served in the traditional style with a contemporary touch.

Below: At The Oak Door, steak is cooked to perfection in dramatic oak wood-burning ovens.

Rooms and amenities

- 389 rooms and suites

Restaurants and bars

- Fiorentina: modern Italian
- Fiorentina Pastry Boutique: cakes, pastries, and chocolates
- The French Kitchen Brasserie and Bar: casual French brasserie with an open kitchen
- Shunbou: Japanese
- Roku Roku: sushi and sashimi restaurant
- The Oak Door and Bar: steakhouse
- Chinaroom: Chinese cuisine with Dim Sum
- Keyakizaka: teppanyaki
- Maduro: live entertainment bar

Facilities

- Nagomi Spa and Fitness
- Pool
- High-tech gymnasium
- High-speed Internet access
- Japanese and Western wedding facilities
- Modern art collection
- Promixity to Roppongi shopping and lifestyle

66-10-3 Roppongi, Minato-Ku, Tokyo, Japan 106-0032
Tel: +81.3.4333 1234 • Fax: +81.3.4333 8123
Email: info@tyogh.com
Website: tokyo.grand.hyatt.com

Mandarin Oriental, Tokyo

Mandarin Oriental, Tokyo was the first hotel in the entire world to be bestowed the six-star Diamond Award by the American Academy of Hospitality Sciences, a true testament to everything outstanding about this exceptional property. Located in the heart of Nihonbashi, the hotel offers an oasis of luxury in a bustling city. Occupying the nine top floors of the glitzy multipurpose Nihonbashi Mitsui Tower, the design of the hotel was conceived as a large tree, the guestrooms being the top branches. Within these branches are triptych floor-to-ceiling windows that offer unrivalled views of the city. East-facing rooms look out over Odaiba, the Sumida River and Tokyo Bay, while West-facing rooms boast views of the Imperial Palace garden, Ginza, Tokyo Station, Shinjuku and Mount Fuji in the distance.

In keeping with the principles of Japanese aesthetics, no single object stands alone in this hotel. There is a harmonious flow in every element, from sumptuous silks on the walls and the rich wood panelling on the floors, to soft arc lights that cast a warm, pleasing glow over it all. At the same time, the very latest in electronic gadgetry complements the sleek flow of the design, with the blinds and drapes operated from control panels, audio jacks for iPods, leather boxed audio-visual kits with laptop and video camera cables, and a 45-inch flat-screen TV with 51 free channels.

With in-room luxuries such as these, it is certainly understandable if guests may prefer to spend the majority of their visit within the luxurious accommodations. But to do so would

Guests can enjoy fragrant tea and a stunning view at Sense Tea Corner.

The floor-to-ceiling windows at the Mandarin Suite reveal a magnificent bird's eye view of the city.

be to miss out on the other attractions that have earned Mandarin Oriental, Tokyo its award-winning reputation.

Located on the 37th and 38th floors, the spa is a beacon of tranquillity and rejuvenation. Experience the spa's Signature Suites with a view of the Sumida River or the old town Asakusa, while a smaller suite offers guests a chance to gaze at the splendour of Mount Fuji. For a unique experience, guests can indulge in a vitality pool within the Heat and Water treatment area, or enter a steam room infused with the energies of an crystal prism before taking a cooling rinse under the rainforest showers. Next comes the dry heat of the sauna, which offers a spectacular view over the bustling city streets. If the heat gets too much for comfort, try the ice-fountain outside for a refreshing cool-down before yet another invigorating dip in the pool.

At mealtimes, seek out one of the hotel's excellent restaurants—Sense for authentic Cantonese cuisine, Signature for modern French, Tapas Molecular Bar for innovative and cutting-edge dining and Ventaglio for Italian.

The pampering continues right up to the point guests doze off on their 450-thread count cotton sheets. While other hotels anoint their pillows with chocolates at turn down, Mandarin Oriental, Tokyo instead places a bottle of aromatherapy oil to calm the senses. Indeed, while the amazing views, splendid interior design and legendary service make this hotel special, it is the many little touches that make it all the more attractive.

Signature serves French-inspired cuisine against a backdrop of the city's dazzling lights.

Rooms and amenities
- 157 guestrooms; 22 suites

Restaurants and bars
- Oriental Lounge: afternoon tea and cocktails
- Tapas Molecular Bar: innovative molecular appetisers
- K'shiki: all-day continental dining
- Signature: French-inspired dining, honoured with one Michelin star
- Sense: Cantonese dining
- Sense Tea Corner: exotic teas
- Mandarin Bar: specialty cocktails
- Ventaglio: Italian dining
- Gourmet Shop: homemade delicacies

Facilities
- 1,180-sq m (12,700-sq ft) premium spa with nine private treatment rooms
- Fitness centre
- Grand ballroom
- Banquet and meeting rooms
- Wedding chapel

Above: The award-winning spa is a haven where guests can indulge in luxurious treatments.
Left: The bedrooms are elegantly furnished with warm wood features and soothing colours.

2-1-1 Nihonbashi Muromachi Chuo-ku
Tokyo 103-8328, Japan
Tel: +81.3.3270 8800 • Fax: +81.3.3270 8828
Website: www.mandarinoriental.com/tokyo

The dramatic lighting, paintings and columns of the Lobby reflect a feeling of warmth, establishing the elegance of the property.

Grand Hyatt Seoul

Like its other Grand Hyatt counterparts throughout the world, the Grand Hyatt Seoul is frequented by countless celebrities, world leaders and royalty, thanks in no small part to its exemplary service and splendid décor which keep patrons coming back for more.

To freshen up its hallmark glass exterior, a multi-million-dollar facelift was initiated in 2003. All guestrooms were fitted with new energy-efficient thermal glass, which allow floor-to-ceiling views of mountain parklands or cityscapes, marked by the Han River's meandering path through the city.

The top seven floors of the Grand Hyatt Seoul are usually reserved for special guests. Here, speciality suites such as the Presidential and Ambassador Suites, with their wood-burning fireplaces and mosaic-tiled jacuzzis, please even the most well-heeled traveller. Grand Rooms, the hotel's standard guestroom, have been newly renovated. Now in classy shades of grey and light brown, their contemporary look is in full harmony with the Grand Club rooms on the exclusive Grand Club Floors, all of which were fully renovated in 2007.

Expansive space has been allocated to Club Olympus, the hotel's signature indoor-outdoor, resort-style recreation facility. The lush landscape is a welcome refuge from the hustle and bustle of the city, and its panoramic views of the Han River are not easily ignored. The pièce de résistance of Club Olympus is its outdoor pool and sundecks which freeze over during the winter months between November and March, morphing into a spectacular ice-skating rink, complete with skate rentals, ice-skating lessons and state-of-the-art technology. The gym was renovated in 2007 and has been totally upgraded. Also new is The Spa Grand Hyatt Seoul, featuring 14 treatment rooms with a botanical garden ambience, offering the utmost in relaxing spa services and poise.

For less strenuous entertainment, the hunting-lodge inspired Lobby Lounge sets the tone for cosy nights, while The Paris Grill, winner of the 'World's Best Hotel Dining Rooms' award in May 2004, serves classic European fare. Fine Asian cuisine is found at Akasaka's Sushi Bar and Teppanyaki Grill or The Chinese Restaurant. Japanese artisans provide a culinary spectacle of flying knives at Akasaka, while The Chinese Restaurant's open kitchen allows diners to marvel at the skilled chefs.

The ultimate treat, if one has a taste for delicate pastries and gourmet foods, is The Deli, the hotel's unparalleled delicatessen. It offers over 600 different items such as hand-made chocolates, marmalades, cheeses, candied fruit and foie gras, and produces more than 50 types of fresh baked goods daily.

Such variety is emblematic of the range of choices available to each guest who stays at the Grand Hyatt Seoul, its illustrious guest list bearing testament to its grandeur.

Rise and shine to breathtaking views of the city or mountains through the floor-to-ceiling windows of the newly renovated Grand Club rooms.

Left: The Paris Grill serves contemporary European cuisine amidst stylish settings and a comfortable ambience.
Below: The hotel's unparalleled Olympic-sized pool and recreation facilities provide resort-like rejuvenation.

Rooms and amenities
- 551 guest rooms
- 50 suites

Restaurants and bars
- Akasaka: Japanese
- The Paris Grill: European
- The Chinese Restaurant: Chinese
- Tenkai: Japanese charcoal grill
- The Terrace: buffet and à la carte
- Jung Won Buffet: international buffet
- Poolside Barbecue: seasonal outdoor barbecue
- JJ Deli: casual European
- JJ Mahoney's: light meals, drinks and entertainment
- Helicon: drinks, snacks and music
- Lobby Lounge: drinks and afternoon tea
- The Paris Bar: drinks and piano music
- The Deli: delicatessen

Facilities
- In-room high-speed Internet access with VPN
- Business and meeting centre with 10 meeting rooms and 4 private computer rooms
- 2 ballrooms with capacity for 2,000 guests
- 5 small to medium-sized function rooms with panoramic views
- Satellite conferencing system
- Fitness centre with gymnasium, indoor and outdoor swimming pools, saunas, tennis courts, squash courts and ice-skating rink
- Spa with 14 luxurious treatment rooms, each featuring a shower, bathroom, grooming area, personal safe and individual music system

747-7 Hannam-Dong, Yongsan-Gu,
Seoul 140-738, South Korea
Tel: +82.2.797 1234 · Fax: +82.2.798 6953
Email: selrs-info@hyatt.com
Website: www.seoul.grand.hyatt.com

Understated elegance shows itself in every line of the Shilla Seoul's lobby.

The Shilla Seoul

The Shilla Seoul takes its name and inspiration from Korea's legendary Shilla Dynasty, a period of phenomenal growth and development for the country. In acknowledgement of that period's standing as a golden age of art and culture, The Shilla Seoul combines award-winning architecture and landscaping with tradition and grace.

Originally built in 1979, the hotel has long set the benchmark for service in the capital city. Through historic events such as the International Olympic Committee meetings of 1988, it has been the face of Korean hospitality and charm for scores of visiting celebrities and delegates. Notable guests include Microsoft chairman Bill Gates, Steve Forbes, and actor Tom Cruise.

No other address in Korea enjoys the privilege of having a 9-hectare (23-acre) private estate within reach of the commercial district. Set in the centre of a wooded parkland, the 23-storey structure enjoys a remarkable view of both progress and nature.

This harmonious approach is perhaps best exemplified in the hotel's Sculpture Garden, created in cooperation with the GANA Gallery. Consisting of over 4 sprawling hectares (10 acres) of forest bordering Jangchung-dan Park, the beautiful garden provides an environment for relaxation, and ample opportunities to enjoy a leisurely stroll or a refreshing jog while admiring over 70 sculptures created through the work of 40 of Korea's finest artists.

In the main building, contemporary interiors created by Peter M Remedios invoke tradition through the use of only the most luxurious materials. As with his previous work on the Four Seasons Hotel New York, Remedios has chosen to incorporate authentic details from the hotel's history. Through the use of granite and lotus flower designs, a rich and instantly recognisable identity has been created, one that belongs wholly to The Shilla Seoul.

The hotel's 431 rooms and 34 suites are immaculate jewels of zen-like calm. Clean, warm colours are married with spacious open plan layouts and exquisite views, while rooms on the Executive Floors enjoy full access to business lounges with a range of exclusive services. Two Presidential Suites, named the North and South Wing Suites, resist being labelled as mere hotel accommodation. At approximately 1,500 sq m (16,146 sq ft) in area and featuring such amenities as full-sized offices and meeting rooms, Finnish dry saunas, and Bulgari products, the suites are palatial masterpieces of grandeur.

No palace is complete without a kitchen, and The Shilla Seoul has five world-class dining venues and a pastry boutique under its roof. Leading the gourmet charge is flagship restaurant, the Continental. From the 23rd floor, one's enjoyment of the standout menu, composed of modern and classic European favourites, is heightened by unmatched views of Mt Namsan and the city's many skyscrapers and gardens below. With The Shilla Seoul, a new golden age may have already begun.

Occupying close to 1,500 sq m (16,146 sq ft) of space, the hotel's Presidential Suites are suitable for even the most distinguished of guests.

Floor to ceiling windows at the Guerlain Spa allow guests to enjoy an unmatched view of the wooded park along with refreshing massage therapies.

Rooms and amenities

- 431 guestrooms
- 34 suites

Restaurants and bars

- Continental: fine European dining
- Library Bar & Lounge: relaxed bar with Korea's largest single malt collection
- The Parkview: all-day dining
- Palsun: elegant Chinese
- Ariake: modern Japanese, with rare sake
- Pastry Boutique: handcrafted cakes and pastries

Facilities

- Fitness centre
- Guerlain Spa
- Indoor golf range
- Indoor and outdoor pools
- Executive Conference Centre with 8 meeting rooms
- The Shilla Arcade
- The Shilla Duty Free Shop
- Sculpture Garden

Formerly the State Guest House, the Yeong Bin Gwan annex is a distinctive part of The Shilla Seoul.

202, Jangchungdong 2-Ga, Jung-Gu, Seoul 100-856, Korea
Tel: +82.2.2233 3131 • Fax: +80.2.2233 5073
Email: reserve@shilla.net • Website: www.shilla.net

The Author's Wing at Oriental, Bangkok offers a calming atmosphere.

The Oriental, Bangkok

The scenic location of The Oriental in Bangkok has been a wellspring of inspiration to many a renowned writer, and authors like Paul Theroux, Tennessee Williams and VS Naipaul have been guests at the hotel at some point in time. So much so that four spacious suites, collectively known as The Authors' Wing, have been named after literary greats Joseph Conrad, Noël Coward, W Somerset Maugham and James L Michener.

The history of this grande dame goes back to 1876, and is rich with literary association. The hotel's heritage is an inextricable part of its identity, and even after a multi-million dollar restoration in late 2003, design elements from its past were retained for a nostalgic touch. The Regency Room is the epitome of old-world elegance. Hand-cut crystal chandeliers, damask-patterned Thai silk walls and period furniture combine to create the rarefied air of a past era.

While dining options abound in the city, The Oriental, Bangkok houses food and beverage outlets that are institutions in their own right. Lord Jim's, named after Joseph Conrad's novel of the same name, is recognised as the city's top seafood restaurant, its fresh culinary offerings served against a background of marine-inspired furnishings and 16-m (52-ft) long aquarium. The China House, long regarded as the mainstay of traditional Chinese cuisine, has been revamped and revived into an avant-garde eatery inspired by the vibrant 1930s Shanghai Art Deco period, serving classic cuisine with a modern twist in a chic space of cutting-edge design. Sala Rim Naam, The Oriental's signature Thai restaurant, has recently been transformed into a mini royal palace serving fine Thai cuisine. Another welcome addition is the Sala Rim Naam Lounge, an open-air pavillion adjacent to the restaurant overlooking the splendid Chao Phraya River, which offers mesmerising Thai dance performances as well. The Bamboo Bar is known for its menu, and for inspiring Morgan McFinn's novel *At The Bamboo Bar*.

Awarded top slot in *Travel + Leisure*'s hotel survey, The Oriental houses one of the world's most highly-acclaimed spas, The Oriental Spa. A stay in the hotel is hardly complete without a pampering session here, whether for a whole day or a mere hour. Traditional Thai and modern Western techniques are utilised in over 50 spa therapies, and guests are guaranteed to emerge cleansed and soothed. Recently the hotel has also unveiled its newest wellness facility, The Oriental Ayurvedic Penthouse. A holistic centre of tranquillity located above The Oriental Spa, the Ayurvedic Penthouse is the first of its kind in Bangkok and offers the most exclusive range of natural healing rituals in the city.

Those keen to learn more about Thai cuisine can do so by enrolling in The Oriental Thai Cooking School. Here, acclaimed chefs impart authentic Thai recipes—a truly unique souvenir of any stay. Another new addition to La Grande Dame is Baan Noi, an exclusive private event area with clear views of the River of Kings.

The living room of the Joseph Conrad Suite opens out onto the chequered floor-tiles of a private terrace.

Right: The panoramic view of the Chao Phraya river from the pool is breathtaking.

Below: A Thai classical performance shown during dinner at the Sala Rim Naam.

Rooms and amenities
- 358 guestrooms
- 35 suites

Restaurants and bars
- Le Normandie: French
- The China House: Chinese
- Lord Jim's: seafood
- Sala Rim Naam: traditional Thai
- Terrace Rim Naam: à la carte open-air Thai
- Ciao: Italian
- The Verandah Coffee Shop: international
- Riverside Terrace: barbeque buffet
- The Bamboo Bar: drinks
- Authors' Lounge: drinks and afternoon tea

Facilities
- 6 function rooms
- Business centre
- The Oriental Boutique
- 25-m (82-ft) swimming and infinity-edge pools
- Spa and fitness centre
- Beauty parlour and barber shop
- Personal butler service
- Ayurvedic Penthouse
- Baan Noi private event area
- Thai cooking school
- Shopping arcade
- Day care centre

48 Oriental Avenue, Bangkok 10500, Thailand
Tel: +66.2.659 9000 • Fax: +66.2.659 0000
Email: orbkk-reservations@mohg.com
Website: www.mandarin-oriental.com/bangkok

The Sukhothai, Bangkok

The Sukhothai was named after the ancient Siamese capital city whose fortuitous location turned it into a trading centre of great beauty and opulence. With its location in Bangkok's central business and embassy district, the hotel does a remarkable job of recreating the splendour and charm of its namesake. Walk the paradisiacal grounds of the modern day Sukhothai, landscaped to tropical perfection with resplendent gardens, reflection pools, and symmetrical colonnades, and one could be forgiven for assuming that the property was designed from actual historic documents.

Echoing the emphatic use of 'Stupa' and 'Chedi' structures in Sukhothai Kingdom-era Buddhist temples, The Sukhothai has the feel of a living artifact. Once inside, guests bear witness to an unfolding of the country's rich history. The sound of a traditional Khim, a zither-like instrument played with two delicate mallets, can often be heard drifting through the lobby, performed live in the lounge. The generous use of luxurious natural materials such as bronze, teakwood, and marble adds to the grand palatial atmosphere.

In each of the 210 guestrooms and suites, the elegance of Thai design meets state-of-the-art modernity and luxury. Rich silks, teak furnishings, and warm tones produce a 21st-century interpretation of royal salons, complete with iPod media connections, flat-screen LCD televisions, wireless Internet access, as well as business desks with fax machines. Perhaps the best indication of the hotel's high standards can be found in the hotel's Sukhothai Suite.

Surrounded by tranquil greenery, the Spa Botanica is an obvious choice for guests wishing to relax.

The conference rooms are fitted with high-tech business amenities, allowing every meeting to run smoothly.

Over 198 sq m (2,132 sq ft), the 'Suite of Kings' features a contemporary Thai style brought into being through the use of rich handwoven Jim Thompson fabrics and other luxurious finishings. Along with a full kitchen, private dining room, study room and a lavish amount of bedroom space, the suite also features a lounge with a grand piano.

One, however, does not need to be a Head of State to appreciate The Sukhothai's brand of indulgence, a fact attested to by the hotel's nomination as 'The Best Hotel in Thailand' by senior international business executives in the magazine, *Institutional Investor*. A crucial factor in this decision may have been The Sukhothai's seven international restaurants and bars, each providing every epicurean reason for lovers of fine dining to rejoice. Celadon, named the 'Best Restaurant in Bangkok' by *Travel and Leisure Magazine*, serves authentic cuisine in a Sala—a traditional Thai open pavilion—surrounded by a tranquil lotus pond.

Guests who wish to experience genuine Thai massages will find skilled practitioners and a menu of signature treatments waiting at the acclaimed Spa Botanica. Set in peaceful garden surroundings, the spa's seven treatment rooms, including a double VIP room with jacuzzi, will rejuvenate any spirit. Along with a fully equipped health and fitness centre, The Sukhothai has all the makings of a world-class resort, albeit one set against the backdrop of a long-lost ancient empire.

The hotel rooms are decorated in warm, rich colours, echoing the royal salons of ages past.

Rooms and amenities
- 128 guestrooms
- 82 suites

Restaurants and bars
- Celadon: Thai fine dining
- Colonnade: all-day dining, Western and Asian, Sunday brunch
- La Scala: contemporary Italian, large wine selection
- Salon: cocktails, coffee and tea lounge, chocolate buffet
- Pool Terrace Café & Bar: light snacks and health drinks
- Thimian: gourmet pastry shop and cafe
- The Zuk Bar: intimate cocktail bar

Facilities
- Wireless Internet access
- Retail shops
- Infinity lap pool
- Squash and tennis courts
- Spa Botanica
- Health centre
- Meeting facilities and ballroom
- Airport transfers
- Mercedes-Benz limousine service

Right: Deluxe Terrace Suites offer their own balcony, allowing guests to enjoy an afternoon of sun in total privacy.
Below: La Scala serves contemporary Italian food with a touch of flair, creating dishes which are perfectly complemented by their selection of fine wines.

13/3 South Sathorn Road, Bangkok 10120, Thailand
Tel: +66.2.344 8888 • Fax: +66.2.344 8899
Email: info@sukhothai.com
Website: www.sukhothai.com

The hotel's outdoor infinity-edge pool offers breathtaking views of the Singapore River.

The Fullerton Hotel Singapore

A bastion of elegance, The Fullerton Hotel presides over the mouth of the Singapore River, offering luxury accommodations as well as unrivalled views in the heart of Singapore's business district. From the impressive Doric columns to the soaring, sunlit atrium lobby, the hotel's neo-classical architecture evokes the grandeur of a bygone era, while its refurbished interiors are tastefully appointed in an elegant, contemporary style.

Though the original 1928 building was not actually designed as a hotel, the space has been re-imagined with guestrooms and suites of various shapes and sizes. Every guestroom is comfortably decorated with warm colours and sophisticated finishes, and is outfitted with high-speed Internet access. Many rooms offer panoramic views of the river or sea, and some also have verandahs where guests may soak up the sun. For further relaxation, a gorgeous outdoor infinity-edge pool and the menu of soothing therapies at The Asian Spa will surely suffice, while a 24-hour fitness centre caters to more active guests.

The suites have also been designed to take full advantage of The Fullerton Hotel's location and architecture. The two-storey Loft Suites offer waterfront views and have an elegant spiral staircase leading to the bedroom upstairs. The Fullerton Suites occupy the top level of the building, with wide terraces that overlook the sea. Naturally, the best is reserved for the Governor and Presidential Suites, the latter featuring an air-conditioned glass verandah, while both offer a 24-hour butler service.

For an even more exclusive experience, The Fullerton Hotel offers the Straits Club, its premier executive club. Guests can enjoy personalised service and private check-ins, as well as a host of other amenities such as a complimentary champagne breakfast. The Straits Club Lounge is decorated in a vintage Peranakan style with Straits Chinese antiques and artefacts to give it a unique local flavour.

Some of Singapore's best fine dining can be found in the hotel. Town Restaurant offers a diverse menu of refined international cuisine, and guests may dine al fresco at tables which overlook the famous Singapore River. In the former lighthouse on the hotel's top floor, the intimate San Marco at The Lighthouse serves exquisite Italian cuisine prepared with modern touches. Jade serves contemporary Chinese delicacies in a refined setting, while guests may enjoy afternoon tea or chocolate buffet at The Courtyard. Post Bar, named after the General Post Office that once occupied the ground floor, still maintains the original ceiling and architectural motifs of the building. Sophisticated and chic, the bar is perfect for after-dinner drinks with friends.

While The Fullerton Hotel may certainly draw upon its rich history in Singapore, it has also established its name in its own right on the international scene: in 2008, it was named a *Condé Nast Traveler* Gold List hotel for the fourth consecutive year. With its distinctive juxtaposition of old and new, stately and modern, The Fullerton Hotel has developed its own stamp of elegant gravitas.

The hotel's interior matches the stately grandeur of Palladian architecture with sleek modern finishes.

Comfort and elegance are expertly paired in the hotel's Governor Suite.

Rooms and amenities
- 371 guestrooms
- 28 suites

Restaurants and bars
- Town Restaurant: international
- The Courtyard: Japanese, Indian, afternoon tea, cocktail and snacks, weekend chocolate buffet
- Post Bar: drinks
- Jade: fine Chinese cuisine
- San Marco at The Lighthouse: Italian

Facilities
- Outdoor infinity-edge pool
- 24-hour fitness centre
- Spa
- 24-hour business centre
- Ballrooms and 8 meeting rooms

Post Bar offers signature cocktails in a contemporary setting with historic touches.

1 Fullerton Square, Singapore 049178 •
Tel: +65.6733 8388 • Fax: +65.6735 8388
Email: info@fullertonhotel.com
Website: www.fullertonhotel.com

Mandarin Oriental, Singapore

A representation of the finest aspects of life in this city-state, Mandarin Oriental, Singapore embraces the five intersecting worlds that give the island nation its character: nature, business, shopping, luxury, and food. Centrally located in the city's fastest developing zone, the hotel lies within both the Central Business District, and a thriving arts and commercial hub that includes the distinctive complex, Esplanade—Theatres on the Bay. Surrounding the property are beautiful landscaped gardens and the lush, omnipresent greenery that Singapore is renowned for.

Many points of interest are only a few minutes away on foot. Taking care of business is Suntec Singapore, one of the largest convention centres and exhibition halls in the Asia-Pacific region. It also features a full-sized shopping centre which connects to the Marina Square Shopping Mall via Citylink Mall—yet another cluster of high-end shops which doubles as an underground passageway connecting the area's buildings. For even more designer label shopping, Singapore's famous Orchard Road is less than half an hour away by public transport. Those who wish for a quiet moment far from the crowds will appreciate the hotel's proximity to the newly completed Singapore Flyer. An observation wheel larger than the London Eye, it offers views of a rarely seen side of the towering skyline, and is just a five-minute walk from the hotel.

Occupants of the hotel's 527 rooms and suites need not go out of their way to enjoy a view, as there are large floor-to-ceiling windows in every room offering incredible views of the

Above: Suites offer incredible views of surrounding landmarks and attractions, such as the newly completed Singapore Flyer.

Left: The Presidential Suite offers the utmost in luxury.

Below: The Mandarin Oriental Club Lounge offers a stylish venue for business travellers to relax and network.

Opposite: Rooms are decorated with fine Oriental touches.

The large outdoor pool is especially inviting on warm afternoons.

city skyline, the wide ocean horizon, or the picturesque harbour of Marina Bay. Recently redesigned in a multimillion-dollar renovation project in 2005, all rooms feature contemporary styling with the high-tech infrastructure that Singapore has built its name on. Suites enjoy separate living spaces with unique artwork, a personalised in-room check-in service, deluxe Molton Brown toiletries, and the lavish use of exquisite materials such as marble and silk. Along with all other guestrooms, they are equipped with high-specification surround sound theatre systems backed by a video-on-demand service and satellite channels.

Business travellers enjoy high-speed fibre optic connections in every room, as well as compatibility with enterprise Virtual Private Networks (VPN). Internet services that often fail when using shared connections, such as videoconferencing and online collaboration, work flawlessly at the hotel.

A number of special Oriental Club rooms offer guests several 'Executive Class' pleasures such as use of an exclusive 481-sq-m (5,177-sq-ft) Oriental Club Lounge. Located on the 19th floor, the lounge boasts an uninterrupted view of the city. Peaceful and relaxed, it is an ideal place to meet with colleagues or catch up on email with the complimentary-use meeting room and wireless Internet access. Twice daily, complimentary food and beverage presentations offer a chance to unwind and take the mind off work. Start the day with a champagne breakfast, and work up an appetite for dinner with evening cocktails and hors d'oeuvres.

Hold a luxurious private banquet at Mandarin Oriental, Singapore.

It's easy to follow that up with the hotel's five superb restaurants, bridging a wide variety of tastes from around the world. At Morton's, The Steakhouse, prime cuts of grain-fed beef and fresh seafood are done to perfection in a fine dining setting that is both chic and lively. Wasabi Bistro serves Japanese cuisine with a Californian influence for a unique experience, while Cherry Garden is a local Cantonese dining favourite. Dark wood panels, slate floors, and dashes of bright red set the scene for an artistic display of dishes served with a wide selection of imported teas.

For a taste of the Mediterranean, look no further than the pool deck where Dolce Vita serves sunny, colourful treats on an outdoor terrace. Should one have trouble deciding, MELT ~ The World Café provides the closest match to 'all of the above'. A buffet restaurant featuring 30 chefs in dynamic show kitchens, it showcases all the tastes of the Orient as well as international highlights. Voted 'Singapore's Best Restaurant' for two years running in *Singapore Tatler*, it offers a feast with few equals.

One final pleasure not to be missed is the hotel's Oriental Spa. Over 620 sq m (6,674 sq ft) of warm walnut flooring, it offers a menu of treatments that combine aromatherapy, touch, and facial renewal regimes using essential oils and natural ingredients. After seeing all that Singapore has to offer, returning to a slow neck rub and soothing cup of herbal tea makes a stay at the Mandarin Oriental, Singapore feel even better than home.

Dolce Vita offers Mediterranean cuisine and is located on an outdoor terrace, so guests may enjoy tropical warmth or the cool night air.

Right: At Axis Bar and Lounge, sip cocktails to the sounds of chic lounge music and views of the Singapore skyline.

Below: Cherry Garden serves genuine Cantonese cuisine in an understatedly elegant setting.

Rooms and amenities
- 452 guestrooms
- 75 suites

Restaurants and bars
- Dolce Vita: Mediterranean
- Cherry Garden: Cantonese
- MELT ~ The World Café: international buffet
- Morton's, The Steakhouse: steaks and seafood
- Wasabi Bistro: Japanese with a Californian influence
- Axis Bar and Lounge: cocktails and chic lounge music

Facilities
- Oriental Spa
- 25-m (82-ft) outdoor pool
- Landscaped gardens
- Wellness Zone fitness centre with yoga sessions
- Meeting and conference facilities
- Internet access
- The Oriental Club

5 Raffles Avenue, Marina Square, Singapore 039797
Tel: +65.6338 0066 • Fax: +65.6339 9537
Email: mosin@mohg.com
Website: www.mandarinoriental.com

The Maharaja's table at Jamavar—the hotel's signature Indian restaurant.

The Leela Palace Kempinski Bangalore

Recreating the architectural splendour of India's Vijaynagar Empire, The Leela Palace Kempinski Bangalore is a vision of traditional Indian beauty. Inspired from the Royal Palace of Mysore, the hotel displays Indo-Saracenic architecture, with elaborate pillars, high pointed arches and grand circular copper domes.

Set in 3.6 hectares (9 acres) of manicured gardens, the hotel's drive to the main entrance is flanked by tall palms that stand proudly at attention. The entrance porte-cochere is the epitome of the stunning architectural flavour that runs through the entire building, with its massive columns supporting the beautifully scalloped arches moulded over with intricately detailed plasterwork and delicate railings that appear like exotic lace wrought of thin metal.

Inside, stately common rooms guarantee a warm stay experience for all guests. The Library Bar, with a separate Billiards Hall and a Cigar Lounge, is wrapped from floor to ceiling in handsome hardwood paneling, hand-knotted carpets and sleekly polished leather couches.

At Jamavar, the hotel's signature restaurant, guests enjoy a meticulously prepared range of traditional Indian recipes carefully selected and sourced from every region of the country. The restaurant's soaring ceilings are crowned with layer upon layer of friezework, sparkling crystal chandeliers, lavish murals and picture windows overlooking the green gardens.

Fine pan-Asian cuisine, including fiery Thai and aromatic Indonesian and Malay dishes, are served in Zen restaurant, where teppanyaki and fresh sushi are also offered

in a cosy Japanese-inspired room. In addition to this, guests may choose to dine around the clock on a wide variety of international favourites, prepared with a flourish in Citrus' open show kitchen.

Guests will find all of the rooms furnished each with hardwood floors, cream-coloured walls with crown mouldings, and wooden lattice screens that lead to private balconies. All rooms have clear views of the gardens for which the Leela group of hotels have become famous. The furniture is made of fine hardwood as well, such as the large desks which provide ample workspace for business travellers, and cabinets housing entertainment units for leisure time. The minibars are fully stocked, and works of local art grace the walls.

At The Leela Health Spa, the hotel has wide range of holistic therapies for in wellness and relaxation. Western therapies are available as well, and all guests have access to saunas, steam baths, whirlpools and body jet showers. For a full workout, the gym is well stocked with the very latest Cyber and Precor cardio training machines, and a full set of weights.

Located near Bangalore's business district with easy access to a neighbouring golf course, it's overwhelmingly clear that The Leela Palace Kempinski, Bangalore is easily the city's premier address for executive accommodations.

Guestrooms are thoroughly modern, albeit with hints of the old Orient in the ornately carved wooden furnishings.

Right: The porch verandah shows off a great view framed by the high scalloped arches that feature through out the hotel.

Below: Zen serves fine pan-Asian cuisine in a spectacular high-ceilinged dining room.

Rooms and amenities
- 257 guestrooms and suites

Restaurants and bars
- Jamavar: classical Indian
- Zen: pan-Asian
- Citrus: 24-hour international brasserie
- Library Bar: drinks and cigars

Facilities
- 2 ballrooms
- 8 meeting rooms
- Fitness centre
- Spa
- Outdoor pool

23 Airport Road, Bangalore 560 008, India
Tel: +91.80.2521 1234 • Fax: +91.80.2521 2222
Email: reservations.bangalore@theleela.com
Website: www.theleela.com

The Leela Kempinski Goa

Situated along the temperate west coast of India, Goa has captured the imagination of countless travelers, from the very earliest Portuguese colonials to the streams of sun seekers who flock to its breezy beaches and colourful culture each year. For well-heeled visitors, The Leela Kempinski Goa is a sanctuary offering a warm and memorable stay with access to everything that Goa has to offer.

Built on 30 hectares (75 acres) of verdant landscaped grounds, the hotel sits between the Arabian Sea and the River Sal. A lazy lagoon snakes throughout the property, carving out micro-islets luxuriant with tropical foliage and towering palms. Overlooking the banks of the lagoon, villas have large balconies and fragrant terraces overhung with flowering bougainvillea. On the inside, marble floors and whitewashed walls keep the heat off in rooms cooled by the languorous drowse of ceiling fans. Meticulously carved hardwood headboards, armchairs and desks, and louvered window shutters add touches of colonial grandeur.

Residents who are seeking the ultimate in exclusivity can check into The Club at The Leela Kempinski Goa, where private suites are luxuriously furnished. An open contemporary design has been created by custom-built furnishings, with space for a Bose Wave System CD player, espresso machine, and LCD flat-screen television with DVD player. Club guests get pampered with their own personal butler and a long list of complimentary services. Club residents also enjoy the exclusive use of a designated lap pool and club lounge.

Deck beds by the beach side—an ideal place for relaxation

A magnificent view of the golf course and the sea beyond

Diners have a number of superb choices at the hotel. At Susegado, fresh seafood is grilled by the beachside beneath the breathtaking sunset over the Arabian Sea. Beside the river, classic Italian favourites are carefully prepared with Mediterranean touches at The Riverside's air-conditioned dining room or al fresco deck. For excellent Indian cuisine, The Leela's signature restaurant, Jamavar, also prepares authentic recipes from Goa's unique culinary tradition. Western and Asian cuisine are also offered through the day at the poolside café.

Guests can while away their days at the pristine beach, where water sports await. Back on solid ground, the par-3, 12-hole golf course is nestled in scenic gardens. To work out kinks at the end of the day, treatments for health and beauty at the spa utilise recipes and wisdom from ancient Ayurvedic medical tradition, and relaxing yoga sessions are also available.

Upon nightfall, the Las Vegas gaming room comes to life with roulette, slot machines and other casino favourites, and Aqua discotheque hosts a party with live DJ dance music, its bar well stocked with fine wines, premium cognac, single malt whiskies and imported cigars.

With so many ways to enjoy a holiday, The Leela Kempinski Goa's guests will literally have to drag themselves away from the hotel's comforts to visit the many nearby sights of historic Goa.

For ultimate exclusivity, guests can check into the Club at The Leela Kempinski Goa.

Right: Ancient Ayurvedic therapies at the spa help guests to work out their tension and enjoy a fully relaxing holiday.

Below: Bedrooms are cosily lit and decorated in neutral earth tones for a classic, elegant look.

Rooms and amenities
- 54 Pavilion Rooms; 66 Conservatory Rooms; 25 Lagoon Suites; 15 Club Suites; 4 Royal Villas; 1 Presidential Suite

Restaurants and bars
- Jamavar: Indian
- The Café: Western and Asian
- The Riverside: Italian
- Susegado: seafood
- Pool Bar: light snacks and drinks
- Yali lounge: cocktails
- Aqua: discotheque

Facilities
- Ballroom and 3 meeting rooms
- Gaming room
- Tennis
- Par-3 12-hole golf course
- Water sports

Mobor, Cavelossim, Goa, India
Tel: +91.832.278 1234 • Fax: +91.832.287 1352
Email: reservations.goa@theleela.com
Website: www.theleela.com

Trident Gurgaon

The city of Gurgaon has been the site of a developmental boom over the last decade as affluent individuals and expanding corporations, both local and multinational, began to look beyond Delhi's crowded boundaries for a new alternative. The original birthplace of India's large outsourcing industry, the city now ranks as a major technological and business service hub in the state of Haryana.

The city is also home to many historic and cultural attractions popular with holidaymakers, and so the five-star Trident Gurgaon hotel deftly blends a host of business-oriented features with the look, feel, and service of a resort destination. It is a formula that has won the Trident Gurgaon accolades from sources such as the World Travel Awards, which handed it the coveted titles of 'India's Leading Hotel' and 'Asia's Leading Meetings Hotel' in 2007.

Conveniently located just 10 km (6 miles) from Indira Gandhi International Airport, the hotel is a five-minute drive from the business district. Those with commitments in Central Delhi will find it a short 26 km (16 miles) journey to the east, which also puts several places of interest within reach, such as Humayun's Tomb, Bahai Temple, the National Museum, and Qutab Minar, the world's tallest brick minaret tower.

Visually impressive, the enormous hotel building by architect Lek Bunnag combines traditional elements of Indian palatial design with a few modern subtleties; amidst the domes, arches, and inner courtyards, one also finds smooth curves and examples of large-scale architectural symmetry. Within the estate,

Above: The high ceiling gives the hotel a sense of limitless space.

Right: The magnificent architecture brings to mind the opulence of ancient palaces.

Opposite: Well-placed lighting gives the Trident Gurgaon a grand feel.

The numerous reflection pools add a tranquil feeling.

Cilantro offers all-day dining with fine international cuisine.

beautiful landscaping, fountains and reflection pools seamlessly merge with stone walkways and long corridors. The lobby atrium is an airy, high-ceilinged affair crowned by a large golden dome. The highlight of the entire structure is at its centre—a heated outdoor pool the size of a football field, inlaid with shimmering blue tiles.

All 129 rooms and seven suites are either garden-facing or pool-facing. Floor-to-ceiling windows allow in plenty of light and bring the splendid views up to within an inch of the bedrooms. Pool-facing rooms and suites enjoy reflection pools that literally extend from the outer edges of their windows to the pool below. Inside, the bedrooms and living areas are richly appointed with stately dark wood furniture and soft, luxurious fabrics.

86 Superior Rooms are furnished with either a single king-sized bed or twin beds, and enjoy all of the standard amenities and business tools that put the Trident hotel group at the top of its category. These range from the essentials: electronic safes, minibars, tea and coffee facilities; to the efficient: dual-line direct-dial telephones, large workdesks, wired and wireless Internet connections; to the sensual: a custom pillow menu, and exclusive designer toiletries. Entertainment options are also a cut above the rest, with satellite channels displayed on large 40-inch flat-screen LCD televisions, and DVD players in some rooms.

A stay at one of the Trident Gurgaon's 43 Deluxe Rooms comes with unusual extras normally associated with suites, such as butler service, walk-in wardrobes, and large bathrooms

with shower stalls and deep soaking tubs. Executive Suites up the ante with separate living rooms, powder rooms, and extra-spacious bedrooms, and the work areas have multifunction printer/copier/fax machines with their own direct lines.

A fully equipped 24-hour business centre serves the call of modern commerce, and also includes a small meeting room. Larger gatherings may make use of four event spaces, which can be combined in pairs to accommodate as many as 195 people.

When the time comes to disconnect from worldly concerns, visit The Spa by Angsana. One of the most recognised names in the spa industry, it promises total renewal in both mind and body through a range of massages, facials, and wraps. A 24-hour fitness centre provides more active possibilities with the latest in gym equipment, while complimentary yoga sessions help to unwind tired muscles.

Dining at the Trident Gurgaon consists of the authentic North Indian fare at Saffron, Japanese specialities like sushi and teriyaki at Konomi, and superb all-day international dining at Cilantro. The latter's menu is centred around a specially designed wood-fired oven which the chef uses to create the time-honoured thin-crust pizzas so popular in Italian cuisine.

For guests without the luxury of time, the Trident Gurgaon emphasises simple pleasures, while others will find that no corners have been cut in making this an opulent, self-contained destination with all the tastes and charms of the region intact.

Above: The gorgeous heated outdoor pool is the centrepiece of the hotel complex.

Left: For guests wishing to stay active, the fully equipped fitness centre provides a range of exercising options.

Deluxe Rooms offer amenities that would only be available in suites at other hotels.

Rooms and amenities
- 129 guestrooms
- 7 suites

Restaurants and bars
- Cilantro: all-day international dining
- Konomi: Japanese
- Saffron: regional and North Indian
- The Bar: cocktails and whiskies
- Pool Bar: light meals and drinks

Facilities
- Spa by Angsana
- Outdoor heated pool
- 24-hour business centre
- Conference facilities
- Wireless and wired Internet access
- 24-hour fitness centre
- Complimentary yoga sessions at 6am every morning
- Valet parking

443 Udyog Vihar, Phase V, Gurgaon, Haryana 122 016, India
Tel: +91.124.245 0505 • Fax: +91.124. 245 0606
Email: reservations@tridenthotels.com
Website: www.tridenthotels.com

The Leela Kempinski Kovalam Beach, Kerala

The Leela Kempinski Kovalam Beach occupies an enviable location along Kerala's fabulously gilded coastline, up the side of a rocky cliff with panoramic vistas of the Arabian Sea. Swaying palms and tropical gardens with exotic blooms invite guests to unwind in one of southern India's most idyllic retreats.

An understated elegance characterises the minimalist design of the resort, which features natural materials such as glossy woods and polished stone, and yet allows small details to shine through. An open-air lobby with vaulted ceilings is cooled by fresh breezes bringing in the bracing sea air. In the sunken lounge area, flickering candle flames illuminate wide bowls of floating flowers. The rich cultural heritage of India's southernmost state is prominent throughout the resort, through local paintings, sculptures and the artful use of textiles.

In order to capture the superb view, all of the resort's public spaces have a stunning view of the sea. At the cliff-top restaurant, The Terrace, guests can dine on a menu of tempting international cuisine while visually feasting on the surrounding flowers and sea view. At Tides, by the beach, fresh seafood is served under a thatch-roofed pavilion, the very epitome of rustic chic. Kovalam Beach's mesmerising sunsets are best savoured from the resort's two bars. Enjoy a cocktail or two by the infinity-edge pool while the sun makes its descent into the horizon—an unforgettable experience.

All of The Leela Kempinski Kovalam Beach's rooms boast magnificent views. Rooms fronting the beach even offer their own generously

The outdoor pool of The Club at The Leela Kempinski Kovalam Beach is absolutely stunning in the twilight.

Poolside dining can be an experience worth waiting for, especially with such a spectacular sunset view.

proportioned private sundecks. High timber ceilings are supported by open beams, with natural themes recurring in the sliding wooden window shutters and the beds' hardwood headboards, some with botanical motifs hand-painted on in traditional local style. Furnishings feature a tropical theme, from plantation chairs with cane seats to colourful silk throw cushions. Bathrooms are handsome in contemporary high-gloss black marble and gleaming chrome.

The Club is reserved for the resort's most exclusive and discerning guests. They enjoy 24-hour butler service, a private club lounge, an exclusive infinity-edge pool, and a fine dining restaurant with customised culinary concierge to ensure their meals are prepared entirely to suit their tastes.

Part of southern India's allure is the promise of health and well-being springing from India's tradition of Ayurveda therapies. The Divya spa offers treatments for beauty and rejuvenation sourced from an ancient medicinal heritage that focuses on harmony of the body and mind. Over 743 sq m (8,000 sq ft), the subtly lit tranquil space is infused with the relaxing scents of aromatherapy oils. The spa also conducts regular yoga sessions for all levels.

The Leela Kempinski Kovalam Beach, on 17 hectares (44 acres) of verdant grounds, blends superb levels of legendary Asian hospitality with the exceptional natural beauty of its surroundings, such that visitors to India's southern Kerala state often find it difficult to tear themselves away from this exotic paradise.

Watch the ocean, read a book or relax to music at The Living Room

Rooms and amenities

- 182 guestrooms and suites
- The Club, with 56 Club Rooms and Suites, The Spa and Gym, The Living Room, The Library and The Café for international cuisine

Restaurants and bars

- The Terrace: international
- Tides: beachside seafood
- The Bar: poolside cocktails
- Sky Bar: lounge

Facilities

- Convention centre and meeting rooms
- Fitness centre
- Ayurveda spa
- Library

Right: The balcony of one of the suites at The Leela Kempinski Kovalam Beach overlooks the glittering Arabian Sea.

Below: Ancient Ayurveda treatments at Divya, the spa

Kerala, Thiruvananthapuram. 695 527 India
Tel+91 471 248 0101 • Fax:+91 471 248 1522
Email:reservations.kovalam@theleela.com
Website:www.theleela.com

Guestrooms boast some of the best views of the surrounding countryside to be had in India.

The Leela Kempinski Mumbai

The Leela Palaces, Hotels and Resorts are synonymous with nature, each Leela property being built on vast acreages of thriving gardens; The Leela Kempinski Mumbai is no different. An escape from Mumbai's bustling urban sprawl, the hotel is built on grounds spanning 4.5 hectares (11 acres), and surrounded by verdant landscaping, rushing waterfalls and calming lotus pools. Nestled within landscaped gardens, the outdoor pool is shaded by towering palms, and the timber poolside deck is the perfect space for an evening cocktail by low candlelight and cascading fountains.

Inside, the hotel's lobby welcomes guests with its cool and contemporary ambience. In the centre, an intricately carved pavilion with a roof of pounded gold-leaf adds a local Indian flavour to the contemporary surroundings. Original Indian artwork is also featured in the lobby and throughout the hotel's public spaces.

Especially perfect for executive travellers, guestrooms combine luxurious relaxation with business functionality. Furnishings in warm-hued woods and plush fabrics, lattice screens and hand-knotted carpets create a haven of comfort, while a practical office area provides ergonomic desk space with Internet access, a plasma-screen TV and executive amenities.

The hotel has also custom-designed mattresses, all dressed in the finest and most comfortable bed linens in order to guarantee a good night's sleep. Within each of the white marble bathrooms are glass-enclosed shower facilities with twin spa-style massaging showerheads for relaxing after a long day.

The Leela's signature Indian restaurant, Jamavar, presents a gastronomic journey through the exotic subcontinent, serving recipes from the country's many and varied culinary traditions. Those with a taste for international cuisine can try Citrus, a 24-hour brasserie with a view of either the airy show kitchen or the greenery outside its floor-to-ceiling picture windows. Also on the menu is authentic Italian at Stella restaurant and a variety of Chinese cuisines at The Great Wall. For the after-hours, one can head to the 6 Degrees, a well-stocked bar specialising in martinis, a variety of beers, and fine wines with signature cocktails, tapas and lounge music .

At The Leela Kempinski Mumbai's health and recreation centre, guests can work up a sweat in a state-of-the-art gym or play a cool game of squash in the air-conditioned court. For relaxation, the hotel offers yoga sessions and Ayurvedic massages.

The Leela Kempinski Mumbai exemplifies the philosophy that drives one of India's most luxurious hotel groups. With this flagship property, The Leela Palaces, Hotels and Resorts introduced world-class luxury accommodations to India, joining forces with Germany's Kempinski Hotels, one of the oldest and most prestigious hospitality groups in Europe. On the anvil are new properties opening in Gurgaon (2008), Udaipur (2009),Chennai (2009), New Delhi (2010), Hyderabad and Pune (2011).

Dark wood furnishings define the luxurious feel of the guestrooms, while soft touches such as the carpets impart an Eastern flavour.

Rooms and amenities
- 390 guestrooms

Restaurants and bars
- Jamavar: Indian
- The Great Wall: Chinese
- Stella: classic Italian
- Citrus: 24-hour international cuisine
- 6 Degrees: cocktails and tapas

Facilities
- Ballroom and 7 function rooms
- 24-hour business centre
- Fitness centre
- Beauty salon
- Shopping arcade

Right: The large outdoor pool is surrounded by palm trees, demonstrating the hotel's close relationship with nature.

Below: An evening outdoor view of the hotel from the poolside.

Sahar, Mumbai 400 059, India
Tel: +91.22.6691 1234 • Fax: +91.22.6691 1212
Email: reservations.mumbai@theleela.com
Website: www.theleela.com

Grand Hyatt Mumbai

At the crossroads of capital and development between the North and South of Mumbai, the centre of India's business activities, lies an entirely new commercial complex like no other in all of South Asia. Stretching over 4 hectares (10 acres) of prime real estate minutes from the new Bandra-Kurla Business District, Grand Hyatt Mumbai is more than just a hotel.

The property is defined by its use of striking contemporary architecture, audaciously paired with Indian influences under the direction of a wholly international design team. Renowned architectural firm Lohan Associates of Chicago collaborated with Californian landscaping gurus SWA Group Sausalito to create the main hotel complex and its magnificent centrepiece: a 12-m- (40-ft-) tall Egyptian-style waterfall square within the hotel itself. Interiors by Chhadha, Siembieda and Remedios of Long Beach, California explore spacious atrium-style public areas and airy, sunlit guestrooms designed to put both the mind and the body at ease. Throughout the complex, a selection of specially commissioned local art curated by Rajeev Sethi erases the line between gallery and public space, provoking thought and inspiring beauty in the most unexpected of places. Spanning over 100 pieces in all, the exhibit deconstructs the myth of Shiva as interpreted by centuries of Indian artists, giving it new meaning in a modern context.

One need not be an art critic to appreciate the luxuries found in the hotel's 547 rooms and suites. Outfitted with floor-to-ceiling windows that give generous views of the courtyard or city skyline, they seem much

Celini comes equipped with a Molteni show kitchen, allowing diners to watch chefs at work.

Above: The Grand Club Lounge is perfect for executives to wind down in after a busy conference.

Right: The rooms are given an airy, spacious feel through their large windows and the light woods used in the décor.

Opposite: Grand Hyatt Mumbai was conceptualised by renowned designers and architects from all over the world.

Simple, comfortable décor characterises 'I–deck', the private area at China House Lounge.

larger than their already sizable dimensions. Grand Rooms are 40 sq m (431 sq ft), while the Presidential Suite gives its occupants 166 sq m (1,787 sq ft) of polished refinement to relax in. All rooms are enhanced with light sycamore wood panels, golden Jaisalmer stone, and marble baths for a look that is both natural and modern.

Business travellers will have good reason to choose the hotel's Grand Club floors. They offer business amenities such as complimentary airport transfers, Internet access, boardroom use, and access to a private lounge. Visitors with long-term business in Mumbai may elect to stay at one of the 147 fully serviced Grand Hyatt Residences. With separate living rooms and kitchen facilities, they offer all the comforts of home with the trappings of an executive suite.

Those who prefer to leave cooking to the experts will be more than pleased with Grand Hyatt Mumbai's five superb restaurants which offer not only regional cuisines, but also specialities from the world beyond. At M, fine dining is given a series of innovative twists that makes the meal unforgettable. Combining a grill, martini bar, and wine library, M is a first-of-its-kind concept in India that serves prime cuts of meat, fresh seafood, and a menu of drinks that boasts over 40 martini variations.

For home-style Italian food served with a dash of theatre, Celini certainly delivers. An authentic wood-fired pizza oven, rotisserie, and charcoal grill in full view of the dining area whet the appetite in an elegantly understated setting. China House specialises in fiery Sichuan cuisine and signature Chinese dishes such as

Peking Duck and handmade noodles. Closer to home, Soma offers Indian cuisine in a tandoor show kitchen complete with all the enticing aromas that one might expect from regional spices. Nearby, the Grand Café serves all-day dining buffets with a combination of Indian and international specialities.

East continues to meet West at the Club Oasis Fitness Centre and Spa. Therapies use exclusive blends of rare oils and a range of massage styles that utilise Asian acupressure philosophies. A state-of-the-art gym welcomes both casual and dedicated exercise enthusiasts, while a range of personal training options and custom exercise programmes are available to help them make the most of their time at Club Oasis. With an area of over 1,000 sq m (10,764 sq ft) containing modern treatment rooms, steam rooms, whirlpools, two outdoor swimming pools, and facilities for tennis and volleyball, the health and well-being needs of guests are well met. Facials, muscle rubs, and workouts aren't the only therapies available at the Grand Hyatt. The Grand Hyatt Plaza, which spans 9,290 sq m (100,000 sq ft), contains enough shopping over two expansive floors of the finest international and local brands to satisfy even the most seasoned retail veterans.

Squarely in the centre of one of the world's fastest developing economies, Grand Hyatt Mumbai offers something for everyone with a taste for the finer things in life. With luxurious comforts, gourmet dining, and a wealth of entertainment pursuits, it has proven itself as the lifestyle capital of Mumbai.

Above: Private rooms at China House are perfect for hosting an intimate dinner party.
Right: The Peking Duck open kitchen at China House, the first of it's kind in India.
Bottom: Enjoy a late-night cocktail while relaxing with friends.

Rooms and amenities
- 547 rooms and suites
- 147 serviced apartments

Restaurants and bars
- M: Grill, martini bar, and wine library
- Celini: Italian
- Soma: authentic Indian and tandoor
- Grand Café: all-day dining buffet
- China House: casual Chinese dining with Sichuan focus
- Gourmet Store: light meals and beverages
- The Bar: wine, whiskies and fine single malts
- China House Lounge: plush lounge and bar

Facilities
- Club Oasis Fitness Centre and Spa
- Christiaan Georgio: ultra-chic salon for men and women
- Wireless Internet access
- Comprehensive meeting and conference facilities and outdoor exhibit space
- Attached shopping arcade
- Business centre
- Two outdoor pools
- Art exhibits

Off Western Express Highway, Santacruz (East), Mumbai 400 055, India
Tel: +91.22.6676 1234 • Fax: +91.22. 6676 1235
Email: grandhyattmumbai@hyattintl.com
Website: mumbai.grand.hyatt.com

The Oberoi, Mumbai

Bustling with life and energy, Mumbai is worthy of its title, 'Manhattan of the East'. Set amidst the skyline of the city and centrally located in the heart of the commercial district, The Oberoi, Mumbai is a magnificent luxury hotel known for its elegance and unfalteringly attentive service. Reflecting the design essence of the hotel, the lobby is a perfect juxtaposition of traditional and modern. Comfortable lounge chairs are upholstered in Indian silk, while 19th-century lithographs that depict hunting scenes adorn the walls. Modern amenities such as wireless and wired Internet access and a well-appointed business centre have made the hotel highly popular with business travellers.

In fact, both business and leisure travellers are given the same indulgent treatment at The Oberoi, Mumbai. From the moment the guest leaves the aircraft, a hotel representative is on hand to personally assist with immigration and customs clearance, after which, the guest is chauffeur-driven to the hotel.

Refreshing fruit juice is presented to each guest by a personal butler upon arrival at The Oberoi, Mumbai, followed by a brief tour of in-room facilities. If the guest so wishes, the butler unpacks the bags, shines the shoes and irons garments, and remains on hand around the clock to attend to any requests, no matter how large or small. In keeping with the hotel's reputation for impeccable personalised service, butlers remain apprised of guests' preferences, so even the smallest details, such as a liking for soft pillows or orange pekoe tea, are remembered for the next visit.

Above: The living room of the Kohinoor Suite, star accommodation at The Oberoi, Mumbai.

Right: True to their name, Luxury Sea View Rooms allow guests to look over the gorgeous Arabian Sea.

Below: The Kohinoor Suite is tastefully decorated with matching florals and greenery.

Opposite: Savour afternoon tea against a panoramic backdrop of the bustling city of Mumbai.

The atrium lobby is a wide, open space with a glorious view of the sea which greets guests in style.

The 333 rooms and suites of The Oberoi, Mumbai are arranged around a vast atrium at the centre of the hotel and overlook either the city skyline, the bay or the magnificent expanse of the Arabian Sea. All guestrooms and suites are spacious, tasteful and luxuriously decorated. Each guestroom features a separate dressing area and bathroom with a separate shower stall and bathtub. Each of the four Presidential Suites are 107 sq m (1,150 sq ft), and consist of a living room, dining room, guest washroom and master bedroom, which offers magnificent vistas of the sea, and includes a walk-in closet. Spread over a lavish 198 sq m (2,131 sq ft), the Kohinoor Suite incorporates some of the finest amenities on this side of the Indian Ocean. Antique objets d'art and a piano take pride of place in the living room, the lavish master bedroom is furnished with a four-poster bed and the bathroom has a jacuzzi and sauna—making this opulent suite the very first choice of the long list of Heads of State, visiting dignitaries and world-famous celebrities who have enjoyed its facilities.

Amongst other leisure facilities, the hotel features an outdoor pool, The Oberoi Spa & Fitness Centre, and restaurants offering a wide range of cuisine. For those seeking a tranquil getaway, The Oberoi Spa & Fitness Centre has a menu featuring non-clinical therapy, massage and beauty treatments incorporating ancient Ayurvedic principles, aromatherapy and Western techniques designed to rejuvenate, relax and pamper. Other items on the menu include exotic body scrubs and floral baths, as well as rejuvenating wellness treatments.

Dining options at the hotel include the popular Tiffin, an all-day dining spot with an informal and warm ambience that offers world cuisine. The restaurant's sushi counter caters to guests who have a liking for such Japanese delicacies as sushi and sashimi. On the other hand, Vetro, the new contemporary Italian restaurant offers fine Italian cuisine, coupled with a choice of the finest Italian wine at Enoteca, its wine repository. For guests who wish to savour exotic cuisine from the Indian subcontinent, Kandahar serves a delectable choice of home-style preparations. The open show kitchen allows diners to view the tandoor and charcoal grill while enjoying their meal, and the gentle, melodic strains of live instrumental Indian classical music serve as a soothing aural backdrop.

The Oberoi, Mumbai is the preferred hotel for both the leisure and business travellers as is evident in it recently being voted best hotel in the city in two separate worldwide readers' polls conducted by *Condé Nast Traveler*, USA, one of the world's leading travel magazines, and *Asiamoney*, among the leading financial monthlies in the Asia Pacific. Moreover, for a stunning three years in succession, The Oberoi, Mumbai has been ranked among the best hotels in the world in surveys conducted by the *Institutional Investor* magazine, USA.

Vetro serves fine Italian cuisine in a modern setting.

Rooms and amenities

- 311 guestrooms
- 22 suites
- Range of Ayurvedic toiletries by Kama

Restaurants and bars

- Kandahar: local and regional
- Tiffin: international
- Vetro: Italian
- The Bayview Bar: single malt whiskies and cigars
- Gourmet Shop and Snack Bar: light meals and snacks

Facilities

- 24-hour Business Centre
- Secretarial services
- 2 meeting rooms
- The Oberoi Spa & Fitness Centre
- Pool
- High-speed Internet access
- 24-hour personalised butler service

Above: Kandahar serves a range of delightful local dishes against the spectacular view as a backdrop.
Left: The live jazz at The Bayview Bar is choice accompaniment for a single malt and fine Cuban cigar.

Nariman Point, Mumbai 400 021, India
Tel: +91.22.6632 5757 • Fax: +91.22.6632 4142
Email: reservations@oberoi-mumbai.com
Website: www.oberoihotels.com

The stately and expansive Presidential Suite.

The Taj Mahal Palace and Tower, Mumbai

One impressive property with two wings of very different appeal, The Taj Mahal Palace and Tower in Mumbai ranks among the finest hotels in the world. The hotel has a proud history dating back more than a century, and some things have not changed—the close attention to detail, superb service and its preferred venue status.

The Taj Mahal Palace wears its Moorish, Oriental and Florentine styles with pride. Rising majestically from Mumbai Harbour right next to the Gateway of India, it's a constant reminder of the subcontinent's glorious heritage.

The grand interior of The Taj Mahal Palace is a feast for all the senses. Priceless artefacts and antiques are placed along the public spaces for all to admire. Guests are pleasantly surprised to come across an old Belgian chandelier or a Goan Christian *objet d'art*, collected over the years.

Each exclusive suite at The Taj Mahal Palace is uniquely and lovingly furnished, and features period furniture, paintings, luxuriant textures and plush rugs. The result is a guestroom fit for for a king. The stunning Presidential Suite comes with a high-domed ceiling, expansive sitting room and separate work area. The best of traditional architecture blends seamlessly with modern conveniences here.

The Taj Club Rooms are a favourite with frequent travellers. Functional, large and comfortable, each room comes equipped with the latest in telecommunications technology.

Luxury is the common theme running through The Taj Mahal Tower as well. The winning combination of luminous alabaster ceilings, onyx columns and floors inlaid with

India
Mumbai

semi-precious stones never fails to elicit gasps of admiration—a reaction which is certainly more than well deserved.

The restaurants at The Taj Mahal Palace and Tower are legendary for their variety of cuisines from around the world. The Zodiac Grill is one of the finest restaurants in the country. Daily, the highly-accomplished chefs oversee preparation of an array of delectable international gourmet dishes, all of which are highly enhanced by the appropriate pairing of vintage wines.

The myriad flavours of India are brought to the fore at Masala Kraft, where recipes for traditional Indian fare are polished to perfection, and then given a modern twist. A must-try is Wasabi by Morimoto, one of India's finest Japanese restaurants. The Chinese restaurant, Golden Dragon, is well known for its spicy Sichuan food, while Souk offers exotic cuisines such as Lebanese, Moroccan, Turkish and Greek. For all-day dining and meals served in a casual setting, head to Shamiana, and if a light snack is what you are looking for, try The Sea Lounge. If a relaxing drink after work or dinner is what you are after, try the elegant Harbour Bar, where a selection of Martinis, Champagnes and cigars are offered against the backdrop of the Gateway of India.

A confirmed way to recover after all that partying is with a visit to Jiva Spa. Choose from an extensive spa menu, and trained therapists will knead, massage and restore your body, mind and spirit. Day packages are available here, as are complete yoga sessions conducted by trained instructors.

The lobby is elegantly formal, yet comfortable and welcoming.

Below: All guestrooms are funished to high levels of luxury.
Right: One is never at a loss for dining options at The Taj Mahal Palace and Tower, Mumbai.

Rooms and amenities
- The Taj Mahal Tower: 209 Superior Rooms; 68 Deluxe Rooms; 1 Luxury Suite
- The Taj Mahal Palace: 24 Luxury Rooms; 134 Grande Luxury Room; 83 Taj Club Rooms; 22 Executive Suites; 8 Luxury Suites; 5 Junior Suites; 9 Grande Luxury Suites; 2 Presidential Suites

Restaurants and bars
- The Zodiac Grill: international
- Masala Kraft: Indian
- Souk: Eastern Mediterranean
- Wasabi: Japanese
- Golden Dragon: Sichuan
- The Sea Lounge: light meals

Facilities
- Jiva Spa
- Taj Luxury Yacht
- pool
- 24-hour fitness centre
- Shopping arcade
- Business high-speed wireless Internet access
- Meeting rooms
- Banquet halls
- Business centre

Apollo Bunder, Mumbai 400001, Maharashtra
Tel: +91.22.5665 3366 • Fax: +91.22.5665 0300
Email: tmhbc.bom@tajhotels.com
Website: www.tajhotels.com

The Claridges,
New Delhi

The hotel's décor is understated and elegant, relaxing guests with soothing earth tones.

Centrally located in the metropolitan heart of modern Indian business and politics, The Claridges, New Delhi has been a recognised landmark of the city for over half a century. Its convenient address on Aurangzeb Road puts it near areas of interest such as the India Gate, Rashtrapati Bhawan and the business district, Connaught Place. Part of the WORLDHOTELS Deluxe Collection, The Claridges, New Delhi has been newly re-envisioned as a chic boutique hotel, and stands proudly as a gateway to India's capital for business travellers as well as those seeking a relaxing getaway.

Built on 1 hectare (3 acres) of prime New Delhi land in the centre of the historic Lutyens' Bungalow Zone, The Claridges, New Delhi recreates the colonial charm of the 1950s. Everything from the architecture to the crisp interiors, period art, atmospheric bars and restaurants, lush gardens lined with palm trees, and good old-fashioned hospitality combine to bring the Old World firmly into the here and now. As one might expect, the 21st-century incarnation of this legendary luxury hotel also provides modern necessities such as wireless Internet access and large plasma screen televisions in every room.

Extravagantly large, even by New Delhi standards, the hotel's guestrooms are some of the most spacious in the city. Deluxe rooms average 30 sq m (323 sq ft) and feature tall windows that increase the sense of space. Some of the hotel's accommodations, such as The Claridges Room, also include a private terrace and overlook the hotel's sparkling pool

Finely decorated with jade carvings, the aptly named Jade offers delicacies from mainland China.

as well as the handsome structures that line the surrounding diplomatic avenue. The hotel's largest room, the Terrace Garden Suite, is 175 sq m (1,884 sq ft) of gracious opulence above the treetops, overlooking the surrounding classic architecture. From its generous sun terrace, guests enjoy some of New Delhi's most serene views, while separate living and bedroom areas offer an entire spectrum of creature comforts.

When the time comes, getting down to work is made an exercise in style with the exclusive The Senate, Executive Lounge. The state-of-the-art boardroom offers the latest in business technologies, and is fully serviced so all events and meetings run smoothly. Refined and sophisticated, the main lounge offers a rare whisky bar and a cigar corner with an extensive collection of cigars and fine cognacs, while the private dining room provides an elegant setting for more intimate gatherings.

Having played host to a number of major political and business summits over the years, the hotel's specialised events team is well-equipped to receive delegates in the stately conference halls. And, with the catering finesse offered by its six dining and entertainment establishments, the hotel more than excels at banquets and private dining functions, no matter what the occasion. Considering the high standards that have been in place since its doors first opened in the 1950s, it is certainly not surprising to learn that The Claridges, New Delhi does just about everything better than most.

The spacious hotel rooms have tall windows, giving them an airy feeling, while fine curtains maintain guests' privacy.

Rooms and amenities

- 125 guestrooms
- 12 suites

Restaurants and bars

- Aura: speciality vodka bar
- Jade: Chinese fine dining
- Pickwicks: multi-cuisine all-day dining
- Sevilla: Mediterranean
- Dhaba: North Indian specialities

Facilities

- Health club with treatment rooms, steam rooms, sauna and jacuzzi
- Gymnasium
- Beauty parlour and hair salon
- Outdoor pool
- Executive lounge
- Shopping arcade
- Wireless Internet access
- Travel desk

Right: Old World elegance characterises The Claridges, New Delhi.

Below: Suites are richly decorated, while still keeping firm sight of the comfort and convenience of the hotel's guests.

12 Aurangzeb Road, New Delhi 110 011, India
Tel: +91.11.4133 5133 • Fax: +91.11.2301 0625
Email: reservations@claridges.com
Website: www.claridges.com

The Oberoi, New Delhi

The city of Delhi is a myriad cocktail of cultures which have influenced and drawn from each other over the course of its lengthy history. Its multifaceted heritage is reflected in the diverse styles of art and architecture found in the city. Located in the heart of New Delhi, close to the commercial, cultural and shopping districts, The Oberoi, New Delhi offers a harmonious juxtaposition of the traditional and modern. Unrivalled efficient and personalised service, meticulous appointments, exquisite interiors, and fine cuisine combine to make it the capital's greatest hotel. It has been greatly lauded, counting among its laurels being voted the Best Business Hotel in New Delhi in the *Asiamoney* Business Travel Poll for three years in succession.

The hotel's 283 elegant rooms and suites are equipped with state-of-the-art amenities and in-room entertainment, essential for discerning business and leisure travellers. The rich tones of ruby, sienna, emerald, and amethyst used generously in the interiors are complemented by expansive views of the fairways of the Delhi Golf Course and the magnificent 16th-century tomb of the ancient Mughal Emperor Humayun.

Executive Suites comprise a dining room, a spacious lounge, and a lavish bedroom, while the Deluxe Suites comprise a spacious lounge and dining room with a private sit-out, bedroom and a well-appointed bathroom with whirlpool. Spread over 150 sq m (1,614 sq ft), the Luxury Suites offer expansive views of the Golf Course and the magnificent Humayun's Tomb. Other suites include bedrooms with king-sized beds and a large living-cum-dining room.

The hotel overlooks the greens of The Delhi Golf Course.

Above: Generously wide picture windows offer guests unprecedented views of the surrounding city.

Right: The hotel's Kohinoor Suite is the height of modern luxury in India.

Opposite The luminous spa pool offers the chance to swim a few relaxing laps.

Fine international dining is available at threesixtyº, where cuisines from all over the world are on the menu.

Now, guests may stay in the opulent Kohinoor Suite, which presents a liberating sense of space with its understatedly elegant interiors complemented by panoramic views. Spread over 334 sq m (3,600 sq ft) of space, it comprises a living room, dining room with service pantry, fully-equipped study, master bedroom, private living room and a relaxation room furnished with a treadmill and massage bed. Adjacent to the suite, the well-appointed Executive Suite and Luxury Rooms are ideal for accommodating additional family members or security and other personnel.

Offering a perfect escape from busy schedules and the rush of a bustling city, the Oberoi Spa & Fitness Centre counts amongst the finest in the city. The spa and wellness centre consists of eight therapy rooms and suites, a state-of-the-art gym, and an indoor heated lap pool—the only one of its kind in the city. The spa menu includes holistic and non-clinical therapies, massages, exotic body scrubs, floral baths and rejuvenating beauty treatments incorporating Western techniques, Ayurveda, and aromatherapy. These soothing treatments are administered in the privacy of luxurious therapy rooms, each with a private treatment and relaxation area and an en-suite steam room and shower.

When adequately refreshed and having worked up a healthy appetite, there is a range of dining options to choose from. Threesixtyº is a bustling restaurant offering world cuisine. The restaurant comprises a sushi station, yakitori grill, genuine wood-fired oven for sumptuous

Mediterranean, and a contemporary tandoor. Travertino offers authentic Italian cuisine with a strong creative element. Enoteca stocks an extensive repository of fine vintage wines to accompany cuisine at threesixty° and Travertino. For fine Cantonese and Sichuan specialities as well as dim sum, try Taipan, or end the day with drinks at the colonial-style Club Bar.

To ensure the safety of all the residents, the most up-to-date security features have been installed. The hotel is also fully prepared to meet the needs of business travellers, with a business centre offering the latest in communication technology and state-of-the-art equipment. Operating 24 hours a day, it offers a number of meeting rooms, from private offices which seat two to boardrooms accommodating up to 16 people. Larger events may be held in one of the opulent banquet rooms or on the rooftop terrace which overlooks the Delhi Golf Course.

With such in-depth attention to guest welfare, offering efficient and uniquely personalised service, luxurious facilities and a wide choice of gourmet cuisine, The Oberoi, New Delhi is the first choice of the business and leisure travelers visiting the city. Recently, the hotel was honoured to be voted as one of the best in the world by the readers of *Travel + Leisure*, one of the world's leading travel magazines. It was also selected to be among some of the top hotels in Asia in a readers' poll conducted by *Condé Nast Traveler*, US.

Above: Travertino's traditional and authentic Italian menu is complemented by an extensive menu of fine wines.

Left: The pace slows down at the lounge, where you can enjoy a range of expertly mixed drinks.

Fully equipped meeting facilities ensure a smooth conference.

Rooms and amenities
- 283 guestrooms and suites
- Kama toiletries

Restaurants and bars
- threesixty°: international all-day dining
- Travertino: Italian fine dining
- Taipan: Sichuan and Cantonese
- The Gourmet Shoppe: delicatessen and espresso bar
- Club Bar: afternoon tea, drinks and cocktails

Facilities
- New fully equipped business centre
- 4 private offices and 6 meeting rooms
- Secretarial services
- Oberoi Spa & Fitness Centre
- Outdoor pool
- Beauty salon
- 24-hour butler service
- 24-hour laundry
- Doctor-on-call
- Babysitting services
- Money changing and banking services
- Valet
- Travel desk

Dr Zakir Hussain Marg, New Delhi 110003, India
Tel: +91.11.2436 3030 • Fax: +91.11.2436 0484
Email: reservations@oberoidel.com
Website: www.oberoihotels.com

Yoga sessions help guests to attain a state of true relaxation.

The Oberoi Udaivilās

Called the 'Venice of the East', Udaipur is as well known for its grand palaces as it is for having miles of beautiful and pristine lakes. One enthralling example is the sprawling City Palace, which enjoys serene views of the Aravalli range from its position on the banks of Lake Pichola. It stands alongside a palace of another kind—created in the image of a classic Mewari royal mansion, the magnificent Oberoi Udaivilās is a modern palatial hotel that combines the best of traditional opulence with contemporary elegance.

From incredible feats of engineering and architecture—the property boasts acres of arches, fountains, and open-air colonnades with a total of 450 hand-carved stone columns—to glorious details such as gold leaf decorations, hand-painted murals, and carefully landscaped gardens, the exclusive resort hotel is an inspired tribute to Old World luxury.

Events and conventions are well served by The Oberoi Udaivilās. Fully equipped with high-tech business facilities, the seven meeting rooms are adaptable to suit virtually all purposes with the help of attentive, highly qualified staff and a complete range of secretarial services. That isn't all the hotel offers, however. These days, technology isn't difficult to replicate, but the surrounding exotic atmosphere and spectacular natural environment are one of a kind, and help to make light work of long business days.

The hotel's rooms and suites feature a blend of traditional Rajput design elements and rich contemporary amenities in exquisitely

private settings. Each of the 63 ground-floor Premier Rooms have their own walled courtyards with seating, while living areas in the 19 Premier Lake View Rooms, with their own semi-private pool, open out to views of Pichola Lake and the hotel's wildlife sanctuary. A step up from those are four very spacious Luxury Suites, and one Kohinoor Suite, with their own private pools. At 107 sq m (1,150 sq ft) each, the Luxury Suites include tented dining pavilions and sweeping views of the City Palace region. For the most lavish experience, the 246-sq-m (2,650-sq-ft) royal Kohinoor Suite is simply without equal, offering its own fountained courtyards, pool, and bedroom with en suite sauna.

A world-class spa experience is available to all guests at the Oberoi Spa by Banyan Tree. Featuring the holistic methods and training programmes devised by the Banyan Tree group, regarded by many as the benchmark for practitioners of Ayurvedic, Thai, and Western massage therapies, the full menu of treatments at the spa are a rejuvenating indulgence. Yoga sessions are also available, as well as a full complement of fitness facilities.

By offering a faithful recreation of palatial Rajasthani living writ large, The Oberoi Udaivilās is in a class of its own in today's business hospitality arena. Sparing no effort in the pursuit of perfection—even the chefs of its three restaurants have been trained by masters from Rajasthan's royal kitchens—this is a place where guests are literally treated like kings.

The hotel's décor mixes traditional influences with contemporary touches designed to appeal to modern tastes.

Rooms and amenities

- 82 guestrooms
- 5 suites

Restaurants and bars

- Udaimahal: traditional Indian
- Surya Mahal: Continental and Indian all-day dining
- Chandni: al fresco dining
- Hotel bar

Facilities

- Oberoi Spa by Banyan Tree
- Two outdoor heated pools
- Fitness centre
- High-speed Internet access
- 24-hour business centre
- Valet service

Right: The Oberoi Udaivilās was built in the style of a palace.
Below: Chefs at the hotel's restaurants create meals which are truly fit for royalty.

Haridasji Ki Magri, Udaipur 31300, Rajasthan, India
Tel: +91.294.243 3300 • Fax: +91.294.243 3200
Email: gm@oberoi-udaivilas.com
Website: www.oberoihotels.com

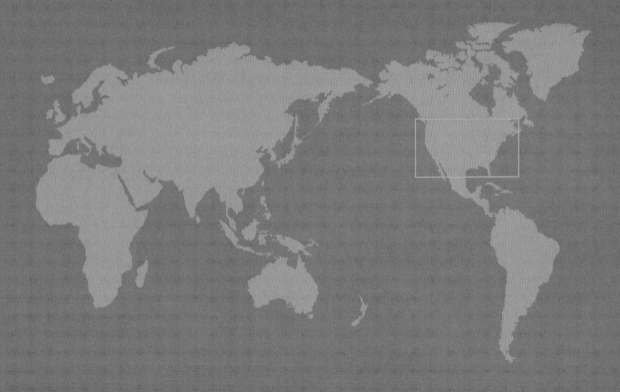

Mandarin Oriental, New York

Towering high above the city that never sleeps, Mandarin Oriental, New York captures all the energy and excitement of midtown Manhattan with sweeping views of Central Park, the Hudson River and the city's breathtaking skyline. Guests are whisked by smooth express elevators from the hectic streets to the hotel's sky lobby on the 35th floor, where they can take in scenes of New York's busy streets far above the maddening crowd, while soaking in an atmosphere that is lush with trappings of Oriental opulence and gracious hospitality.

The chic Lobby Lounge of the hotel welcomes guests with cosy furnishings infused with rich Asian motifs and textiles mixed with contemporary artwork from some of New York's finest artists. An island bar made of hammered nickel—the focal point of the MObar—replicates the classic style of the 1930s and 1940s, and hints at other Art Deco touches throughout the hotel. Mandarin Oriental, New York takes advantage of its command of the city's skyline at every turn, with stunning views of the Hudson River from the spa to that of Central Park from Asiate.

The hotel's pièce de résistance—The Spa at Mandarin Oriental, New York—and the hotel have been awarded the Five-Star award by *Mobil Travel Guide*. And it is easy to see why it is one of only two spas in the US to be given this prestigious rating. Furnished with bamboo, water features and stones, this tranquil paradise offers guests a generous variety of exotic spa therapies and treatments.

Asiate offers a truly stunning sky-level dining experience with the best of French and Japanese cuisine.

The Spa at Mandarin Oriental, New York has been awarded five stars by *Mobil Travel Guide*.

From its vantage point on the 35th storey of the hotel, Asiate offers a spectacular view of Central Park and the Manhattan skyline as guests enjoy exquisite cuisine offering all the best elements of Asian influences, in keeping with the hotel's East-meets-West theme. The elegant dining room—the work of renowned designer Tony Chi—includes personal booths with city views, a private dining room, and a glass wall cabinet displaying a fantastic selection of fine wines.

Guests dreaming of Oriental luxury won't be disappointed. Guestrooms on the 35th through 54th floors are dressed in either sleek black and gold or radiant red and silver colour palettes, with Asian and Art Deco-inspired furnishings, Chinese art, and floor-to-ceiling windows. Some rooms even have large bathtubs situated under windows, which allow guests to admire New York's skyline while taking a relaxing soak. In addition, busy executives and business travellers alike will appreciate the large workspaces, which are outfitted with all the latest and the best of communication and entertainment technology.

The guests at Mandarin Oriental, New York are never far from the action of the city, as the hotel's central location provides easy access to the rest of the Big Apple. In addition, luxury shopping, world-class dining, and the performance hall for Jazz at Lincoln Center are all just steps away, each of them located within the same building as the hotel.

The spectacular view of Columbus Circle.

Right: The breathtaking panoramic view of Manhattan's skyline from one of the luxurious bathrooms.

Below: Treatments fit for royalty amidst soothing settings will take all stress away.

Rooms and amenities
- 202 guestrooms
- 46 suites

Restaurants and bars
- Asiate: Asian influences
- MObar: cocktails
- Lobby Lounge: light fare and drinks

Facilities
- Business centre
- 3 banquet/meeting rooms
- Spa and fitness centre
- Concierge services

80 Columbus Circle at 60th Street
New York, NY 10023, USA
Tel: +1.212.805 8800 or +1.866.801 8880 ·
Fax: +1.212.805 8888
Email: monyc-reservations@mohg.com
Website: www.mandarinoriental.com/newyork

Millenium Hilton, New York

Part of the ongoing philosophy firmly held at the Millenium Hilton, New York is that "Travel should take you places." This, indeed, makes it a very fine thing when one's travels land in New York City, the exhilarating doorstep of countless journeys of discovery offered by the glamorous city that never sleeps.

Standing tall in the very heart of New York City's world-renowned Financial District, the magnificent high-rise Millenium Hilton boasts breathtaking window views—from Manhattan's legendary skyline and famed Statue of Liberty to the spectacular Brooklyn Bridge and scenic Hudson River harbour.

Following a highly extensive US$32 million refurbishment and redesign several years ago, the Millenium Hilton is looking particularly fresh. Its spacious guestrooms and luxurious suites are all swathed in eye-soothing neutral shades and hues, and each room has been fitted out with all the little conveniences that, over the years, one has come to expect from Hilton—and even more. Standard features in every guestroom include the trademark Hilton Serenity® bedding experience—adorned with plush down comforter, abundance of pillows and complementary fine linen, guaranteeing all a restful night's sleep. The hotel's impressive marble baths also feature a pulsating massage shower as well as fragrant Crabtree & Evelyn Le Source® bath amenities.

Every guestroom—including the 98 luxurious suites—offers an array of modern amenities, such as 42-inch flat-screen plasma televisions, wired high-speed Internet access,

The Millenium Hilton offers breathtaking window views of New York's most beloved landmarks, including the Statue of Liberty.

The hotel's rooms are designed to ensure that every guest enjoys a comfortable night.

dual-line cordless phones with personalised voicemail, Cuisinart® dual-cup coffeemakers, and the innovative Hilton Family Clock with radio and MP3 connectivity, allowing guests to wake up to the sounds of their choice.

Elsewhere in the high-rise boutique hotel, a refreshing workout is available at the newly renovated and fully equipped Hilton Fitness by Precor® centre, which features premium cardiovascular equipment with personal entertainment and numerous strength-training machines. Guests may also enjoy an invigorating swim in the beautiful 12-m (40-ft) glass-enclosed heated indoor pool, or relax in the sauna available on the hotel's 5th floor.

Come evening, the chic lobby bar Liquid Assets proves to be the perfect spot for people watching, friendly conversation, or perhaps a celebratory cocktail (any excuse will suit, as long as carried off with true New York style and panache). And at the hotel's premier in-house brasserie, Church & Dey, sumptuous Americana dishes with a gourmet twist fill the menu for breakfast, lunch and dinner.

Just steps from Wall Street, the New York Stock Exchange and World Financial Center, Battery Park Promenade and the South Street Seaport, and a brief stroll to the trendy hotspots of Tribeca, Soho, and West Village, the Millenium Hilton's unique location offers exclusive shopping, cultural institutions, fine dining and entertainment options, making it an obvious choice for every traveller's New York City experience.

The Millenium Hilton's heated indoor pool is perfect for those who want a swim without having to depend on the weather.

Right: The Millenium Hilton is situated in Manhattan, right in the heart of the bustling financial district of New York City.

Below: The lobby is decorated in warm earth shades, echoing the sense of welcome each guest feels at the hotel.

Rooms and amenities
- 471 guestrooms
- 98 suites

Restaurants and bars
- Church & Dey: American brasserie
- Liquid Assets: classic cocktails
- Children and special diet menus available

Facilities
- Indoor heated pool
- Fitness centre
- Business centre
- 6 Conference rooms

55 Church Street, New York, NY 10007, USA
Tel: +1.212.693 2001 • Fax: +1.212.571 2316
Email: nycml_fo@hilton.com
Website: www.newyorkmillenium.hilton.com

An aerial view of The Villard Mansion Grand Courtyard leading into The New York Palace Hotel.

The New York Palace Hotel

Beginning life as a high-profile collection of residences commissioned by wealthy financier Henry Villard in 1882, The New York Palace Hotel is steeped in Manhattan Island history. Over the last century, the Villard Mansion's timeless design by Messrs McKim, Mead & White has become an iconic presence on Madison Avenue, first as residences, then as prestigious commercial space. The landmark residences were finally united with a new 55-storey building in 1980 to create one of the most distinguished luxury properties in what is often called the greatest city on Earth.

The hotel is instantly recognisable by its large, street-facing courtyard, inspired by 15th century Italian cathedral design. A hallmark of the address since 1882, the elegant welcome of its wrought-iron gates is indicative of the typically Old World opulence within. A grand gilded staircase leads the way down to halls of crystal chandeliers, towering columns, floors of polished marble, and ornate classical details. Modern touches have been judiciously applied throughout—often subtle and occasionally surprising, but never in such a fashion that they appear unnecessary.

Over the hotel's 893 rooms and suites, the seamless combination of rich indulgence and 21st century style continues with exceptionally furnished spaces and the provision of deluxe amenities like oversized marble bathrooms, and no less than three phone lines. A lounge on the 39th floor gives guests of the Executive Club accommodations a spectacular view of St Patrick's Cathedral and the city, as well as food and beverage presentations throughout the day in a business-friendly environment. In addition to the lounge's three meeting rooms, the hotel has 2,044 sq m (22,000 sq ft) of function space, able to accommodate events of up to 1,000 attendees.

From the 41st to the 54th floors, an exclusive luxury hotel-within-a-hotel caters to guests desiring the ultimate in privacy. With its own reception area, The Towers at The New York Palace Hotel is the highest point of luxury in New York, offering unobstructed views of the Manhattan skyline and beyond. Few experiences can top the ones offered by the four Triplex Penthouse Suites, each of them boasting 5-m- (18-ft-) tall windows and a private outdoor terrace.

While it would certainly be difficult for anybody to tire of in-room dining with a view, the striking decor and attentive service offered at fine dining restaurant, Gilt, and the chic brasserie-style Istana make a fantastic case for venturing out. Chef Christopher Lee of Gilt expresses not just culinary skill, but time itself in his cuisine—his eclectic New American style menus are designed around the turning of the seasons and the availability of fresh produce, and are changed eight times yearly. A fusion of classic simplicity and rewarding invention, his signature style has one thing in common with The New York Palace Hotel: the results are unforgettable.

A King Bed room at The New York Palace Hotel.

Rooms and amenities
- 807 guestrooms
- 86 suites

Restaurants and bars
- Gilt Restaurant & Bar: modern American fine dining
- Istana: brasserie-style restaurant

Facilities
- Fully-equipped fitness centre
- Day Spa with in-room massage services
- Executive Club Lounge
- Business centre
- High-speed Internet access
- Meeting and event facilities

Right: Guests may enjoy a relaxing tea break at the hotel's Executive Lounge.

Below: Gilt Bar at The New York Palace Hotel is the perfect place for a stylish rendezvous over cocktails.

455 Madison Avenue, New York, NY 10022, USA
Tel: +1.212.888 7000 • Fax: +1.212.303 6000
Email: info@nypalace.com
Website: www.newyorkpalace.com

The Ritz-Carlton
New York, Battery Park

As the place where America's first colonists landed over five centuries ago, and a symbol of freedom and promise for millions of immigrants since, Lower Manhattan has long been one of New York's most beloved and treasured districts. In 2002, the opening of The Ritz-Carlton New York, Battery Park revitalised the area, bringing new attention and contemporary luxury to a historic neighborhood.

As Manhattan's only waterfront luxury hotel, the 39-storey Ritz-Carlton New York, Battery Park enjoys a first-class view of the Statue of Liberty and New York Harbour. Over 14 points of interest lie in the immediate vicinity of the hotel, each telling an integral part of the city's story. From its beginnings as the very first neighbourhood and site of the nation's first capital, to the rise of Wall Street as an international financial centre, attractions nearby such as the South Street Seaport, Ellis Island Immigration Museum and the chic Soho precinct chart the grand history and culture of Lower Manhattan.

Developed at a cost of US$210 million, the glass and brick tower designed by Polshek Partnership and Gary Handel & Associates is a striking addition to the waterfront skyline. Inside, Art Deco-style influences create an atmosphere that marks the emergence of the hotel as a modern-day art gallery. Exhibited throughout its guestrooms and public spaces is an extensive art collection representing the work of over 100 of New York's most talented artists. Two impressive masterpieces hang on display in

Opposite: Enjoy a light breakfast in the hotel before heading out for a busy day of business meetings or touring the New York sights.
Right: The hotel bathrooms feature deep-soaking tubs and decadent Bulgari toiletries.
Below: Taking full advantage of their location, harbour-facing rooms come equipped with a high-powered telescope.

Below: As Manhattan's only waterfront luxury hotel, The Ritz-Carlton New York, Battery Park offers superb views of the New York Harbour and the Statue of Liberty.

Enjoy cocktails and casual refreshments throughout the day in the cosy Lobby Lounge.

the main lobby, by the grand staircase—a specially commissioned piece by Ross Bleckner in his signature style, and a profound Joseph Stashkevetch meditation.

Another first for the hotel industry is the incorporation of an acclaimed museum into the building. Occupying a large, permanent exhibition space on the ground floor since 2004, the Skyscraper Museum celebrates the city's rich architectural culture and heritage. Further up, on the 14th floor, the award-winning Rise Bar and Terrace offers sweeping, panoramic views of the Manhattan skyline. Featuring a menu of highly sought-after signature concoctions such as the Libertini and The PHAT Apple, Rise is an after-hours icon on an island that is renowned for its world-class dining and entertainment.

Downstairs, French Master Chef Jacques Sorci heads the culinary team responsible for 2 West Steakhouse, a restaurant whose name should be familiar to connoisseurs across the country. Pairing prime steaks and seafood with classic French sauces, 2 West infuses the tastes of the great American grill with a gourmet touch. Tellingly, the establishment is one of only three restaurants in New York City which serve the highest grade of beef available in the United States: Certified Angus Beef Prime.

True to the easy-going intellectualism of New York City, the hotel features an updated aesthetic that its owners call 'next generation Ritz-Carlton'. Its Frank Nicholson-designed interiors are strictly 21st century, with lighter woods and tones that suggest a youthful, bounding energy. The hotel's 259 rooms and 39 suites are all open and spacious, appointed in shades of sage, buttercream, and beige. Luxurious details such as 400 thread-count Frette linens, feather beds, goose down pillows, and Bulgari bath amenities are standard.

The rooms' sleek lines complement the modernity to be found upon closer inspection. High-speed wireless Internet access, large 27-inch televisions, dual-line cordless telephones with voicemail, and Bose Wave CD clock radios are only some of the thoughtful amenities included. In addition, a dedicated Technology Butler ensures that guests have their personal computers and devices seamlessly connected and working upon arrival, taking the pain out of business travel.

Guests also enjoy the use of a 760-sq-m (8,180-sq-ft) fitness centre with similarly superb views. The health club features a weights room, a gymnasium with high-end computerised workout machines, and a spa. Significantly, the Ritz-Carlton Spa utilises exclusive Prada Beauty Special Care products for its range of skin treatments. A menu of Prada Beauty Spa Experiences unite skincare, massage, and body wraps with unique high-touch techniques, shiatsu, and pre-treatment breathing exercises for optimal absorption and benefit. With the best views in Manhattan, and total dedication to providing guests with a superior New York experience, it should come as no great surprise that The Ritz-Carlton New York, Battery Park has been named an AAA Five Diamond hotel for six years running.

Above: Stylish and romantic, the award-winning Rise is a nightlife landmark in chic New York City.

Right: The Ritz-Carlton New York, Battery Park is an instantly recognisable addition to the Manhattan waterfront skyline.
Below: At 2 West Steakhouse, French and American influences are combined with premium ingredients to deliver the best in grilled steak and seafood.

Rooms and amenities
- 298 guestrooms and suites

Restaurants and bars
- 2 West Steakhouse: French-American steaks and seafood
- Rise: rooftop bar and terrace
- The Lobby Lounge: all-day dining and cocktails

Facilities
- Fitness Centre
- Spa with Prada Beauty Treatments and Massage
- Ritz-Carlton Club floors with private lounge
- Wireless Internet access
- Bath Butler service
- Technology Butler service
- Limousine service
- Business centre

Two West Street, New York, New York 10004, USA
Tel: +1.212.344 0800 • Fax: +1.212.344 3801
Email: mady.cohen@ritzcarlton.com
Website: www.ritzcarlton.com

The Ritz-Carlton
New York, Central Park

The hotel boasts an unmatched location at the corner of New York's iconic Central Park.

Club Lounge guests enjoy exquisite caviar service in addition to a number of other exclusive luxuries.

Located on the island of Manhattan, on the corner of Central Park South and Sixth Avenue, overlooking all 341 hectares (843 acres) of Central Park, The Ritz-Carlton New York, Central Park needs no introduction as one of the most prestigious addresses in the city. For years, its guests have enjoyed unrivalled access to some of the most iconic attractions on the East Coast, including famed shopping thoroughfare Fifth Avenue; Carnegie Hall, the musical venue against which all others are compared; the influential Museum of Modern Art, and the unmatched artistic hub, Lincoln Center—all of which are within walking distance.

Behind the 33-storey building's distinctive façade, Old World details such as antique chandeliers, polished wood-panelled walls, and charming floral arrangements create a refined residential feel that is only enhanced by the hotel's collection of modernist paintings. Centred on the work of renowned American artist Samuel Halpert, who spent much of his life in New York, the hotel's collection easily rivals that of a museum's.

That level of resplendent luxury is also present in the upper floors, where custom bedspreads and fine 400 thread-count linens accompany exquisite European-style furniture in the hotel's 259 guestrooms and suites. Featuring panoramic views of Central Park and the city beyond, these spacious havens of repose have been designed in peaceful shades of celadon, taupe, and pale rose to accentuate their truly top-of-the-world locations. Even the simplest of pleasures are elevated to greater heights, one example of which can be seen in every bathroom: toiletries from celebrated beauty and hair care brand, Frédéric Fekkai. In the interest of fairness, even infants receive Bulgari baby amenities.

As is typical of New York, The Ritz-Carlton New York, Central Park works as hard as it plays. Offering over 185 sq m (2,000 sq ft) of meeting space to business-minded guests, it provides the latest in high-tech videoconferencing services, while a Conference Concierge ensures every event runs smoothly. With boardrooms that offer a sweeping view over a canopy of treetops, it hosts corporate and social functions with a grace that few others can muster.

Further executive comforts await at the exclusive Ritz-Carlton Club Lounge, a tranquil relaxation and meeting venue with wireless Internet access and six food and beverage presentations daily. Although the Club Lounge requires key access, all guests are welcome to enjoy French-inspired dining on an outdoor patio at the BLT Market restaurant. With a focus on seasonal ingredients from farmers' markets, chef Laurent Tourondel serves the freshest ingredients at their very best. It is fitting, then, that this new venture for the acclaimed restaurateur should be situated in a hotel that lets visitors to New York savour the passing of the seasons so visually. Since its opening in 2002, a stay at The Ritz-Carlton New York, Central Park has become synonymous with a magnificent view that defines the complex beauty of America's greatest city.

The hotel suites are designed with classic Old World opulence.

Rooms and amenities
- 212 guestrooms
- 47 suites

Restaurants and bars
- BLT Market: seasonal American
- Star Lounge: stand-up bar and lounge with afternoon tea

Facilities
- La Prairie at The Ritz-Carlton Spa
- Ritz-Carlton Club Lounge
- Fitness centre
- Complimentary Bentley/Mercedes-Benz limousine service
- Meeting space
- Technology Butler
- Wireless Internet access
- 24-hour in-room dining

Right: The Star Lounge is strikingly appointed with rich, dark wood and artwork on the walls.

Below: BLT Market serves only the freshest ingredients, with monthly menus and weekly blackboard specials designed to reflect the seasonal offerings at farmers' markets.

50 Central Park South, New York, NY 10019, USA
Tel: +1.212.308 9100 • Fax: +1.212.207 8831
Website: www.ritzcarlton.com

Guestrooms and suites are decorated in classic European style, as exemplified by the elegant Deluxe Room.

Taj Boston

In a city as prominent in history and renowned for its arts, culture and high society as Boston, Massachusetts, visitors naturally look to a hotel that reflects this excellence. Filling this hallowed spot is none other than the iconic 1927 Boston landmark building at the corner of Newbury Street and the Public Garden, Taj Boston.

While the hotel first opened its doors in 1927 and has been in continuous service ever since, the 2007 announcement that Taj Hotels Resorts and Palaces was assuming operations has brought levels of service to a new standard with the addition of the legendary Taj flair.

The classic lobby, clad in marble and rich wood panelling, welcomes guests to a world of elegance and subtle luxury that extends throughout the hotel. The 273 rooms and suites are enhanced with indulgent touches such as plush linens, crystal chandeliers and pampering bath amenities, not to mention windows that offer wide, clear views of the city. Suites are at even higher levels of indulgence, with individual wood-burning fireplaces that Fireplace Butlers will be glad to assist with, picking out just the right wood for a lovely fire on a cold evening.

Taj Boston was extensively restored in 2002, and its list of facilities and services now includes on-request babysitting, Fireplace or Bath Butlers, in-room massage therapy, and 24-hour room service, as well as a prized collection of art and antiques on display throughout the hotel.

Guests have a plethora of dining options, for the wide streets of Boston are overflowing with fine dining establishments. Those who prefer to stay within the comforts of the hotel, however,

The Roof—dramatic setting overlooking Boston's skyline available for private events.

will find plenty to their liking in the restaurants of Taj Boston. The Café has remained a Boston favorite for 55 years reflecting changing culinary trends. It offers a menu of classics and innovative surprises. The windows in The Café that overlook fashionable Newbury Street are often filled with equally fashionable people dining before or after the theatre. The Lounge has an intimate drawing room air and a view of Newbury Street, presenting the charms of Afternoon Tea with an accompanying harpist to set the mood. The Bar is a celebrated social venue with a club atmosphere, glowing fireplace, a view of the Public Garden and a pianist in the evenings. Since the 1930s it has been noted for its martinis, classic cocktails and delectable light-dining menu.

Those on a packed business schedule will be well looked after, with the latest technology available in rooms and the business centre. Express check-in and check-out services bring convenience to guests when they most need it, at the oft-time pressed beginning and end of each stay. A complimentary car service to the financial district and recreational exercise facilities gild the near-perfect whole.

With an unparalleled location in the city, surrounded by art galleries, high-end retail boutiques and restaurants, Taj Boston is right where one wants to be in this historic city. It's no wonder that locals and visitors alike have made this hotel one of the definitive symbols representing the best of Boston.

The lobby of Taj Boston is resplendent in warm tones of wood and pale marble.

Below: The rich yellow hues of the Winston Churchill Suite form a harmonious blend with the dark wood furnishings while the wood-burning fire casts a wam glow.

Right: The Lounge—a Boston tradition for Afternoon Tea.

Rooms and amenities
- 273 guestrooms and suites

Restaurants and bars
- The Café: fine Western dining
- The Lounge: afternoon tea and evening drinks
- The Bar: cocktails and light dining menu

Facilities
- 24-hour Front Desk
- 24-hour room service
- Airport services available on request
- Babysitting
- Business center
- Exercise room
- Express Check-In & Checkout
- Fitness centre
- Handicap-accessible Facilities
- In-room massage
- Laundry/Valet service
- Meeting and Event Facilities
- Fireplace and Bath Butler
- Translation services/multilingual staff

15 Arlington Street, Boston, MA 02116, USA
Tel: +1.617.536 5700 • Fax: +1.617.536 1335
Email: taj.boston@tajhotels.com
Website: www.tajhotels.com

Directory

ASIA & THE PACIFIC

CHINA

Grand Hyatt Beijing
Beijing Oriental Plaza
1 East Chang An Avenue, Beijing 100738
Tel: +86.10.8518 1234
Fax: +86.10.8518 0000
Email: grandhyattbeijing@hyattintl.com
Website: beijing.grand.hyatt.com

The Shangri-La Hotel, Beijing
29 Zhizhuyuan Road, Beijing 100089
Tel: +86.10.6841 2211
Fax: +86.10.6841 8002
Email: slb@shangri-la.com
Website: www.shangri-la.com/beijing

The Westin Beijing, Financial Street
9B Financial Street, XiCheng District
Beijing 100032
Tel: +86.10.6606 8866
Fax: +86.10.6606 8899
Email: reservation.beijing@westin.com
Website: www.westin.com/beijingfinancial

JW Marriott Hotel Shanghai
399 Nanjing West Road, Shanghai 200003
Tel: +86.21.5359 4969
Fax: +86.21.6375 5565
Email: mhrs.shajw.reservations
        @marriotthotels.com
Website: www.marriotthotels.com/shajw

Park Hyatt Shanghai
100 Century Avenue, Pudong New Area
Shanghai 200120
Tel: +86.21.6888 1234
Fax: +86.21.6888 3400
Email: shanghai.park@hyatt.com
Website: www.parkhyattshanghai.com

The Portman Ritz-Carlton, Shanghai
1376, Nanjing Xi Lu, Shanghai 200040
Tel: +86.21.6279 8888
Fax: +86.21.6279 8800
Website: www.ritzcarlton.com/en/
        properties/shanghai

The St Regis Shanghai
889 Dong Fang Road, Pudong District
Shanghai 200122
Tel: +86.21.5050 4567
Fax: +86.21.6875 6789
Email: stregis.shanghai@stregis.com
Website: www.stregis.com/shanghai

The Westin Bund Center Shanghai
88 Henan Central Road
Shanghai 200002
Tel: +86.21.6335 1888
Fax: +86.21.6335 2888
Email: rsvns-shanghai@westin.com
Website: www.westin.com/shanghai

Conrad Hong Kong
Pacific Place, 88 Queensway, Hong Kong
Tel: +852.2521 3838
Fax: +852.2521 3888
Email: hongkonginfo@conradhotels.com
Website: www.conradhotels.com/hongkong

Four Seasons Hotel Hong Kong
8 Finance Street, Central, Hong Kong
Tel: +852.3196 8888
Fax: +852.3196 8899
Website: www.fourseasons.com/hongkong

Grand Hyatt Hong Kong
1 Harbour Road, Hong Kong
Tel: +852.2588 1234
Fax: +852.2802 0677
Email: info.ghhk@hyattintl.com
Website: www.hongkong.grand.hyatt.com

Island Shangri-La, Hong Kong
Pacific Place, Supreme Court Road
Central, Hong Kong
Tel: +852.2877 3838
Fax: +852.2521 8742
Email: isl@shangri-la.com
Website: www.shangri-la.com

The Landmark Mandarin Oriental, Hong Kong
15 Queen's Road Central, The Landmark
Central, Hong Kong
Tel: +852.2132 0188
Fax: +852.2132 0199
Website: mandarinoriental.com/landmark

Mandarin Oriental, Hong Kong
5 Connaught Road,Central, Hong Kong
Tel: +85.2.2522 0111
Fax: +85.2.2810 6190
Email: mohkg-reservations@mohg.com
Website: mandarinoriental.com/hongkong

The Peninsula Hong Kong
Salisbury Road, Kowloon, Hong Kong
Tel: +852.2920 2888
Fax: +852.2722 4170
Email: phk@peninsula.com
Website: hongkong.peninsula.com

The Ritz-Carlton, Hong Kong
3 Connaught Road Central, Hong Kong
Tel: +852.2877 6666
Fax: +852.2877 6778
Website: www.ritzcarlton.com/en/
        properties/hongkong

Grand Hyatt Taipei
2, Song Shou Road, Taipei, Taiwan 11051
Tel: +886.2.2720 1234
Fax: +886.2.2720 1111
Email: grandhyatttaipei@hyattintl.com
Website: taipei.grand.hyatt.com

JAPAN

The Ritz-Carlton, Osaka
2-5-25 Umeda, Kita-ku, Osaka 530-0001
Tel: +81.6.6343 7000
Fax: +81.6.6343 7001
Website: ritzcarlton.com/en/properties/osaka

Four Seasons Hotel Tokyo at Chinzan-so
0–8, Sekiguchi 2-chome
Bunkyo-ku, Tokyo 112-8667
Tel: +81.3.3943 2222
Fax: +81.3.3943 2300
Website: www.fourseasons.com/tokyo

Grand Hyatt Tokyo
6-10-3 Roppongi, Minato-Ku, Tokyo 106-0032
Tel: +81.3.4333 1234
Fax: +81.3.4333 8123
Email: reservation@tyogh.com
Website: tokyo.grand.hyatt.com

Imperial Hotel, Tokyo
1-1 Uchisaiwai-Cho 1-Chome, Chiyoda-Ku
Tokyo 100-8558
Tel: +81.3.3504 1111
Fax: +81.3.3581 9146
Website: www.imperialhotel.co.jp

Mandarin Oriental, Tokyo
2-1-1 Nihonbashi Muromachi Chuo-ku
Tokyo 103-8328
Tel: +81.3.3270 8800
Fax: +81.3.3270 8828
Website: mandarinoriental.com/tokyo

New Otani, Tokyo
4-1 Kioi-Cho, Chiyoda-Ku, Tokyo 102-8578
Tel: +81.3.3265 1111
Fax: +81.3.3221 2619
Website: www.newotani.co.jp/en/tokyo

Okura, Tokyo
2-10-4 Toranomon, Minato-ku, Tokyo 105-8416
Tel: +81.3.3582 0111
Fax: +81.3.3582 3707
Website: www.okura.com/tokyo

KOREA

Grand Hyatt Seoul
747-7 Hannam-Dong, Yongsan-Gu
Seoul 140-738
Tel: +82.2.797 1234
Fax: +82.2.798 6953
Email: selrs-info@hyatt.com
Website: www.seoul.grand.hyatt.com

The Shilla Seoul
202 Jangchung-dong 2-ga
Jung-gu, Seoul 100-856
Tel: +82.2.2233 3131
Fax: 80.2.2233 5073
Email: reserve@shilla.net
Website: www.shilla.net/seoul

The Westin Chosun, Seoul
87 Sogong-Dong, Jung-gu, Seoul 100-070
Tel: +82.2.771 0500
Fax: +82.2.752 1443
Email: email@westinchosun.co.kr
Website: www.westin.com/chosunseoul

THE PHILIPPINES

Makati Shangri-La Hotel, Manila
Ayala Avenue at Makati Avenue
Makati City, Manila 1200
Tel: +63.2.813 8888
Fax: +63.2.813 5499
Email: slm@shangri-la.com
Website: www.shangri-la.com/en/
        property/manila/makatishangrila

VIETNAM

Hotel Sofitel Metropole Hanoi
15 Ngo Quyen Street, 10000 Hanoi
Tel: +84.4.826 6919
Fax: +84.4.826 6920
Email: sofitelhanoi@hn.vnn.vn
Website: www.sofitel.com

THAILAND

Four Seasons Hotel Bangkok
155 Rajadamri Road, Bangkok 10330
Tel: +66.2.250 1000
Fax: +66.2.253 9195
Website: www.fourseasons.com/bangkok

The Oriental, Bangkok
48 Oriental Avenue, Bangkok 10500
Tel: +66.2.659 9000
Fax: +66.2.659 0000
Email: orbkk-reservations@mohg.com
Website: mandarinoriental.com/bangkok

The Peninsula Bangkok
333 Charoennakorn Road
Klongsan, Bangkok 10600
Tel: +66.2.861 2888
Fax: +66.2.861 1112
Email: pbk@peninsula.com
Website: bangkok.peninsula.com

The Sukhothai
13/3 South Sathorn Road,Bangkok 10120
Tel: +66.2.344 8888
Fax: +66.2.344 8899
Email: info@sukhothai.com
Website: www.sukhothai.com

MALAYSIA

Mandarin Oriental Kuala Lumpur
Kuala Lumpur City Centre
Kuala Lumpur 50088
Tel: +60.3.2179 8818
Fax: +60.3.2179 8659
Email: mokul-reservations@mohg.com
Website: mandarinoriental.com/kualalumpur

SINGAPORE

The Fullerton Hotel
1 Fullerton Square, Singapore 049178
Tel: +65.6733 8388
Fax: +65.6735 8388
Email: info@fullertonhotel.com
Website: www.fullertonhotel.com

Mandarin Oriental Singapore
5 Raffles Avenue, Marina Square
Singapore 039797
Telephone: +65.6338 0066
Facsimile: +65.6339 9537
Email: mosin@mohg.com
Website: mandarinoriental.com/singapore

Raffles Hotel Singapore
1 Beach Road, Singapore 189673
Tel: +65.6337 1886
Fax: +65.6339 7650
Email: singapore-raffles@raffles.com
Website: singapore-raffles.raffles.com

The Ritz-Carlton, Millenia Singapore
7 Raffles Avenue, Singapore 039799
Tel: +65.6337 8888
Fax: +65.6338 0001
Email: rc.sinrz.reservations@ritzcarlton.com
Website: www.ritzcarlton.com/en/
      properties/singapore/

The Shangri-La Hotel Singapore
22 Orange Grove Road, Singapore 258350
Tel: +65.6737 3644
Fax: +65.6737 3257
Email: sls@shangri-la.com
Website: www.shangri-la.com/en/property/
      singapore/shangrila

INDIA

The Leela Palace Kempinski, Bangalore
23, Airport Road, Bangalore 560 008
Tel: +91.80.2521.1234
Fax: +91.80.2521.2222
Email: reservations.bangalore@theleela.com
Website: www.theleela.com

The Leela Kempnski Goa
Mobor, Cavelossim, Goa
Tel:+91.832.287.1234
Fax: 91+832.287.1352
Email: reservations.goa@theleela.com
Website: www.theleela.com

The Leela Kempinski Kovalam Beach, Kerala
Kerala Thiruvananthapuram 695 527
Tel: +91.471.248.0101
Fax: +91.471.248.1522
Email: reservations.kovalam@theleela.com
Website: www.theleela.com

The Leela Kempinski, Mumbai
Sahar, Mumbai 400 059
Tel: +91.22.6691.1234
Fax: +91.22.6691.1212
Email: reservations.mumbai@theleela.com
Website: www.theleela.com

Grand Hyatt Mumbai
Off Western Express Highway
Santacruz (East), Mumbai 400 055
Tel: +91.22.6676 1234
Fax: +91.22.6676 1235
Email: grandhyattmumbai@hyattintl.com
Website: www.mumbai.grand.hyatt.com

The Taj Mahal Palace and Tower, Mumbai
Apollo Bunder, Mumbai 400001
Tel: +91.22.5665 3366
Fax: +91.22.5665 0300
Email: tmhbc.bom@tajhotels.com
Website: www.tajhotels.com

The Oberoi, Mumbai
Nariman Point, Mumbai 400 021
Tel: +91.22.6632 5757
Fax: +91.22.6632 4142
Email: reservations@oberoi-mumbai.com
Website: www.oberoihotels.com

The Claridges, New Delhi
12 Aurangzeb Road, New Delhi 110 011
Tel: +91.11.4133 5133
Fax: +91.11.2301 0625
Email: reservations@claridges.com
Website: www.claridges.com

The Oberoi, New Delhi
Dr Zakir Hussain Marg, New Delhi 110 003
Tel: +91.11.2436 3030
Fax: +91.11.2436 0484
Email: reservations@oberoidel.com
Website: www.oberoihotels.com

The Oberoi Udaivilás
Haridasji Ki Magri, Udaipur 31300
Tel: +91.294.243 3300
Fax: +91.294.243 3200
Email: gm@oberoi-udaivilas.com
Website: www.oberoi-udaivilas.com

AUSTRALIA

Four Seasons Hotel Sydney
199 George Street, Sydney, NSW 2000
Tel: +61.2.9238 0000
Fax: +61.2.9251 2851
Website: www.fourseasons.com/sydney

Grand Hyatt Melbourne
123 Collins Street, Melbourne, VIC 3000
Tel: +61.3.9657 1234
Fax: +61.3.9650 3491
Email: melbourne@hyatt.com.au
Website: www.melbourne.grand.hyatt.com

EUROPE

UK

Four Seasons Hotel Dublin
Simmonscourt Road, Dublin 4
Tel: +353.1.665 4000
Fax: +353.1.665 4099
Website: www.fourseasons.com/dublin

Andaz Liverpool Street, London
40 Liverpool Street, London EC2M 7QN
Tel: +44.0.20.7961 1234
Fax: +44.0.20.7961 1235
Email: info.londonliv@andaz.com
Website: www.andaz.com

Claridge's, London
Brook Street, Mayfair, London W1K 4HR
Tel: +44.20.7629 8860
Fax: +44.20.7499 2210
Email: info@claridges.co.uk
Website: claridges.co.uk

Dukes, London
St James's Place, London SW1A 1NY
Tel: +44.20.7491 4840
Fax: +44.20.7493 1264
Email: bookings@dukeshotel.com
Website: www.dukeshotel.com

Four Seasons Hotel London
Hamilton Place, Park Lane, London W1A 1AZ
Tel: +44.20.7499 0888
Fax: +44.20.7493 1895
Website: www.fourseasons.com/london

Hilton London Paddington
146 Praed Street, London W2 1EE
Tel: +44.207.850 0500
Fax: +44.207.850 0600
Email: reservations.paddington@hilton.com
Website: www.hilton.com/paddington

Langham Hotel, London
1C Portland Place, Regent Street, London W1B 1JA
Tel: +44.20.7636 1000
Fax: +44.20.7323 2340
Email: lon.resv@langhamhotels.com
Website: london.langhamhotels.com

Mandarin Oriental Hyde Park, London
66 Knightsbridge, London SW1X 7LA
Tel: +44.20.7235 2000
Fax:+44.20.7235 2001
Email: molon-info@mohg.com
Website: mandarinoriental.com/london

Renaissance Chancery Court London
252 High Holborn, London WC1V 7EN
Tel: +44.20.7829 9888
Fax: +44.20.7829 9889
Website: www.renaissancechancerycourt.co.uk

The Ritz Hotel London
150 Piccadilly, London W1J 9BR
Tel: +44.20.7493 8181
Fax: +44.20.7493 2687
Email: enquire@theritzlondon.com
Website: www.theritzlondon.com

Savoy, London
Strand, London WC2R 0EU
Tel: +44.20.7836 4343
Email:savoy@fairmont.com
Website: www.fairmont.com/savoy

The Berkeley, London
Wilton Place, Knightsbridge, London SW1X 7RL
Tel: +44.20.7235 6000
Fax: +44.20.7235 4330
Email: info@the-berkeley.co.uk
Website: www.the-berkeley.co.uk

The Dorchester, London
Park Lane, London W1K 1QA
Tel: +44.20.7629 8888
Fax: +44.20.7629 8080
Website: www.thedorchester.com

SPAIN

Hotel Arts Barcelona
Marina 19-21, Barcelona 8005
Tel: +34.93.221 1000
Fax: +34.93.221 1070
Website: ritzcarlton.com/en/properties/barcelona

Hotel Claris, Barcelona
Pau Claris 150, Barcelona 08009
Tel: +34.93.487 6262
Fax: +34.93.215 7970
Email: claris@derbyhotels.com
Website: www.hotelclaris.com

Hotel Urban, Madrid
Carrera de San Jerónimo 34, Madrid 28014
Tel: +34.91.787 7770
Fax: +34.91.787 7799
Email: urban@derbyhotels.com
Website: www.derbyhotels.com

Hotel Villa Real, Madrid
10 Plaza de Las Cortes, Madrid 28014
Tel: +34.91.420 3767
Fax: +34.91.420 2547
Email: villareal@derbyhotels.com
Website: www.derbyhotels.com

FRANCE

Four Seasons Hotel George V, Paris
31, avenue George V, Paris 75008
Tel: +33.1.4952 7000
Fax: +33.1.4952 7010
Email: reservation.paris@fourseasons.com
Website: www.fourseasons.com/paris

Hôtel de Crillon, Paris
10 place de la Concorde, Paris 75008
Tel: +33.1.4471 1500
Fax: +33.1.4471 1502
Email: crillon@crillon.com
Website: www.crillon.com

Hôtel Le Bristol, Paris
112 rue du Faubourg Saint-Honoré, Paris 75008
Tel: +33.1.5343 4300
Fax: + 33.1.5343 4301
Email: resa@lebristolparis.com
Website: www.lebristolparis.com

InterContinental Paris Le Grand
2 Rue Scribe, Paris 75009
Tel: +33.1.4007 3232
Fax: +33.1.4266 1251
Website: www.paris.intercontinental.com

Le Meurice, Paris
228 rue de Rivoli, Paris 75001
Tel: +33.1.4458 1010
Fax: +33.1.4458 1015
Email: reservations@lemeurice.com
Website: www.lemeurice.com

Park Hyatt Paris–Vendôme
5 rue de la Paix, Paris 75002
Tel: +33.1.5871 1234
Fax: +33.1.5871 1235
Email: vendome@hyatt.com
Website: www.paris.vendome.hyatt.com

DENMARK

Copenhagen Hotel D'Angleterre
34, Kongens Nytorv, PO Box 9077
Copenhagen K DK-1022
Tel: +45.3312 0095
Fax. +45.3312 1118
Email: dangleterre@dangleterre.dk
Website: www.dangleterre.com

NORWAY

Grand Hotel Oslo
Karl Johans Gate 31, Oslo NO-0159
Tel: +47.23.212 000
Fax +47.23.212 100
Email: grand@rica.no
Website: www.grand.no

FINLAND

Hotel Kämp
Pohjoisesplanadi 29, Helsinki 00100
Tel: +358.9.576 111
Fax: +358.9.576 1122
Email: hotelkamp@hotelkamp.fi
Website: www.hotelkamp.fi

SWEDEN

Grand Hotel, Stockholm
Södra Blasieholmshamnen 8
PO Box 16424, Stockholm 103 27
Tel: +46.8.679 3500
Fax: +46.8.611 8686
Email: info@grandhotel.se
Website: www.grandhotel.se

ITALY

Four Seasons Hotel Milan
Via Gesù, 6/8, Milan 20121
Tel: +39.02.77 088
Fax: +39.02.7708 5000
Website: www.fourseasons.com/milan

SWITZERLAND

Mandarin Oriental Hotel du Rhône, Geneva
Quai Turrettini 1, Geneva 1201
Tel: +41.22.909 0000
Fax:+41.22.909 0010
Email: mogva-enquiry@mohg.com
Website: mandarinoriental.com/geneva

Baur Au Lac, Zürich
Talstrasse 1, Zürich 8001
Tel: +41.44.220 5020
Fax: +41.44.220 5044
Email: info@bauraulac.ch
Website: www.bauraulac.ch

BELGIUM

Conrad Brussels
Avenue Louise 71, Brussels 1050
Tel: +32.2.542 4242
Fax: +32.2.542 4200
Email: brusselsinfo@conradhotels.com
Website: www.conradhotels.com/brussels

LUXEMBOURG

Hotel Le Royal
12 Boulevard Royal L-2449
Tel: +352.241 6161
Fax: +352.225 948
Website: www.hotelroyal.lu

THE NETHERLANDS

InterContinental Amstel Amsterdam
Professor Tulpplein 1, Amsterdam 1018 GX
Tel: +31.20.622 6060
Fax: +31.20.622 5808
Email: amstel@ihg.com
Website: amsterdam.intercontinental.com

AUSTRIA

Hotel Imperial, Vienna
Kaerntner Ring 16, Vienna 1015
Tel: +43.1.501 100
Fax: +43.1.5011 0410
Email: hotel.imperial@luxurycollection.com
Website: www.starwoodhotels.com

GERMANY

Hotel Adlon Kempinski
Unter den Linden 77, Berlin 10117
Tel: +49.30.22610
Fax: +49.30.2261 2222
Email: hotel.adlon@kempinski.com
Website: www.hotel-adlon.de

The Ritz-Carlton, Berlin
Potsdamer Platz 3, Berlin 10785
Tel: +49.0.3033 7777
Fax: +49.0.3033 777 5555
Email: berlin@ritzcarlton.com
Website: ritzcarlton.com/en/properties/berlin

Steigenberger Parkhotel
Königsallee 1a, Düsseldorf 40212
Tel: +49.211.13810
Fax +49.211.1381 592
Email: duesseldorf@steigenberger.de
Website: www.steigenberger.com

Steigenberger Frankfurter Hof, Frankfurt
Am Kaiserplatz, Frankfurt 60311
Tel: +49.69.215 02
Fax: +49.69.215 900
Email: frankfurter-hof@steigenberger.de
Website: frankfurter-hof.steigenberger.de

Bayerischer Hof, Munich
2-6 Promenadeplatz, Munich 80333
Tel: +49.89.21200
Fax: +49.89.2120 906
Email: info@bayerischerhof.de
Website: www.bayerischerhof.de

CZECH REPUBLIC

Four Seasons Hotel Prague
Veleslavinova 2a/1098, Praha 1, 110 00
Tel: +420.221.427 000
Fax: +420.221.426 000
Website: www.fourseasons.com/prague

TURKEY

Çırağan Palace Kempinski, Istanbul
Çırağan Caddesi No. 32, Besiktas 34349
Tel: +90.212.326 4646
Fax: +90.212.259 6687
Website: www.kempinski-istanbul.com

Four Seasons Hotel Istanbul
Tevkifhane Sokak No 1
Sultanahmet-Eminönü, Istanbul 34110
Tel: +90.212.638 8200
Fax: +90.212.638 8210
Website: www.fourseasons.com/istanbul

The Ritz-Carlton, Istanbul
Suzer Plaza, Elmadag, Sisli, Istanbul 34367
Tel: +90.212.334 4444
Fax: +90.212.334 4455
Email: rc.istrz.reservations@ritzcarlton.com
Website: ritzcarlton.com/en/properties/istanbul

RUSSIA

Ararat Park Hyatt Moscow
4 Neglinnaya Street, Moscow 109012
Tel: +7.495.783 1234
Fax: +7.495.783 1235
Email: moscow@hyatt.com
Website: moscow.park.hyatt.com

Moscow Marriott Royal Aurora Hotel
Petrovka St-Bld 11/20, Moscow 107031
Phone: +7.495.937 1000
Fax: +7.495.937 1001
Website: www.marriott.com

The Ritz-Carlton, Moscow
Tverskaya Ulitsa 3, Moscow 125009
Tel: +7.495.225 8888
Fax: +7.495.225 8400
Email: moscow.inquiries@ritzcarlton.com
Website: www.ritzcarlton.com

Swissôtel Krasnye Holmy, Moscow
Kosmodamianskaya Nab 52, Building 6
Moscow 115054
Tel: +7.495.787 9800
Fax: +7.495.787 9800
Email: moscow@swissotel.com
Website: www.moscow.swissotel.com

KUWAIT

Sheraton Kuwait
Safat 13060, Fahd Al-Salem Street
PO Box 5902 Safat, Kuwait City 13060
Phone: +965.242 2055
Website: www.starwoodhotels.com

OMAN

Al Bustan Palace InterContinental
PO BOX 1998, Muttrah 114, Muscat
Tel: +968.2479 9666
Fax: +968.2479 9600
Website: www.ichotelsgroup.com

UNITED ARAB EMIRATES

Emirates Palace Abu Dhabi
PO Box 39999, West End Corniche, Abu Dhabi
Tel: +971.2.690 9000
Fax: +971.2.690 9999
Website: www.emiratespalace.com

Grand Hyatt Dubai
PO Box 7978, Dubai
Tel: +971.4.317 1234
Fax: +971.4.317 1235
Email: reservations.grandhyattdubai
@hyattintl.com
Website: dubai.grand.hyatt.com

Jumeirah Beach Hotel
PO Box 11416, Dubai
Tel: +971.4.348 0000
Fax: +971.4.301 6800
Email: JBHinfo@jumeirah.com
Website: www.jumeirahbeachhotel.com

Jumeirah Emirates Towers
PO Box 72127, Dubai
Tel: +971.4.330 0000
Fax: +971.4.330 3030
Email: JETinfo@jumeirah.com
Website: www.jumeirahemiratestowers.com

The Palace – The Old Town
The Old Town Island, Downtown Burj Dubai
PO Box 9770, Dubai
Tel: +971.4.428 7888
Fax: +971.4.428 7999
Email: h6230-re@accor.com
Website: www.sofitel.com

SAUDI ARABIA

Four Seasons Hotel Riyadh
Kingdom Centre, P.O. Box 231000, Riyadh 11321
Tel: +966.1.211 5000
Fax: +966.1.211 5001
Website: www.fourseasons.com/riyadh

AFRICA

EGYPT

Four Seasons Hotel Cairo at Nile Plaza
1089 Corniche El Nile, PO Box 63
Maglis El Shaab, Garden City 11519, Cairo
Tel: +20.2.2791 7000
Fax: +20.2.2791 6900
Website: www.fourseasons.com/caironp

SOUTH AFRICA

Mount Nelson Hotel
76 Orange Street, Cape Town 8001
Tel: +27.21.483 1000
Fax: +27.21.483 1001
Email: reservations@mountnelson.co.za
Website: www.mountnelson.co.za

NORTH AMERICA

USA

Arizona Biltmore, Phoenix
2400 East Missouri Avenue, Phoenix, AZ 85016
Tel: +1.602.955 6600
Fax: +1.602.381 7600
Email: reservations@arizonabiltmore.com
Website: www.arizonabiltmore.com

Phoenician, Phoenix
6000 East Camelback Road
Scottsdale, AZ 85251
Tel: +1.480.941 8200
Email: info@thephoenician.com
Website: thephoenician.com

The Beverly Hills Hotel
9641 Sunset Boulevard, Beverly Hills, CA 90210
Tel: +1.310.276 2251
Fax: +1.310.887 2887
Website: www.thebeverlyhillshotel.com

Beverly Wilshire (Four Seasons)
9500 Wilshire Boulevard, Beverly Hills, CA 90212
Tel: +1.310.275 5200
Fax: +1.310.274 2851
Website: fourseasons.com/beverlywilshire

Four Seasons Hotel Los Angeles
300 South Doheny Drive, Los Angeles, CA 90048
Tel: +1.310.273 2222
Fax: +1.310.859 3824
Website: www.fourseasons.com/losangeles

Four Seasons Hotel San Francisco
757 Market Street, San Francisco, CA 94103
Tel: +1.415.633 3000
Fax: +1.415.633 3001
Website: www.fourseasons.com/sanfrancisco

Hotel Bel-Air, Los Angeles
701 Stone Canyon Road, Los Angeles, CA 90077
Tel: +1.310.472 1211
Fax: +1.310.909 1611
Email: sales@hotelbelair.com
Website: www.hotelbelair.com

Mandarin Oriental, San Francisco
222 Sansome Street, San Francisco, CA 94104
Tel: +1.415.276 9888
Fax: +1.415.433 0289
Email: mosfo-reservations@mohg.com
Website: mandarinoriental.com/sanfrancisco

Shutters on the Beach, Los Angeles
1 Pico Boulevard, Santa Monica, CA 90405
Tel: +1.310.458 0030
Fax: +1.310.458 4589
Email: info@shuttersonthebeach.com
Website: www.shuttersonthebeach.com

The Fairmont San Francisco
950 Mason Street, San Francisco, CA 94108
Tel: +1.415.772 5000
Fax: +1.415.772 5013
Email: sanfrancisco@fairmont.com
Website: www.fairmont.com/sanfrancisco

The Ritz-Carlton, Marina del Rey, Los Angeles
4375 Admiralty Way, Marina del Rey, CA 90292
Tel: +1.310.823 1700
Fax: +1310.823 2403
Website: ritzcarlton.com/en/
              properties/marinadelrey

The Ritz-Carlton, San Francisco
600 Stockton Street at California Street
San Francisco, CA 94108
Tel: +1.415.296 7465
Fax: +1415.291 0288
Website: ritzcarlton.com/en/
              properties/sanfrancisco

Four Seasons Hotel Washington, DC
2800 Pennsylvania Avenue NW
Washington, DC 20007
Tel: +1.202.342 0444
Fax: +1.202.944 2076
Website: www.fourseasons.com/washington

Mandarin Oriental, Washington DC
1330 Maryland Avenue SW
Washington, DC 20024
Tel: +1.202.554 8588
Fax: +1.202.554 8999
Website: mandarinoriental.com/washington

The Hay-Adams, Washington, DC
1 Lafayette Square, 16th & H Streets NW
Washington, DC 20006
Tel: +1.202.638 6600
Fax: +1.202.638 2716
Website: www.hayadams.com

Willard InterContinental Washington
1401 Pennsylvania Avenue NW
Washington, DC 20004
Tel: +1.202.628 9100
Fax: +1.202.637 7326
Email: washington@interconti.com
Website: washington.intercontinental.com

Four Seasons Hotel Miami
1435 Brickell Avenue, Miami, FL 33131
Tel: +1.305.358 3535
Fax: +1.305.358 7758
Website: www.fourseasons.com/miami

Four Seasons Hotels Atlanta
75 Fourteenth Street, Atlanta, GA 30309
Tel: +1.404.881 9898
Fax: +1.404.873 4692
Website: www.fourseasons.com/atlanta

The Ritz-Carlton, Atlanta
181 Peachtree Street NE, Atlanta, GA 30303
Phone:+1.404.659 0400
Fax: +1.404.688 0400
Website: ritzcarlton.com/en/properties/atlanta

Halekulani, Honolulu
2199 Kalia Road, Honolulu, HI 96815
Tel: +1.808.923 2311
Fax: +1.808.926 8004
Website: www.halekulani.com

Four Seasons Hotel Chicago
120 East Delaware Place, Chicago, IL 60611-1428
Tel: +1.312.280 8800
Fax: +1.312.280 1748
Website: www.fourseasons.com/chicago

Park Hyatt Chicago
800 North Michigan Avenue
Chicago, IL 60611
Tel: +1.312.335 1234
Fax: +1.312.239 4000
Email: communicationschiph@hyatt.com
Website: parkchicago.hyatt.com

The Peninsula Chicago
108 East Superior Street (at North Michigan
Avenue), Chicago, IL 60611
Tel: +1.312.337 2888
Fax: +1.312.751 2888
Email: pch@peninsula.com
Website: chicago.peninsula.com

The Ritz-Carlton (Four Seasons), Chicago
160 East Pearson St. at Water Tower Place
Chicago, IL 60611-2124
Tel: +1.312.266 1000
Fax: +1.312.266 1194
Website: www.fourseasons.com/chicagorc

Boston Harbor, Boston
70 Rowes Wharf, Boston, MA 02110
Tel: 617.439.7000
Fax: 617.330.9450
Email: reservations@bhh.com
Website: www.bhh.com

Four Seasons Hotel Boston
200 Boylston Street, Boston, MA 02116
Tel: +1.617.338 4400
Fax: +1.617. 423 0154
Website: www.fourseasons.com/boston

Taj Boston
15 Arlington Street, Boston, MA 02116
Tel: +1.617.536 5700
Fax: +1.617.536 1335
Email: taj.boston@tajhotels.com
Website: www.tajhotels.com

The Ritz-Carlton, Boston Common
10 Avery Street, Boston, MA 02111
Tel: +1.617.574 7100
Fax: +1.617. 574 7200
Website: ritzcarlton.com/en/
              properties/bostoncommon

Four Seasons Hotel New York
57 East 57th Street, New York, NY 10022
Tel: +1.212.758 5700
Fax: +1.212.758 5711
Website: www.fourseasons.com/newyorkfs

Mandarin Oriental, New York
80 Columbus Circle at 60th Street
New York, NY 10023
Tel: +1.212.805 8800 or +1.866.801 8880
Fax: +1.212.805 8888
Email: monyc-reservations@mohg.com
Website: mandarinoriental.com/newyork

Millenium Hilton, New York
55 Church Street, New York, NY 10007
Tel: +1.212.693 2001
Fax: +1.212.571 2316
Email: nycml_fo@hilton.com
Website: www.newyorkmillenium.hilton.com

The Peninsula New York
700 Fifth Avenue at 55th Street
New York, NY 10019
Tel: +1.212.956 2888
Fax: +1.212.903 3949
Email: pny@peninsula.com
Website: newyork.peninsula.com

The St Regis New York
2 East 55th Street, at Fifth Avenue
New York, NY 10022
Tel: +1.212.753 4500
Fax: +1.212.787 3447
Email: stregisny.res@stregis.com
Website: www.starwoodhotels.com/stregis

The New York Palace Hotel
455 Madison Avenue, New York, NY 10022
Tel: +1.212.888 7000
Fax: +1.212.303 6000
Email: info@nypalace.com
Website: www.newyorkpalace.com

The Pierre, New York
Fifth Avenue at 61st Street, New York, NY 10021
Tel: +1.212.838 8000
Fax: +1.212.940 8109
Email: thepierre.ny@tajhotels.com
Website: www.tajhotels.com

The Ritz-Carlton New York, Battery Park
Two West Street, New York, NY 10004
Tel: +1.212.344 0800
Fax: +1.212.344 3801
Website: ritzcarlton.com/en/
properties/batterypark

The Ritz-Carlton New York, Central Park
50 Central Park South, New York, NY 10019
Tel: +1.212.308 9100
Fax: +1.212.207 8831
Website: ritzcarlton.com/en/
properties/centralpark

Bellagio
3600 Las Vegas Boulevard South
Las Vegas, NV 89109
Tel: +1.702.693 7111
Email: roomres@bellagioresort.com
Website: www.bellagio.com

Four Seasons Hotel Philadelphia
One Logan Square
Philadelphia, PA 19103-6933
Tel: +1.215.963 1500
Fax: +1.215.963 9506
Website: www.fourseasons.com/philadelphia

Rosewood Mansion on Turtle Creek, Dallas
2821 Turtle Creek Boulevard, Dallas, TX 75219
Tel: +1.214.559 2100
Fax: +1.214.528 4187
Email: themansion@rosewoodhotels.com
Website: www.mansiononturtlecreek.com

Grand Hyatt Seattle
721 Pine Street, Seattle, WA 98101
Tel: +1.206.774 1234
Fax: +1.206.774 6120
Website: www.grandseattle.hyatt.com

CANADA

Four Seasons Hotel Toronto
21 Avenue Road, Toronto, ON M5R 2G1
Tel: +1.416.964 0411
Fax: +1.416.964 2301
Website: www.fourseasons.com/toronto

Pan Pacific Vancouver
Suite 300-999 Canada Place,
Vancouver, British Columbia V6C 3B5
Tel: +1.604.662 8111
Fax: +1.604.685 8690
Website: vancouver.panpacific.com

MEXICO

Four Seasons Hotel Mexico City
Paseo de la Reforma #500, Colonia Juárez
México, DF 06600
Tel: +52.55.5230 1818
Fax: +52.55.5230 1808
Website: www.fourseasons.com/mexico

SOUTH AMERICA

ARGENTINA

Alvear Palace, Buenos Aires
Av Alvear 1891, C1129AAA Buenos Aires
Tel: +54.11.4808 2170
Email: info@alvearpalace.com
Website: www.alvearpalace.com

BRAZIL

Copacabana Palace, Rio de Janeiro
Avenida Atlântica 1702
Rio de Janeiro 22021 001
Tel: +55.21.2548 7070
Fax: +55.21.2235 7330
Email: reservas@copacabanapalace.com.br
Website: www.copacabanapalace.com.br

GROUPS

Conrad Hotels & Resorts
Tel: +800.00.266 723
Website: www.conradhotels.com

Photo credits

The publisher would like to thank the following for permission to reproduce their photographs:

AFP/Getty Images 53
Al Maha Desert Resort & Spa 28 top
Bob Handelman /Getty Images 60
Château Les Crayères 32
Cocoa Island Maldives 38 top
Copacabana Palace Hotel 26
Desert Rangers Dubai 42 top
The Dorchester, London 62
Four Seasons Hotel New York 18
Four Seasons Hotel, Hong Kong 24, 116
Gary John Norman/Getty Images 43
Geostock/Getty Images 46
Getty Images 54, 62
The Gleneagles Hotel 39
The Hay-Adams, Washington DC 19 top
Hiroyuki Matsumoto/Getty Images 47
Hotel Adlon Kempinski

Hotel Bel-Air, Los Angeles 5, 30
Hotel Caruso Ravello (Hotel Caruso Belvedere) 31
Hotel Claris 44, 51
Hotel Côté Cour SL 58
Hotel Goldener Berg 34
House By The Park 57 top
Huka Lodge 33
Huvafen Fushi, Maldives 42 bottom
InterContinental Amstel Amsterdam 23 right
Jeff Spielman/Getty Images 8
Jembisa 38 bottom
Juergen Stumpe 16
Jumeirah Beach Hotel 41
Jumeirah Emirates Towers 50
Lan, Beijing 56
Lanson Place 6
Le Meurice, Paris 19 bottom

Le-Dung Ly/Getty Images 45
Maia, Seychelles 27
Mandarin Oriental Dhara Dhevi 28 bottom, 35
Mandarin Oriental, Hong Kong 23 left
The New York Palace Hotel 4
Noah Clayton/Getty Images 36
One&Only Resorts 37
Panoramic Images/Getty Images 48–49
Raffles Beijing Hotel 57 right
Ray Laskowitz/Lonely Planet Images/Getty Images 52
Red Gate Gallery 59
The Ritz-Carlton New York, Battery Park 9, 10
Royal Malewane 29
Steigenberger Frankfurter Hof 20
The Sukhothai, Bangkok 12–14
Tom Bonaventure/Getty Images 55
Villa San Michele 40